Marx against Marxism

Marx against Marxism

Julius I. Loewenstein

translated from the German by
Harry Drost

Routledge & Kegan Paul
London, Boston and Henley

First published in German in 1970
as Vision und Wirklichkeit
Revised edition published as Marx contra Marxismus
by J.C.B. Mohr (Paul Siebeck) Tübingen
© Julius I Loewenstein 1976
This English translation first published in 1980
by Routledge & Kegan Paul Ltd
39 Store Street, London WC1E 7DD,
9 Park Street, Boston, Mass. 02108, USA and
Broadway House, Newtown Road, Henley-on-Thames, Oxon RG9 1EN
Set in IBM Press Roman 10 on 11 pt by Columns
and printed in Great Britain by
Redwood Burn Ltd
Trowbridge & Esher
English translation © Routledge & Kegan Paul 1980

British Library Cataloguing in Publication Data

Loewenstein, Julius I.

Marx against Marxism.
1 Historical materialism
2 Weber, Max
I Title
335.4'11 D16.9 80-40573

ISBN 0 7100 0562 8

In memory of Karl Jaspers

Contents

Preface to the first German edition (1970)

A few years after the end of the First World War Thomas Mann wrote:[1]

> Our socialism, which has all too long allowed its spiritual life
> to languish in the shallows of a crude economic materialism, has
> no greater need than to find access to that loftier Germany . . .;
> but it will not rise to the height of its natural task until — if I
> may be allowed the extravagance — Karl Marx has read Friedrich
> Hölderlin: a consummation which, by the way, seems in a fair
> way to be achieved.

Such a consummation seemed possible in the 1920s, when open-minded young Marxist intellectuals like Georg Lukács, Karl Korsch, and Ernst Bloch began to relax party doctrine and align it to the tradition of European humanism. But it did not happen. The leaders of the communist parties suppressed any 'revisionist' aspirations and instead extended the inferior dogmatism into the even more anti-intellectual and intolerant system that was to split the world into two hostile camps. Today, after the end of the cold war, as intellectuals are deprecating both the dogmatism of Marxism and the complacency of the capitalist consumer society, the task of reconcilement once again obtrudes itself.

Intellectuals believe they have found a socialist humanism in the early works of Marx, which had been discovered in the meantime, and with this intellectual weapon they try to counter the inhuman Soviet ideology. But Marx's early socialism was still steeped in dogmatic philosophical speculation. Marx became Marx only after he had unequivocally renounced 'futile speculation', as he would later call it; for this renunciation paved the way to his truly scientific analysis of society. What survived from the earlier speculative phase was the doctrine of the dialectic; and although Marx himself began to extricate himself from it in stages, his followers adopted the doctrine and made it into a dogma that was to have a momentous influence.

Max Weber was the only one able to divorce Marx's work from its doctrinaire Procrustean bed and make it *scientifically* fruitful. But the narrow-minded Marxist school dissociated itself from this great scholar; only Lukács would admit that Weber had taught him the first lessons of social science.[2]

This study concludes that only an approach starting from Marx's *later* work can break the magic circle of fateful dogmatism and recover the humanist and political goals and scientific content of Marx. This came as a surprise to me. To show that the result is not based on an arbitrary interpretation, I have let the sources speak largely for themselves.

The philosophically untrained reader may skip the methodological discussions, for example on Hegel (chapter 5) and on Marx's dialectic (the last section of chapter 8). Although they are necessary to the argument, it can be understood without them.

Of the enormous literature on Marx and his school I have used only works that are indicative of Marx's influence.

Preface to the second German edition (1976)

When I began this study, the great disappointment with the political systems erected in the name of Marx had stunned many intellectuals. At that time I was concerned to show that sterile Marxist dogmatism could be exploded by using the views of the later Marx — hence the book's title, *Marx against Marxism*. When the study was concluded, the New Left movement raised its protest against both the stifling bourgeois-rationalist establishment and the intolerant Marxist systems. (For this reason I have amended the first editions with a few comments warning against an inaccurate interpretation of the young Marx.) The influence of the New Left may have declined in the last few years, but it has clearly brought about a change in the political and intellectual climate: its new standards are replacing the hitherto prevailing materialist and utilitarian attitudes. The additional chapters on the New Left will discuss to what extent the new world-view, which even theoreticians and politicians ideologically far removed from the New Left find stimulating, has anything in common with Marx.

Preface to the English edition

The teachings of Karl Marx very quickly became a part of the official programmes of all continental socialist parties. His doctrines were attractive for socialists because they seemed to solve, at the same time, the riddles of past history and the serious social problems of the day. To the dispossessed proletariat Marx promised a unique historical mission; to the estranged intelligentsia he brought a whole new *Weltanschauung*.

In the Anglo-Saxon countries, however, Marx was regarded as a very different phenomenon precisely because of his apparently absolute assumptions and fanciful predictions. The British and Americans tended to be sceptical of panaceas, whether metaphysical or political. They preferred the empirical methods of the sciences which were proving so successful; and they preferred to establish free institutions not on the basis of theoretical assumptions but by trial and error. Edmund Burke, a champion of freedom for Ireland and the American colonies, firmly rejected the 'abstract' democracy of the French philosophers and the Jacobin revolutionaries. It is not surprising then that the Fabian Society shied away from Marx's 'panacea' against all evils of human society, and that John Maynard Keynes wondered how 'a doctrine so illogical and so dull can have exercised so powerful and enduring an influence over the minds of men'.[3]

But there is more to Marx than his prescriptions for salvation. He threw fresh light upon the economic aspect of human culture. The British and Americans were slow to accept the Marxian analysis; but that attitudes have changed is clear: such otherwise dissimilar scholars as Joseph Needham, Richard Hoggart, and George Steiner all admit that they learned to appreciate the inescapable implications of sociology through the Marxist approach. Marx's sociology now attracts much attention in the Anglo-Saxon countries.

It is my contention that scholars would find the challenge posed by Marx more rewarding if they approached Marx's sociology through Max Weber, who presented Marx's essential and enduring thought stripped of its philosophical dogmatism. By rejecting the monocausal explanation of history, Weber made the very fruitful Marxist doctrine of historical materialism available to empirical studies.

Without a doubt there is much in Marx that must be reconsidered and re-examined. In this book I have tried to open a new aspect to the study of Marx, simply by extending the discussion to include Weber. It is my hope that an approach to Marx through Weber — an approach free of party doctrine of any kind — will be of value to an English-speaking audience.

Part one

Antecedents

Chapter one

The intellectual setting

German humanism

In 1818, the year in which Karl Marx was born, the classical epoch of German humanism reached its zenith. In that year Goethe wrote the *Westöstlicher Divan*; Beethoven composed the *Missa Solemnis*; Schelling became president of the Munich Academy of the Sciences; Schopenhauer published *The World as Will and Idea*, his main work; and Hölderlin was still writing poetry though already in the throes of madness. German humanism was part of the eighteenth-century European Enlightenment which freed man from his political immaturity and the authority of the ossified churches. The new self-confidence of the Enlightenment intellectuals, grounded in a new feeling of responsibility and independence, effected a break with the past. Goethe noted in retrospect that during this period 'poetic genius' became aware of its power to 'create its own conditions, and lay the foundation for a dignified independence'.[1]

But particularly in Germany external conditions constrained the activities of scholars and artists. They were cut off from public life by the absolutist regimes of the German princes. In addition, owing to the prolonged economic recession in Germany after the discovery of America and the Thirty Years War, patronage was difficult to secure for many artists. These factors explain why Goethe remarked that the artists and intellectuals, 'Judging by their creative activities, may without hesitation be called great, but in relation to the world at large they remain unimportant; and their economic success was insignificant compared to that gained in a more active life.'[2] Only the road to spiritual internalization remained open to the energies unleashed in the Enlightenment. The inner lives of most intellectuals were as excessively rich as their outer, active lives were poor. While the social ideal in England was the gentleman, and in France the cavalier, German society exalted the man of culture (*Bildung*).

Pietism, which had created the foundation of German culture, encouraged the striving for spiritual fulfilment. German pietism gave rise to the *Bildungsroman* and the music of Bach, and its appeal to inner experiences inspired the thought of Lessing, Kant, and Schleiermacher. (In contrast, English Calvinism impelled people to work indefatigably and disdain pleasure, thereby suffocating the spirit of the old society, its art and its music.) But most German humanists showed no inclination to study the external world of economic and political activity. Goethe was one of the few German thinkers of the classical period who possessed an ever-active drive for general education. He was interested not only in the internal world of the arts but also in the external world of commerce and science. For him, a man's duty was to fulfil 'the demands of the hour'.[3] Nevertheless, he still considered himself a 'liberator' of the Germans because through him they realized 'how people can and should live from within'.[4]

German intellectuals were no less moved by the libertarian ideals of the Enlightenment than their British and French contemporaries. All — Goethe was perhaps the sole exception — celebrated the French Revolution as the event that proved '(because of its disinterestedness) that man has a moral character, which gives hope for human improvement. The revolution has aroused in the hearts and desires of all spectators ... a *sympathy* which borders almost on enthusiasm', as the usually imperturbable Kant put it.[5] At the outbreak of the French Revolution the young friends Hölderlin, Hegel, and Schelling planted a 'liberty tree'. Hegel never changed his view of the revolution as a great mental dawn, not even when the old political order was restored after 1815. But *actively* to take part in the political struggle for freedom? 'Argue as much as you like about whatever you like, but obey!' — this was, as Kant himself noted, the 'strange and unexpected' conclusion of his essay *What is Enlightenment?* Luther had taught the people to entrust the reins of government to their rulers. In Germany the prophets of the Enlightenment remained loyal subjects and were content to note that the spirit of freedom was spreading because 'Our rulers have no interest in assuming the role of guardians over their subjects.'[6] While everywhere in the West free men felt a new responsibility for the welfare of the community and rebelled against autocratic rule with both words and actions, the men of the German Enlightenment kept aloof from politics and even wanted to justify their political impotence.[7] Only a German could have written 'A filthy song! Fie! A political song!'[8]

A wider interest in politics was first aroused in Germany during the Napoleonic wars. But the mass of the population took no part in this awakening, and the political aims of the few (mainly students) were romantic and unrealistic. The inchoate attempts to draft liberal constitutions were cut short by the restoration of the old order after the

Congress of Vienna. It is indicative of the superficial nature of the political involvement at this time that the loss of political freedom was accepted almost unopposed. The intellectuals consoled themselves by diverting their energies to the cultivation of education, intellectual tolerance, and the incorruptible civil service. Hegel, although he showed greater interest in politics than most, none the less regarded the Prussian state as 'constituted on the principle of intelligence'.[9] After isolated demonstrations and book-burnings the patriotic students withdrew from the political arena. They returned to their academic studies divorced from reality; some even preferred to escape into a world of fable and myth. Only a few deplored the prevalent unwillingness to face reality. Surprisingly enough it was Hölderlin who, while he submitted to the 'creative genius of our people', saw that 'we are poor in actions and rich in thoughts'.[10] And Goethe complained that young German intellectuals were 'short-sighted, pale, with sunken chest, young without youthfulness, ... only disposed to be interested in the highest problems of speculation. With them there is no trace of healthy senses and pleasure in the sensuous.'[11] There were no signs that these students erudite in philosophy and theology would become the political revolutionaries whose ideas were to rock the world.

The degeneration of the bourgeoisie to cultural philistinism

There exists a misconception that at the time of the great poets and thinkers their works were read and assimilated by a growing public – after all, in Germany *Bürgertum* denoted the bourgeoisie as the social class of culture, education, and property. Goethe investigated the previous century's many-faceted concern for the German language and literature. This, he wrote, 'is now of benefit to the whole nation, especially a certain middle class, as I would like to call it in the best sense of the term' (the Prussian educational reforms had made a humanist education available to a much wider section of the population). 'And yet', he continued, 'because every individual leads a mediocre life, he likes to be stimulated only by average feelings and wants to be confronted only with average situations.'[12] Indeed, with the exception of his early works, the poetry of Goethe and that of the other great writers remained unknown to the German public. Goethe himself was not surprised: 'My things can never be popular. He who thinks about it and strives for it is in error.'[13] The educational reforms had encouraged non-committal aestheticism and professional erudition, but not humanist ideals. It even came to the point where, as Goethe had also foreseen, 'Every mediocre talent can conveniently and mindlessly avail himself of the present thoughts and ideas.'[14]

The vacuity of culture coupled with a lack of political responsibility bred a kind of cultural philistinism that incensed the following generation. Many young intellectuals complained about the accumulation of indifferent and tasteless culture and the hypocritical moral self-confidence of the German bourgeoisie. In a letter to Arnold Ruge the young Marx wrote dejectedly that 'even if one can feel no national pride, one does feel national shame'; and in his reply Ruge quoted Hölderlin, who had been particularly harsh: 'I cannot think of any nation more divided than the Germans. You see craftsmen, but no people; you see thinkers, but no people.'[15]

From contemplativeness to political activism

Within the space of a decade the young intellectuals descended from their ivory towers to become radical political activists. They were shaken out of their contemplativeness by the July Revolution of 1830 in France. There were isolated attempts at rebellion in Germany, but after the arrest of the 'demagogues' law and order were soon restored. Then Hegel and Goethe died in successive years, 1831 and 1832. With them almost a whole cultural epoch was buried. The intellectual youth felt orphaned. Yet now the spell of the great masters seemed to be broken. The young students discovered that the ideas of freedom that Hegel had proclaimed *ex cathedra* had not been put into practice in the German states and had not even been accepted by a wide section of the bourgeoisie. The intellectuals became estranged from the bourgeoisie. Out of a feeling of indignation at the stupidity of the philistine bourgeoisie and the absence of political freedom, the intelligentsia – a term coined by Russian revolutionaries at the end of the last century, describing specifically that group of intellectuals which breaks its links with the bourgeoisie – renounced romantic dreams and speculative philosophy and turned enthusiastically to a life of political activism. The Hegelians grew impatient with their master's dictum that 'what is rational is actual', and gave it a new and revolutionary turn: 'What is rational must be!' Young writers calling themselves Young Germany began to proclaim ideas of political freedom only a few years after the death of Hegel and Goethe. Engels, who when he was sixteen thought that poetry was his vocation, published political poems under the pseudonym 'Young German'. Georg Gottfried Gervinus, who published a comprehensive history of German literature in 1835, announced the end of the poetic epoch and exhorted the Germans 'to venture onto the great market of life'.[16] And the aesthetic philosopher Friedrich Theodor Vischer demanded: 'We have had enough of the cultural struggles of the individual in his private situation. We want to see struggles of whole nations.'[17]

In the same year that the first volume of Gervinus's history appeared, David Friedrich Strauss questioned the validity of the concept of a transcendent God in his book *The Life of Jesus*. It provoked a heated debate among theologians and philosophers; and eventually a group of 'Young Hegelians' split off from the orthodox Hegelian school. Strauss raised the issue of the conflict between the Christian faith and modern science: reason rebelled against the authority of the churches. The critique of the ecclesiastical principle of bondage was followed by the critique of political bondage. The philosophical Young Hegelians also became the political Left Hegelians.

We can judge the impact made by the politically committed young writers from the reactions of those who opposed them. Although the writer Franz Grillparzer was full of contempt for the political writers of Young Germany, he admitted they possessed a commendable quality which 'at the moment is very much absent in Germany, . . . namely honesty, albeit a clumsy honesty'.[18] At first Heinrich Heine, like many German romantics, scoffed at the idea of the 'muses' performing patriotic services 'almost like the market women of freedom'.[19] But only a few years later he too had been infected by political enthusiasm and began to write *Zeitgedichte*, or topical poems:[20]

> The virgin Europe is betrothed
> To the most beautiful genius of freedom.
> They lie in each other's arms,
> They revel in their first embrace.

Looking back on this period, he wrote to Rahel Varnhagen:[21]

> The new generation will enjoy and be active in the visible; we, the old generation, bowed humbly before the invisible. . . . The millennium of the romantics is at an end, and I was its last fable king. . . . You, like me, have helped to bury the old epoch and act as a midwife for the new.

In order to illustrate fully the intellectual environment in which Marx grew up, let me add to the above comments of contemporaries the judgment of a modern historian:[22]

> The magnitude of the liberating energy which at the time emanated from Germany is shown by the influence it had on the young Jacob Burckhardt. Even he, the Swiss who tended towards scepticism and pessimism, was enraptured, carried away by a noble intoxication, so that in retrospect it appeared to him as if he had lived only then, with young people whose views he did not share.

Goethe would probably have been pleased with a young generation that showed such delight in the sensuous; but he would have been repelled by its political radicalism. Heine sensed the unpredictability of the forces unleashed. 'Yes, we brought it to life, and now we are frightened', he wrote in the same letter in which he spoke of his role in the birth of the new epoch. The change in attitude was unprecedentedly radical, and the descent from the contemplative heights of poetry into harsh political reality was unprecedentedly sudden.

Chapter two

Marx's philosophical apprenticeship

First political studies

Marx began his academic study in 1835, the year in which the books of Gervinus and Strauss appeared. In the second semester he transferred to the University of Berlin, which even after Hegel's death was still regarded as the centre of intellectual life in Germany. Besides studying law he attended lectures on political history and literary criticism. He also wrote poems to his fiancée, Jenny von Westphalen. The philosophy of Hegel fascinated him: at first its 'grotesque craggy melody did not appeal to me', but after a year's study in which 'I got to know Hegel from beginning to end, together with most of his disciples, I became even more firmly bound to the modern world philosophy from which I had thought to escape.'[1] He remained bound, like Engels, to Hegelian philosophy all his life.

While at Berlin he became a member of the *Doktorklub*, where radical Young Hegelians discussed philosophical and political issues. He quickly gained the respect of the other members of the group. The ideas of the *Doktorklub* became more and more radical in response to the political events of the day. Prussia was still living on the glory of the reforms and the wars of liberation, and even on its reputation for enlightened government acquired under Frederick the Great. Altenstein, the minister for education, promoted Hegelian philosophy and permitted the academic appointments of Ruge (who had been arrested as a 'demagogue' in 1830) and the anti-clerical Bruno Bauer. But in 1837 the new king of Hanover, supported by Prussia, set aside the liberal constitution. In protest seven eminent professors from the University of Göttingen refused to take the oath of loyalty. They were summarily dismissed. The show-piece of liberalism had been discarded, and the 'most repulsive despotism stands revealed for all the world to see', as Marx observed.[2]

One year after the events in Hanover and after the German diet in Frankfurt had banned the works of Young Germany, August Cieszkowski coined the slogan of 'the descent of philosophy from the heights of theory into the fields of practice'.[3] Philosophy, which Hegel had compared to the 'owl of Minerva' spreading its wings only with the falling of dusk, became for Marx the 'lightning of thought' ushering in the new age.[4]

But as early as 1840, when he was writing his doctoral dissertation, Marx progressed from philosophical theory to political practice in a manner which set him apart from his fellow Young Hegelians. Both he and they were 'liberals', but whereas for the Young Hegelians the realization of freedom was a moral task, Marx insisted that it was a historical necessity. A moral justification of political demands was 'simple ignorance'. Instead, the contradiction between reality and Hegel's idea of freedom should be viewed objectively as an 'inverted relationship of philosophy to the world'. And the necessary dialectical 'turn-about' from the contemporary political state — in which negativity existing in itself has become negation — into a future free state should be seen under this aspect of the inverted relationship. Marx adopted the Hegelian dialectical method — 'the torrent which . . . tears down the independent forms' — not to justify the course of history in a quietistic manner, as Hegel had done, but to change it through political activity. The discussion of Epicurean philosophy in his dissertation was to show that there are 'nodal points' in history:[5]

> moments when philosophy turns its eyes to the external world, and no longer apprehends it, but, as a practical person, weaves, as it were, intrigues with the world. . . . So philosophy casts its regard behind it . . . when its heart is set on creating a world; . . . as Prometheus, having stolen fire from heaven, begins to build houses and to settle upon the earth, so philosophy turns against the world of appearance.

Marx's revolutionary spirit, already apparent in his doctoral dissertation, was expressed some years later, when he had become a communist, in the striking comment that 'philosophers have until now *interpreted* the world in various ways; the point is to *change* it'.[6]

Marx finished his dissertation in 1841, and he intended to embark upon an academic career. But events thwarted his hopes. In the previous year both the king of Prussia and his liberal minister of education had died. Although the new king, Friedrich Wilhelm IV, proclaimed an amnesty for all political prisoners upon his accession to the throne, he soon afterwards began to expel the 'pantheistic dragon-seed' of the Hegelians from his universities. Bruno Bauer, among others, was dismissed. Denied the possibility of gaining an academic post, Marx accepted an offer to become the editor of the new *Rheinische Zeitung* in the autumn of 1842. He came into conflict with the censorship laws almost immediately. According to official Prussian documents (discovered much later), the censor reported to Berlin that Marx's 'ultra-democratic opinions are in utter contradiction with the principles of the Prussian State'.[7] Marx tried in vain to keep clear of the stumbling-block of censorship: he was forced to leave the paper only five months after his appointment. After the suppression of the *Rheinische Zeitung* he was caricatured in the popular press as 'Prometheus bound'. He had not lost hope, however. The paper's suppression was a 'definite advance of political consciousness', he wrote to Ruge at the time.[8]

Even though his material existence which he had sought to secure for his marriage was once again in ruins, he accepted the blow with composure: 'It is truly fortunate that scandals of a public nature make it impossible for a man of character to be irritated over private ones.'[9] At this point Ruge, who was planning to start a journal in Paris, suggested to Marx that he take on the editorship. Marx accepted, and he was at last in a position to get married. In 1843 he moved to Paris to prepare the new journal, the *Deutsch-Französische Jahrbücher*.

Discovery of the 'European importance' of communism

Marx was confronted for the first time with economic problems while covering debates in the Rhineland Provincial Assembly for the *Rheinische Zeitung*. It is a strange coincidence that his editorial colleague, Moses Hess, tried to convert him to socialism at this particular time. Marx immersed himself in the new ideas and studied them thoroughly. Did socialism provide the chance to abolish political bondage and social misery? A few months later he wrote in the paper that communism was not only important for France and England, but that it had a 'European importance'. Nevertheless, he dissociated himself from communism. He could not accept that communist ideas 'in their present form' possessed even theoretical reality; consequently he could not 'desire their practical realisation'. He concluded his article with the announcement that he would subject communist ideas to 'a thoroughgoing criticism'.[10]

But what did the theory and practice of communist ideas consist of? Since they originated as a countermovement to modern capitalism, they must be considered in connection with its development in modern society.

Chapter three

Modern capitalism

Early unrestrained capitalism

Modern capitalism differs from all other forms of capitalism, which has existed at all times, in the rational form of the economy: in the separation of household and business, the rational organization of businesses, rational accounting, and the rational attitude to work. It owes its dynamic development to this rational form of organization. The traditional economic forms of manorial agriculture and the guild system were gradually dissolved when the artisans within the guild became merchants and distributors and the landed gentry dependent on sheep-farming became purveyors of wool. These two groups pushed through legislation in the English parliament which was aimed to free the market from the restrictions imposed by the feudal and guild system and the protectionist mercantile system. This resulted in a social upheaval that affected, above all, the peasants and the craftsmen: once their bonds of feudal duty were dissolved, the peasants were driven off the common lands; and once the protective structure of the guild system was destroyed, the small masters and journeymen became impoverished.

The invention of the spinning-machine and the steam-engine towards the end of the eighteenth century sparked a truly revolutionary development. The use of the steam-engine made mining more efficient, especially the mining of the coal required for the smelting of iron. This in turn produced the preconditions for revolutionary changes in textile and metal production. The affluent class of traders and merchants that had accumulated capital after the dissolution of the medieval economic system was able to appropriate the new machines. But at the other end of the social spectrum the emancipated but impoverished peasants and craftsmen were forced to sell their labour to the factory-owners in order to survive. The number of factories multiplied rapidly and new machines were installed — and thousands of workers were almost literally shackled to the machines and incarcerated in the factories. The industrial revolution had begun.

But why did it begin in Britain, when after all there was an even greater accumulation of capital in Spain owing to the imports of precious metals from the colonies? Max Weber found the reason for this in the 'Protestant ethic'. The Calvinist doctrine of predestination, by implying that economic success is a mark of God's favour, impelled the Puritans in England to be both industrious and ascetic. This produced the methodical and rational way of life that prepared the ground for the rational economic attitude and the specifically capitalist concept of business. The Puritan entrepreneurs considered themselves merely the custodians of the wealth granted by God, and they despised its enjoyment. In capitalist activity they saw a duty, a divine calling in which the person exists for the sake of the business and not the other way around. Weber described the idea of money-making as an end combined with a strict avoidance of all the natural pleasures of life paradoxically but accurately as 'worldly asceticism'.[1] But his thesis that the ethic of worldly asceticism produced the spirit of capitalism even *before* does not wish to suggest (as is often assumed) that it *caused* the development of capitalism, but rather that the spirit of the professional ethic acted as an incentive to economic development. The pressure — unmitigated by any confession — of the Puritan's question as to whether he was chosen or damned encouraged the ascetic way of life required by the capitalist system because it provided a very specific and significant psychological reward for thrift.

The practical consequences of this world-view are evident in, for instance, Daniel Defoe's *Robinson Crusoe*, which articulated the glorification of work and success. Defoe also wrote a typical pamphlet in which he argued that charity was detrimental because it hindered production, and that employment of the poor was detrimental because it created overproduction. Here Puritanism is merely carried to its logical conclusion, for when the successful man is *ipso facto* among the 'chosen', the unsuccessful man must be among the damned and should therefore be left to his own devices. Thus Defoe could write "Tis the Men that *wont work*, not the Men that *can get no work*, which makes the numbers of our Poor.'[2]

While a few accumulated unprecedented wealth, the masses became proletarianized and demoralized. The population of England, which had remained stable for centuries, quadrupled between 1700 and 1850, even with large-scale emigration. Industrial expansion transformed the towns into squalid and unhealthy slums. The proletarian masses were forced to work fourteen hours a day or even longer for starvation wages; women and children slaved themselves to death; and children leading vagabond lives were locked up in workhouses and often cruelly treated. The human deprivation of the working class was no less terrifying than its material misery. The worker on the machine lost any relation to his product (which even the most menial craftsman had possessed). Labour was degraded to a commodity. Working-class children received no education, many vegetated without family names in the slums. At the time when Marx and Engels published their *Communist Manifesto* Disraeli noted that Britain was divided into 'two nations'.[3]

Classical political economy

The science of economics, which originated in the attempt to analyse the new economic system, has its roots in the natural law theory of the Middle Ages. The Christian schoolmen accepted the concepts of the just price and the guaranteed livelihood as 'natural' in the economic sphere. This theory, derived from the truth of divine revelation, was seriously shaken during the Renaissance, when the battle for the affirmation of *this* world against the demands of the other world was fought intellectually. The earliest exponents of the modern secular natural law theory — Hobbes and Locke — agreed, despite many differences between them, in principle on the rejection of the Christian concept of 'fallen nature'. They condemned the Christian view of the natural order as unnatural and instead posited free competition as the natural state of affairs.

The theoreticians of the free market economy were not economists in the strict sense but instead philosophers. The Enlightenment philosophers believed in a natural order of things which could be explained by reason. Leibniz presupposed a 'pre-established harmony' in the universe, and Kant presupposed a 'natural purposiveness' in political society. Analogously, Adam Smith, the first of the classical economists, presupposed the existence of a 'hidden hand' in the economy.[4]

Smith's *Inquiry into the Nature and Causes of the Wealth of Nations*, published in 1776, is justly regarded as a classic, not because it formulated original ideas but because it summarized the then prevalent view of the sources of the new wealth. Smith's demand for economic freedom was inspired by, and an extension of, the British tradition of political freedom. His arguments advocating a free market as an element of the free play of the forces of nature and condemning the mercantilist monopolies of the crown are as much political and moral arguments as they are economic. Because he thought within this political tradition, his theories do not add up to a sanctioning of an economic free-for-all but present the freedom of the individual in the economic and political sphere in conjunction with a responsibility for the common good. Smith was imbued with the spirit of the English merchants who compared themselves, not without reason, to Roman citizens. He subordinated self-interest to the patriotic 'martial spirit', and the egoistic interests of society to the national interest of the state. Defence, he argued, is more important than 'opulence'.[5] When monopolies restrict free competition they are to be eliminated through state intervention. The rate of interest is to be regulated by the state. The lower classes should be educated in state schools lest the 'nobler parts' of the human character be 'obliterated and extinguished'.[6] Only through education will the masses be able to form their own opinions, as is appropriate to a free nation.

Smith's moral philosophy provided the foundation for his claim that self-interest can be reconciled with a commitment to the welfare of the state. Even when his attempt to reconcile the two mainsprings of sympathy and self-interest did not reach the level of Kant's practical philosophy, he was still more a political philosopher in the tradition of the Stoa and Kant than the economists who succeeded him.

Whereas Smith still saw the whole man, his successors, Say, Ricardo and Malthus, knew only the self-interested *homo oeconomicus*. They abstracted and limited the notion of the free play of natural forces, which had been a guiding principle for the Enlightenment philosophers, into an economic law as deterministic as Newton's laws of physics. David Ricardo's discovery of the laws regulating wages and governing 'the happiness of far the greatest part of every community' was without a doubt a major scientific breakthrough.[7] But the deterministic way in which he and others formulated the economic laws precluded human freedom and reduced active man to the homuncule of *homo oeconomicus*. The nobility of the human character and the welfare of the community, the standards which Smith had always applied, were forgotten. The economic laws transformed human dignity into exchange-value. Moreover, the 'happiness' invoked by Ricardo in his elegant formulation of economic laws was enjoyed not by the great majority of the people but only by a small elite.

When Smith had studied the economy, in the initial phase of the factory system, more attention was paid to the origin of the wealth of the factory-owners than to the misery of the working class, which in any case was then still quite small. But in the period between the publication of Smith's *Wealth of Nations* and Ricardo's *Principles of Political Economy and Taxation* (1817), the number of factories and the size of the proletariat had increased manifold. The tenor of the two books differs accordingly. In Ricardo's analysis the masses are forced to sell their labour according to the 'natural price', which is that price 'necessary to enable the labourers, one with another, to subsist and to perpetuate their race, without either increase or diminution'.[8] The law regulating wages states that the price of labour cannot exceed the subsistence level of the worker. It cannot rise because the accumulation of capital is already put at risk as a result of the falling rate of profit. Higher labour costs would only reduce production and so make it impossible to maintain the subsistence and perpetuation of the labour force.

Thomas Malthus, arguing along the same lines as Ricardo, had a harsh fate in store for the worker who could not find work. Science, he decided, could reply to the question only as follows: if society no longer requires a man's labour, then he has 'no claim of right' to any subsistence.[9] He deleted this remarkable prescription in later editions of his *Essay on the Principle of Population*, presumably because it was thought to be too offensive. However, contrary to appearance, he was not a cynic; he was in fact very much concerned with the lot of the poor. One of the first to recognize the abject poverty of the working classes (the obverse of the optimistic belief in the 'happiness' achieved in the free economy), he wrote the book in order to research a means of 'essentially and permanently bettering the condition of the poor'.[10] Like Ricardo, he regarded the economic laws as immutable laws of nature, 'the laws of God', which brook no interference.[11] But if, as Malthus hoped, the poor could be made to realize the true nature of their situation, they could extricate themselves from their misery. Thus, if they defer marriage and exercise 'moral restraint' (i.e. sexual restraint), the poor will produce less children. This is the prerequisite for an improvement, since 'Withholding the supplies of labour is the only possible way of really raising its price.'[12] But those unfortunates who are too many in the world and who are not needed by society have no right to demand employment or maintenance; they should receive assistance from private charity and public institutions.[13]

The deterministic interpretation of the newly discovered economic laws had grave consequences. This system of laws established that wages could not rise above subsistence level, and it discountenanced any intervention in the laws of nature it had established. These principles determined the scope of the new science of economics of the classical school no less than the Marxist school. They also fascinated public opinion: a parliamentary report of 1810, for instance, stated that 'No interference of the legislature with the freedom of trade . . . can take place without violating general principles of the first importance to the prosperity and happiness of the community.'[14] State intervention (e.g. by means of a poor law) was considered detrimental to society. The state was no longer placed above society but subordinated to it. This liberal ideal of the non-interventionist state can be appropriately described as a 'night-watchman state' (a phrase attributed to Ferdinand Lasalle).

The first social reforms

In the first half of the nineteenth century the British parliament enacted the first social reforms. They constituted the beginnings of a system of social legislation which gradually altered the character of competitive society. It speaks for the British virtue of compromise that these reforms were adopted in defiance of the maxim of *laissez-faire*, which appeared to have a scientific foundation; but what is most remarkable is that they were adopted against the opposition of the bourgeoisie, which defended its economic interests uncompromisingly and saw no need for reform — success and failure being attributable in the Puritan world-view to individual application and fate.

The planned reforms proposed by Smith suffered a setback when the London riots of 1780 frightened off the bourgeoisie. These riots, a protest against the emancipation of the Catholics that degenerated into drunken orgies and anarchy, temporarily thwarted any policy of social and political reform. The Napoleonic wars detracted fully from the need for reforms. Agitation resumed after 1815, but demonstrations were ruthlessly dealt with by the authorities.

Eventually, however, a number of forces combined successfully to push through reforms. Ricardo's opponents and his disciples (e.g. Godwin and Thompson) inferred from the labour theory of value that the worker is entitled to a share of the product of his labour — a corollary which Ricardo himself had never recognized. Economists thus undermined the immutability and conservatism of their own laws. The utilitarians agitated for reform with the argument of the greatest happiness for the greatest number. Many others provided moral arguments for improving the lot of the demoralized and pauperized masses: John Stephens, the Methodist preacher; William Wilberforce, the abolitionist; Robert Owen, the utopian socialist; and Charles Kingsley and Frederick Maurice, both Christian socialists. The laments over the loss of the old virtues in the vulgar and materialistic new society expressed by Byron, Shelley, Coleridge, and Carlyle indirectly influenced public opinion. The Young England group around Disraeli translated Burke's critique of abstract political principles on to the economy.[15] They also proposed the integration of the proletarian masses into the community. Dickens's description of the wretched social conditions shook the social conscience of the affluent bourgeoisie and indirectly lent support to the reform movement (he advocated the establishment of private charities rather than state intervention). Thus the most diverse groups united in a movement proposing extensive reforms to control the excesses of unrestrained competition.

One of the first reforms, enacted in 1819, regulated the reduction of working hours for children in the cotton mills; the repeal of the

Combination Acts (1824) legalized the organization of the workers in trade unions; the Reform Bill of 1832 extended the franchise, albeit not as radically as had been hoped. Also in 1832 a budget for education was passed for the first time, although it was only a fraction of the sum allocated for the maintenance of the royal stables. But the reforms were too minimal to satisfy the working class, and the Chartist movement gave expression to the growing dissatisfaction. Parliamentary and private inquiries were set up. Their reports revealed for the first time the horrifying working conditions in the factories and the social misery in the slums. (Later, Marx was to use these reports as the raw material for his studies.) These reports, the revolutionary class movement of the Chartists, a serious economic crisis, and the co-operative experiments and educational work of Robert Owen, prompted further legislation after 1841. A law restricting the working day to ten hours, a poor law, and the establishment of the Public Health Board, were approved. Peel, prime minister at the time, also revived income tax — which had been in force for a short period during the Napoleonic wars — partly to finance the new social services. In 1846 the controversial Corn Laws were repealed.

The social and moral condition of the working class improved slowly. Around the middle of the century wages began to rise as migration to the industrial towns dropped drastically and exports increased. The gap between the 'two nations' was gradually bridged. The new social laws stole the revolutionary movement's thunder. Therefore, when revolution broke out in 1848 in France and spread across Europe, Feargus O'Connor, the feared revolutionary who had split off from the Chartists, assured the government that his followers would not incite to violence.

Chapter four

The emergence of socialism

British and French socialism

More or less concurrent with the first attempts to curb the excesses of
the free market economy by political reforms, a movement which
aspired to transform capitalist society as a whole emerged independently
in Britain and France: socialism. The first socialists (Owen, Saint-Simon,
Fourier) proceeded like Smith and Ricardo from the Enlightenment
view that man is capable of establishing a natural society. But they
resented the idea that self-interest constituted the natural social order,
for it dissolved social unity into atomized and self-centred individuals.
Opposed to a society founded on individualism, they posited as an ideal
of natural society the social co-operation of all producers, be they
workers or capitalists, be they productive in agriculture, industry, or
the arts. They comprised these disparate groups within the term 'industrious classes' (Owen) or '*industriels*' (Saint-Simon). Some socialists
imagined the emergence of the new society in small co-operative
associations variously called 'villages of co-operation' (Owen), 'phalan-
stères' (Fourier), and 'Icaria' (Cabet); others, especially the followers of
St Simon, strove for a reorganization of the whole economy.

The term 'socialist' was intended to contrast the new society with
the old society and its individualist principle of the free market
economy. When in the *Essay on Natural Law* Hegel referred to systems
of natural law 'which are called anti-socialistic and posit the being of
the individuals as the primary and supreme thing', he had in mind the
natural law theories of Hobbes.[1] He used the negative concept of 'anti-
socialistic' by way of contrast to the positive concept of public welfare.
Its usage must have been relatively common, since Hegel saw no need
to define it. The positive term 'socialist', which Hegel himself never
employed, suggested itself for the new society. It first appeared in the
1820s.

In Britain and France, where the political revolutions had divorced
the economy from the sphere of government and state control, the

independence of the economy was as self-evident to the socialists as it was to the political economists. Neither desired to regulate the economy by artificial restrictive practices; but the socialists intended to replace the free market economy held together by the blind self-regulation of individual interests by a new society in which the associated producers would co-operate on the basis of rational regulation. And therefore they did not see the foundation of the new society in 'nationalization' — this concept appeared much later in Germany — but in 'socialization', because the producers themselves, not the state, were to achieve the transformation of individualistic society. Whereas the ideal of classical political philosophy from Plato to Smith and Hegel had been participation in public life (and in case of emergency, in war), socialist philosophy championed the peaceful union of all working people for the common good.

Long before Marx and Engels, then, the early socialists, like the *laissez-faire* economists, showed little interest in the political state. They considered economic reform more important than political reform. That is why Owen did not participate in the political movement of Chartism. Saint-Simon experienced how between 1789 and 1815 the French constitution was altered ten times, while industrial society was developing quite independently of political changes. A political constitution seemed to him a peripheral legal form; and the parliamentary system was merely a manifestation of the intermediate phase between the feudal system and the socialist society of the future. In socialist society politicians would be replaced by engineers, bankers, self-nominated priests, and above all by men of science who were supposed to supervise the development of the new society through 'positive science'. Although Saint-Simon first formulated the concept of scientific socialism, his socialism lacked the historical perspective subsequently added by Marx. Saint-Simon was more influenced by the mechanistic spirit of modern natural science, which is still influential today in what is called 'social engineering'.

As we saw earlier, the social reformers had inferred from Ricardo's labour theory of value that the worker is entitled to a share of his own labour. The socialists went further and demanded the abolition of the property of all non-working people, those parasites who lived off the exploitation of the labour of others. Proudhon's essay *What is Property?* (1840) caused a sensation because in its provocative answer — 'property is theft' — all unearned property was equated with theft. But most socialists had no objections to the property of the working entrepreneur, and they even allowed the entrepreneur to have a larger income than the worker without capital. They knew nothing of a class struggle between capital and labour. Quite the opposite. They believed that once the industrialists had been convinced with rational arguments, they could together with them build the new society. Owen, himself a successful textile factory-owner, wanted to demonstrate with his model factory that productivity would increase and employees would take an interest in their work and in the maintenance of the machines when they had a share in the business, the education of their children was guaranteed, and working hours were reduced. The first generation of socialists were active during the post-Napoleonic restoration of the rule of the reactionary aristocracy. They still fought together with the bourgeoisie against the remnants of feudalism, especially in France.

From socialism to communism in France

In France the transition from feudalism to the system of free enterprise did not occur through centuries of struggle, as in England, but overnight in a National Assembly decision to annul all feudal rights and privileges (on 4 August 1789). The French bourgeoisie, which took over from the *ancien régime* economically in 1789 and politically in 1830, did not adopt the ideals of the old upper class, as the English bourgeoisie had done in the previous century. Nor did they perceive the capitalist profit motive as an ascetic professional duty. Lacking any sense of tradition, they shamelessly exploited their newly acquired position of power to pursue particular interests — 'enrich yourselves!' — and prevent any reforms intended to improve the conditions of the working class. As a result, anti-bourgeois sentiment grew not only among the workers and peasants who were being exploited by urban wholesalers and financiers but also among intellectuals. The intellectuals, including many not committed to socialism, despised the baseness of the bourgeoisie (this rift between intelligentsia and bourgeoisie still exists in France today). The great French writers wanted to expose the bitter truth about their society. Balzac and Stendhal depicted with total contempt the new world of the bourgeoisie in which, to quote the protagonist of Balzac's novel *Old Goriot*, 'The rich lived beyond the jurisdiction of law and public opinion, and found in success the *ultima ratio mundi*.'[2] Honoré Daumier caricatured the vulgar faces of the bourgeoisie. Those writers who did not want to make common cause with the proletariat because they were repelled by raw fists (e.g. Mallarmé, Verlaine, Baudelaire, Rimbaud) escaped into bohemianism and sought a substitute for religious salvation in the esoteric cult of pure art. But even if they did not actively take part in the socialist movement, they did sympathize with it. Baudelaire, for instance, had fought on the barricades during the revolution of 1848 but withdrew from politics after the disappointment of the revolution's collapse.

The old socialism lived on only among the Fabians in Britain, where state reforms and the realization of Owen's ideas in trade unions and co-operatives began to mitigate class distinctions. On the whole British socialists rejected the millenarian and revolutionary aspect of socialism. They retained the notion of a gradual and peaceful reorganization of society with the aim of eliminating existing inequalities in the distribution of wealth.[3]

In France, however, the class struggle intensified. Although the second generation of socialists did not produce works of the same scientific and philosophical calibre as their intellectual predecessors, they did infuse a new revolutionary element into the socialist idea. Saint-Amand Bazard, a disciple of Saint-Simon, postulated the inevitability of class struggle between the propertied class and the working class as early as 1829. A book on the forgotten communist Babeuf conspiracy of 1797 published by Filippo Buonarotti, a comrade-in-arms of Babeuf, exercised a great influence. Had Babeuf not shown that the political revolution must be completed by a social revolution? Impressed by the arguments in this book, many republicans converted to Babeuvism. Louis Blanc, who joined Buonarotti, demanded the right to work in his essay *Organisation du travail*, which met with a lively response. (It influenced the organization of a work-relief scheme — the 'national workshops' — during the revolution of 1848.) Auguste Blanqui introduced into socialist literature the concept of dictatorship as a temporary, and necessary, phase. In the early 1840s, the revolutionary socialists began to call themselves 'communists' to distinguish themselves from the old socialists.[4]

Heine's account in *Lutezia*, written in 1843, provides an insight into the socialist ferment of those days. He portrayed the communists, 'the only party in France deserving attention', as[5]

> a small community, reminiscent of the Christian church in the first century, at present despised and persecuted, but which still produces a propaganda with a zeal and dark destructive will that also reminds one of those Galilean beginnings. . . . Sooner or later the scattered family of St Simon and the whole . . . of the Fourierists will join the growing army of communism. They will then properly articulate the raw needs, taking on the role of the Fathers of the Church, as it were.

Ruge made a similar point in a letter from Paris written at about the same time. He reported that one heard only two topics of conversation: 'first, the downfall of the bourgeoisie; and second, the dawn of the millennium of true freedom and equality'.[6]

During these years, when communist ideas were discussed in newspapers and pamphlets, at social gatherings and in cafes, the young Marx arrived in Paris. He was already aware of the European importance of communism and was convinced that the revolution was imminent.

German communism

The interest in communism shown by Marx and Engels was not an isolated instance in Germany. In the 1830s Eduard Gans, a student of Hegel, had propounded ideas derived from Saint-Simon, while other writers had taken up the ideas of Fourier. Many intellectuals published communist pamphlets. Between 1840 and 1842 only eight socialist publications appeared in Germany, but between 1843 and 1845 as many as fifty-five.[7] But apart from those who are known to us from the history of the socialist movement (Weitling, Büchner, Grün, Hess, Lüning, Becker, and others), there were many respected politicians, writers and intellectuals who in their youth had been communists: Johannes von Miquel, for instance, was a member of the Communist League in the 1840s and subsequently became Prussian minister of finance. Many intellectuals had communist leanings: Eduard Lasker, later a liberal member of the Reichstag; Rudolf Virchow, the anatomist and liberal politician; Bettina von Arnim, author of *Goethes Briefwechsel mit einem Kinde*; and Richard Wagner and his friend August Röckel. This is now forgotten because their revolutionary enthusiasm dissipated after the collapse of the revolution of 1848 and when a growing prosperity in the 1850s gave rise to more optimistic ideas of progress. Even so, in the 1840s, when Marx and Engels embraced communism, socialist and communist ideas had gained wide currency within German intellectual circles.

Political and social radicalism were not yet divorced in Germany as they were in France and Britain. Feuerbach declared himself a communist in 1845, then joined the bourgeois republicans in 1848. Some liberal politicians briefly pinned their hopes on the emerging working class because they doubted the ability of the philistine bourgeoisie to galvanize itself into political action. Until the revolution of 1848, which proved to be a watershed, many politicians felt united in a great coalition of the left. Marx himself urged the workers to participate in the revolution of the German bourgeoisie in 1848 because he thought the proletariat was too weak for independent action.

The German socialists and communists differed from their British and French counterparts in their blissful ignorance of both the functioning of the modern capitalist economy and the plight and role of the proletariat. 'Political economy', Marx noted as late as 1873, 'remains a foreign science in Germany up to this very moment'; it was interpreted by its professors 'in the sense of the petty bourgeois world surrounding them, and therefore misinterpreted'.[8] The early German socialists misinterpreted the economy and idealized the proletariat in the same way. Karl Grün, one of the most prominent socialists of the period, expected the proletariat to inaugurate the epoch of a 'new true culture' that would achieve 'the salvation of humanity'.[9] Richard Wagner believed that the communist revolution was 'The ever-rejuvenating, ever-creating Life . . . the dream, the balm, the hope of all those who suffer.'[10] Moses Hess, the socialist teacher of Marx and Engels, stressed that German socialism 'did not spring from the needs of the stomach' and was unique in its inclusion of the 'idea of humanism'.[11]

In the *Communist Manifesto* Marx would ridicule the German literati who 'completely emasculated' the French socialist and communist literature because they were more interested in the unreal 'truth of man in general' than in the 'true' economic conditions.[12] Communist ideas were emasculated in Germany because the German socialists and communists had been reared on the abstract speculative tradition of philosophy; consequently they did not know the first thing about economics and politics. They had all studied at German universities and had been exposed only to German philosophy. Their opponents saw the differences between them and the British and French socialists clearly. The sociologist Wilhelm Riehl pointed out that the German communists had become 'the prophets of the fourth estate' with their 'cosmopolitan philanthropy' and 'poetic and philosophical universalism reconciling all social differences'.[13]

What disturbed the German humanists about the development of capitalism was not so much the social tensions it produced (these were as yet hardly noticeable in Germany), but more the threat it posed to the intellectual and spiritual tradition. At the very time that British economists welcomed the introduction of advanced machines as a contribution to technological progress, romantic German economists, Adam Müller foremost among them, portrayed the elementary division of labour as the root of all evil. Goethe feared the spread of mechanization: 'It is like a storm brewing, slowly, slowly; but it has taken its course: one day the storm will break, and it will hit hard.'[14] A few years before his death he suggested that 'We may be the last representatives . . . of an era that will not easily come again. . . . Wealth and speed are what the world admires, and what all are bent on.'[15]

For the German intellectuals the striving for wealth implied the end of the old epoch. They condemned the division of labour and feared mechanization because spiritualism, 'living from within' (Goethe), could not be reconciled with the new rational attitudes of capitalism. The English conceived of the capitalist drive as a divine command, but the Germans considered it degrading. The contrast between the two traditions is strikingly illustrated in a controversy between two Swiss writers, Gottfried Keller, a Lutheran from Zurich, and Jeremias Gotthelf, a Calvinist from Berne. Keller objected to the fact that in Gotthelf's novels the pious man is always economically successful, for 'There is nothing in the Gospel which says that the devout Christian should be a

rich Bernese farmer.'[16] The fear of economic liberalism was widespread
in Germany during the period leading up to the revolution of 1848. It
was felt not only by the humanist and romantic intellectuals but also
by the bourgeoisie. The revolution failed in Germany partly because the
bourgeoisie, despite its political liberalism, did not desire a liberalization of the economy and consequently participated only half-heartedly
in the revolution.

In Britain too the forces of tradition had defended themselves
against modern capitalism. The political and intellectual debate between
the conservatives — Bolingbroke, Swift, Pope — and the progressives —
Walpole, Defoe, Mandeville — was illustrative of this struggle. The
former defended the old organic society against the encroachment of
the capitalist free market society. In Britain, however, the declining
organic society was not represented by an inward-looking pre-capitalist
petty bourgeoisie, as in Germany, but by financiers who wished to
preserve mercantilist monopoly capitalism. In Germany the difference
between the old world and the new was so enormous that capitalism
was feared and thought to be sinister.

Goethe was one of the few Germans who took their political and
economic responsibilities as seriously as their writing. He was a government minister in Weimar and administrator of the iron-ore mine at
Ilmenau. And in *Wilhelm Meister* he discussed economic problems
(which already went too far for the romantics). The development of
capitalism still distressed him, however; he feared it but resigned
himself to it. The romantics, on the other hand, refused to acknowledge
the inevitability of capitalism; they wanted to roll back the wheel of
history. Some seriously hoped that the factories would be closed down
and the masses would return to agricultural work. Because the romantics could not cope intellectually with the fateful development of
capitalism, their attitude became pathological — 'the romantic' is 'the
diseased', Goethe told Eckermann[17] — and they branded capitalism as
Western and Jewish. Those later romantics who turned to politics
substituted a narrow-minded nationalism for the cosmopolitan humanism
of Lessing and their predecessors. Such unrealistic sentiments were to
dominate the whole spectrum of German intellectual life during the
nineteenth century. Even respected scholars who should have known
better fell prey to this romanticism: Werner Sombart, for instance,
contrasted the Germans as an 'Heroic people' with the English as a
'Trading people'.[18] The nineteenth-century German writers who glorified the old *Bürgertum* failed to notice that they had 'slept through
the transformation of the burgher into the bourgeois', as Thomas
Mann observed aptly.[19]

The German socialists and communists of the 1840s drew from the
same intellectual tradition. They missed, even more so than Goethe

and Hegel, the significance of capitalism as the inexorable force of the age. While the romantics tried nostalgically to escape from it into the past, the socialists ignored it and pointed to a better future. Marx was no exception in this respect. He related communism to the economic developments of the period only after Engels had introduced him to the economics of capitalist society.

In the *Economic and Philosophical Manuscripts* of 1844 Marx extricated himself fully from unrealistic romanticism. He retained the ideals of German humanism, from which he borrowed the concepts for a critique of capitalism and the formulation of the goal of communism. He quoted Shakespeare, who in *Timon of Athens* had called gold 'the common whore of mankind', and concluded:[20]

> A dwelling in the *light*, which Prometheus describes in
> Aeschylus as one of the great gifts through which he
> transformed savages into men, ceases to exist for the worker.

The religious element in communism

At this point a digression must be made to illustrate the aspect of socialism that gave it a special dynamic, namely its messianic or millenarian element. Before the advent of socialism, messianic expectation had inspired both the American and the French Revolution: the English Puritan colonists saw their experiment of the new commonwealth as a heaven-sent New Jerusalem; and the French revolutionaries may have considered themselves the descendants of the Roman citizens — their glorification of virtue was derived from classical political philosophy — but their belief in the realm of fraternity had its roots in the Bible.

The Biblical concept of salvation assigned to activity in the world a degree of importance which it did not possess outside the Judaeo-Christian tradition. It conferred on the West a specific dynamic. The belief in the kingdom of heaven was still a powerful spiritual force in the secularized eighteenth century. Franz Rosenzweig, himself a practising Jew, commented that 'The demands of the kingdom of God begin only now to be genuinely transformed into temporal demands. . . . Liberty, equality, and fraternity, the canons of faith, now become the slogans of the age.'[21] The idea of the natural world order was, like the idea of the natural order of the free economy, both a rational conception and the expression of a secularized messianic faith. This secularized faith was evident in the calls for economic and political liberalization. The question of free trade was for many of its advocates not so much an economic argument as a religious precept, a matter of faith. The same faith was evident in the political demands for liberty, equality, and fraternity. The religious character of the French Revolution and the priestly character of the Jacobins has been stressed by many historians. As de Tocqueville put it succinctly: 'The French Revolution operated in reference to this world in exactly the same manner as religious revolutions acted in view of the other world.'[22] The transformed faith was also the motive force in the philosophy of history of Lessing, Kant and Hegel, and later in Condorcet's belief in progress. 'It will come, it will certainly come, the time of consummation', when human reason will 'attain its full enlightenment', Lessing wrote in his *Education of the Human Race*.[23]

Religious enthusiasm also affected the founders of socialism. Owen's followers sang 'community is happiness, community is heaven'. Fourier expected that millions of people would become poets like Homer and mathematicians like Newton (indeed, much later Trotsky would go so far as to suggest that the average man would rise to the heights of Aristotle, Goethe and Marx[24]). Their rapturous hopes are evocative of the early Christians' belief in the apocalypse. The early socialists believed in the advent of the kingdom of humanity with the same religious fervour as once the Christian and Jewish sects had believed in the imminent kingdom of heaven. For them, as for Comte and Marx in the next generation, the concept of humanism possessed an almost explicitly millenarian significance. The conservative Lorenz von Stein, the first German to make a serious study of French socialism, noticed that the socialists hoped for 'the establishment, through the rule of labour, of the kingdom of heaven on earth. . . . Thus, socialism turns from a mere science . . . into a religion.'[25] It is no coincidence that many prominent German socialists − Grün, Becker and Feuerbach, to name but a few − had originally studied theology. Their religious feelings found a home in socialism. Wilhelm Weitling, the first German socialist, accepted communism as 'the Gospel' and 'the faith based on nature and the teachings of Christ'.[26] Mikhail Bakunin proclaimed 'the cause of stamping out all evil . . . with fire and sword'.[27] In the nineteenth-century United States, where the socialist movement did not gain a foothold because opportunities for material success were plenty, early Christian visions influenced some of the founders of the labour unions. Charles Litchman of the Knights of Labor prophesied that 'As God is mercy and love, in His own good time the toiler will be free.'[28] Instances of such 'religious' socialism can also be found in this century. Leonhard Ragaz, a Lutheran pastor, became a socialist because 'One cannot preach the New Heaven without preaching the New Earth at the same time.'[29] And André Gide turned to communism because he hoped it would fulfil the teachings of Christ after the Christian church had failed.[30] In conclusion, Arthur Koestler's description of an encounter with a young Jewish communist may be adduced to illustrate the powerful force of messianic expectation in communism. While travelling by boat from Haifa to Trieste in 1929, he made friends with a young girl. She had decided that 'The messiah of humanity is Lenin' and had left her kibbutz in Galilee to go to Soviet Russia, the promised land.[31]

The Jews, who had been expecting the Messiah for more than two millennia, were especially predestined to become the prophets of socialism. Above all, those Jews who had renounced Judaism endeavoured to give a new contemporary meaning to the traditional content of messianic expectation. The 'sole function' of the new (secular) kingdom of heaven was for Moses Hess 'the furtherance of human dignity'.[32] The young Marx saw in the modern proletariat a sphere with 'a universal character because of its universal suffering', whose redemption would require and entail 'the total redemption of humanity'.[33]

The relative predominance of Jews in the socialist movement can also be attributed to the special situation of the Jewish assimilation. Since the social position of the first generation of assimilated Jews in Europe was comparable to that of the Westernized liberals in Russia, Dostoyevsky's analysis of the psychology of the 'Westerners' may be adduced here to illustrate the psychology of the Jewish socialists. 'As soon as we Russians reach the shore', he wrote in *The Idiot*, 'we are so glad of it that we lose all sense of proportion'; the Russian liberal, to whom he was referring, 'has found his motherland at last . . . and rushes to kiss it!'.[34] Elsewhere he wondered why the majority of the Westernized intellectuals adopted the extreme left-wing views questioning the values of the very society they were striving to emulate. He explained this as the unconscious protest of the Russian soul against European culture, which 'in many of its manifestations had always . . . been hateful and had always been alien' to it; the Russian soul protested 'because it conserved in itself something loftier and better than that which it perceived through the window'.[35] The assimilated Jews felt the same ambivalence towards Western society.

A number of modern historians have tended, after the horrifying experiences of this century, to blame political messianism for the emergence of totalitarian systems.[36] This analysis is, however, too. simplistic. It is not religious enthusiasm as such that leads to terror but its correlation with dogmatism or demonism. Kierkegaard judged more accurately than these historians when he wrote that the strength in communism 'obviously is the same ingredient demonically potential in religiousness, even Christian religiousness'.[37] Kierkegaard defined 'demonic' as the drive for the absolute in a relative world. In this sense political fanatics are demonic, because they want to establish a perfect world on earth. They consider those of a different opinion to be misguided and try to convert them through coercion, 'to force them to be free' (Rousseau). The politician in whom the religious ingredient is not combined with the demonic lives, in contrast, in the tension between the religious goal and the relativities of this world. Kant expressed this tension when he observed that *summum bonum* can never be fully attained in this life, 'yet the progress towards it is possible and necessary'.[38] Weber reiterated this in his paradox of the politician who must reconcile in practice the irreconcilable imperatives of the 'ethic of intention' and the 'ethic of responsibility'.[39]

Religious motivation gives political action its strength. It leads to disaster only when it is combined with a dogmatic or demonic element. What causes both the Christian gospel of love and the socialist prophecy of the end of all oppression to produce their opposites is invariably a dogmatic abstraction: in the one case the doctrinaire falsification of Christ's command 'Go out into the highways and hedges, and compel them to come in' (Luke 14.23) into ecclesiastical coercion; in the other case the orthodox interpretation of the dialectical movement of history as a historical necessity which renders freedom and morality superfluous. This does not mean that from doctrine intolerance *must* develop, but that it *may* do so.

The 'advantage' of Marx's communism

We left Marx after he had discovered the importance of communism, even though he was still doubtful about its theory and practice. After a consideration of the communist ideas prevalent at the time we can understand his objections. The communist ideas encountered by Marx were also dependent on the hypothesizing and moralizing which he had observed and rejected in the ideas of his Young Hegelian friends. He had demanded of them to study objectively the contradictions of the given political reality in order to expose the historical necessity of the dialectical inversion. He reproached his communist predecessors and contemporaries in the same way for failing to recognize the historical conditions of the emancipation of the proletariat. However,[40]

> this very defect turns to the advantage of the new movement,
> for it means that we do not anticipate the new world with our
> dogmas but instead attempt to discover the new world through
> the critique of the old.

Finding the new world in a critique of the old required, in Marx's view, a study of the political state in the 'conflict between its ideal vocation and its actually existing premises. This internecine conflict within the political state enables us to infer the social truth.'[41] He was able to do this by applying Hegel's dialectical method in the analysis of society.

It was the knowledge of the dialectic which in his eyes constituted the 'advantage' of his brand of communism over all others. Marx's own formulation of communism can therefore only be understood in conjunction with the Hegelian dialectic.

Chapter five

The Hegelian dialectic

The rationalization of the dialectic

By means of the dialectical method Hegel succeeded in integrating the whole of Western philosophy into a closed rational system. At first, however, the dialectic was not inherently rational. In his early writings it expressed the 'mystery' of the 'reciprocal give and take' in the love of Romeo and Juliet. The dialectical unity in love was for the young Hegel 'a miracle which we cannot comprehend'.[1] Spirit (*Geist*) is differentiated from dead matter by this dialectic. In the world of matter the various parts are not connected and the whole is only the unity of the parts.

Man, as Hegel later said in the *Phenomenology of Spirit*, becomes man only in 'losing himself', by alienating himself (*sich entfremden*); 'for the self . . . without having alienated itself from itself, is without substance'.[2] We find the same idea in one of Goethe's poems:[3]

> And when you do not have
> This 'Die and Become!',
> You are only a dreary guest
> On a dark earth.

The dialectic became of paramount importance to Hegelian philosophy once it had been transformed into the cognitive method for the understanding of world-history. How Hegel succeeded in this can be indicated only very briefly in this context. Greek philosophy began with the attempt to advance from the sensuous and transient world to eternal and liberating being not through myth but through rational concepts. Time and again Western metaphysics has endeavoured to comprehend in thought the true essence of things behind their transient appearances. It was Kant's great achievement to establish the futility of such attempts. Finite consciousness is separated from the thing it perceives, Kant argued, subject is detached from object. The relationship of subject and object and the transcendental basis for their unity

[handwritten margin note: INADEQ. EXPLANATION]

remain an impenetrable mystery. But free will is independent and can reach the absolute denied to knowledge. Fichte took this further. He tried to invest theoretical reason with the same autonomy by conceiving it as self-consciousness. In self-consciousness the ego is the identity of subject and object. Therefore, he concluded, the object is not given to the ego from outside but posited by the ego itself. Hegel in turn proceeded from this and explained self-consciousness in terms of the dialectic which he had found in spirit. Spirit also developed in the dialectical movement of self-consciousness, from immediate subjective unity through division into subject and object to the unity of self-consciousness.

The transformation of the dialectic of the life of spirit into the act of cognition led to a rationalization of the dialectic. Whereas the dialectic was originally the medium explaining the secret of historical life, it now became a scientific method for the resolution of the mysterious relationship of subject and object, and ultimately the key to the resolution of all the mysteries of knowledge. Hegel was quite clear about this. In the introduction to the *Science of Logic* he wrote:[4]

> I know that it is the only true method. This is self-evident simply from the fact that it is not something distinct from its object and content; for it is the inwardness of the content, the dialectic which it possesses within itself, which is the mainspring of its advance. It is clear that no expositions can be accepted as scientifically valid which do not pursue the course of this method.

The implications of the rationalized dialectic

Hegel's rationalization of the dialectic has certain consequences which are also found in Marx, even though in his view the dialectic operates only in history. A rationalized dialectic implies, in short, 1 the hubris of a comprehensive explanation of history; 2 determinism; 3 hypostatization of one factor; and 4 the expectation of a harmonious synthesis.

1   The dialectical movement that resolves the mystery of knowledge also reveals for Hegel the secret of world-history. Because his philosophy is still rooted in the Biblical tradition of the divine purpose of history, the process of world-history is explained dialectically as follows: God 'resolves' to let nature go forth from him and to alienate himself from it, in order to find himself in it and achieve full self-consciousness.[5] In this scheme, logic is the exposition of God 'in his external essence before the creation of nature and the finite mind';

and the philosophy of history is the 'transition from the notion of God to his existence', that is, God, 'as living God, and still more as absolute spirit is known only in his *activity*'.[6]

Hegel never doubted that the purpose of the world-spirit can be apprehended in thought and that its true significance can be exactly explained. Kant, on the other hand, was aware of the limits of human knowledge, and asked whether nature had not treated man in a 'step-motherly fashion' in this matter. He thought a combination of humility and self-respect appropriate to man: 'The unsearchable wisdom by which we exist is not less worthy of admiration in what it has denied than in what it has granted.'[7] Hegel mocked Kant's 'false idea' of Christian humility and modesty.[8] Against it he set his claim that he could explain the world and its secrets in '*a system of totality*'.[9] A new tone entered philosophy — hubris. It can be found in Marx, who like Hegel was convinced he knew the secret of history, and also in his disciples from Lenin to Adorno (the latter explicitly justified Hegel's rebellion against 'the regressive and violent aspect of Kantian humility'[10]).

2   Kant perceived that if man could know God's will, he would have no choice but to obey — the course of history would be determined and freedom of will would be lost. Exactly that happened in Hegel's philosophy. He had to admit that 'individuals in general come under the category of means rather than ends'.[11] The individuals are mere instruments in the hands of the world-spirit; they 'produce and effect altogether differently from what they themselves intend and accomplish in the process of gratifying their own interests'.[12] As we shall see, Marx would demand in the same way that the working class pursue its interests without ideals and so realize the goal of history — the new society.

3   However, the irrational world defies rational explanation. Hegel, who knew God's thoughts, explained away those matters that did not correspond to what should happen as mere coincidences indicative of the impotence of nature. Only that reality that can be comprehended is true. In this way spirit is hypostatized and everything else devalued. This hypostatization of a single factor reappears in Marx, though in inverted form: the factor which for him determines the course of history is the economic base, and consciousness is relegated to the ideological superstructure.

4   Since Hegel assumed the existence of the dialectical movement of thesis to antithesis and finally to synthesis, a harmonious synthesis of the divine realm of freedom is achieved at the end of history. Marx rightly saw the importance of the dialectic in its negativity as the moving and producing principle; but he failed to see that in Hegel's optimistic conception the dialectical movement comes to a standstill

at the end of historical development in a synthesis, in the negation of the negation. This faith in eventual harmony he adopted blindly.

The ambivalence in Hegel's historical dialectic

The dialectical and rationalistic view of history should not be interpreted as a means of, in Hegel's own words, 'labelling all that is in heaven and earth with the few determinations of the general schema' so that this construction looks like 'a skeleton with scraps of paper stuck over it'.[13] His derision for this procedure, which he found in Fichte, is obvious. He attempted, rather, to fathom the divine plan of history through empirical analysis. The unique character of his philosophy of history consists precisely in the conjunction of an *a priori* historiography and an *a posteriori* empirical procedure. Hegel studied an enormous amount of empirical material, had a sharp eye for political forces and intellectual influences, and wrote in a graphic and imaginative style. He had a better grasp of historical connections than any historian of his time. He also recognized the impact of modern capitalism, hardly noticeable in early nineteenth-century Germany, long before the German political economists. He was versed in all fields of knowledge, from ancient Chinese philosophy and Egyptian hieroglyphics to the British Reform Bill of 1832 and colonial expansion in America. When one of his interpretations or theories was refuted by the latest research and discoveries, he modified it to fit the facts. The dialectical method was supposed to elicit a meaningful unity of history from the endless emergence and decline of states and cultures.

Nevertheless, there exists an ambivalence in the dialectic. It is revealed in the concept of *Er-Innerung*. In the sense of 'memory' it means that we understand the past, communicate with it, and exclude or adopt that which is still present to our minds or not. The great deeds and works of the past, Hegel wrote, have become 'dumb':[14]

> The statues are now only stones, from which the living soul has flown. . . . They have become what they are for us now —
> beautiful fruit already picked from the tree . . . , only the veiled recollection (*Er-Innerung*) of that actual world.

But in the sense of 'internalization' it means not our recollection but the *re*-collection of the divine spirit. Internalization into self is then the transcendental march of God through history in the process of achieving self-consciousness. To this extent history is not what it is for us — memory or recollection — but that which 'proceeds for us, as it were, behind the back of consciousness', behind the back of the historical object.[15] In this case the philosopher perceives the divine providence and partakes of the divine internalization. The synthesis of these two aspects, history and the science of knowledge (or phenomenology), forms the recollection of absolute spirit.[16] Here the two sides of Hegel's dialectic are revealed as the true dialectic of human historical consciousness and as a dialectical construction of a transcendent movement in history. Marx later criticized the logical mysticism of the dialectic which takes place 'behind the scenes', and he consequently translated the dialectic from heaven to the earth. But as we shall see later, the ambivalence characteristic of the Hegelian dialectic reappears in Marx.

The Hegelians

Hegel's disciples were fascinated by a system that comprehended all that was known to the human spirit. One of them, Rudolf Haym, remarked (after he had already rejected Hegelianism):[17]

> I still think that a number of those living today remember well
> the time when all the sciences drew from the rich legacy of
> Hegel's wisdom, . . . where one was either a Hegelian or a
> barbarian and an idiot. One has to recall this period to know what
> the supremacy of one philosophical system actually implies.

The epigones singled out part of the system while ignoring its internal dialectical correlations. Marx saw in this philosophical charlatanry of the Hegelians the signs of the system's decay: 'When the last spark of its life had failed, the various components of this *caput mortuum* began to decompose.'[18]

Marx was one of the few Hegelians who started from the living dialectic. 'The dialectic is the inner, simple light, the piercing eye of love, the inner soul, . . . the vehicle of vitality', he wrote in his youth.[19] Throughout his life it remained for him the vehicle of active life. He reflected on his intellectual development in 1873: 'I . . . openly avowed myself the pupil of that mighty thinker' at a time when educated circles in Germany were treating Hegel 'like a "dead dog".'[20]

The dialectical method became *scientifically* fruitful for Marx only after its inversion from Hegelian idealism into materialism, since this, he would later claim, eliminates the 'mystification' which the Hegelian dialectic suffered from.[21] It was Feuerbach who set about this task of inversion in his *The Essence of Christianity*, which appeared in 1841, about the time when Marx and Engels were converted to communism.

Chapter six

Feuerbach's inversion of the dialectic

Feuerbach's materialism

Ludwig Feuerbach originally studied theology. He too was at first spell-bound by Hegel's philosophy, and he tried to explain religious views in terms of the concepts of reason. But Hegel's concepts did not satisfy him for long. He found that in them the truth of religion had been sacrificed to the reason of philosophy. The point of religion is not that man thinks about God but that he lives a religious life, Feuerbach declared. In the tales of God's love and suffering man's own experiences of love and suffering are objectified. But why does man transfer his subjective experiences on to an objective God? The loving man is prepared to die for his loved ones; in love he feels a force that conquers death. This infinite force, without which he cannot exist, he attributes to God. In the first stage religious consciousness, the childish and immediate consciousness, imagines its own experiences as the love of God. In the second stage, progressive consciousness makes God into the object of reason. In this conception of God man is alienated from himself. It is only in the third stage that man recognizes in the object his own love, and so returns to himself out of alienation. Up to this point the Hegelian method is correct. History is the progress towards self-consciousness — but not, as Hegel had assumed, towards the self-consciousness of God but towards the self-consciousness of the finite human being of flesh and blood. Accordingly, 'The essence of Theology is Anthropology.'[1]

Feuerbach himself had passed through the three stages of self-recognition revealed in the history of man. 'God was my first thought, reason my second, and man my third and final thought.'[2] In the early *Todesgedanken* (1830) he condemned the attempt to obscure the fact of one's own death by invoking ideas of immortality as 'most immoral, most pitiable'.[3] 'Only when [man] admits the truth of death, when he no longer denies the fact of death, will he be capable of true religious feeling, true self-denial.'[4] It is therefore man's task to realize himself within the confines of nature.

Because, according to Feuerbach, the anthropomorphic attributes of the divine essence are objectifications, alienations of human essence, these attributes must be brought back to the subject in order to achieve their truth. Theology is to be transformed into anthropology. The infinity expressed in the divine essence is to be recognized as the infinity of man's own essence. Man only becomes man when he relinquishes his natural self-consciousness and finds himself in the other, in the love of the other. 'The true dialectic is not a monologue of the lonely thinker with himself, it is a dialogue between I and You.'[5] Religion is also a dialogue, supposedly with God but actually with oneself. Feuerbach thus recovered the true dialectic of the loving man that had been Hegel's starting-point in his youth (he did not know of Hegel's early works, which were not published until the turn of the century).[6]

The concept of love should not be misinterpreted as a renunciation of rational thought and an appeal to irrational feeling; it is, rather, a critique of the baseless speculation of Hegelianism. Just as Pascal had juxtaposed the *logique de coeur* to the *logique de raison*, so Feuerbach juxtaposed 'the head, the source of activity and freedom' to 'the heart, the source of suffering, finiteness, need and sensualism'.[7] This can be expressed theoretically as the union of thought and intuition. In the polemic against Hegel, Feuerbach stressed 'sensualism', or as he said provocatively against Hegelian idealism, 'materialism'. Materialism asserts that 'Thought is out of being, but being is not out of thought.'[8] Marx later proceeded from this axiom, and he would repeat it almost word for word.

It should be noted that the materialism of Feuerbach has nothing in common with what is usually understood by this term. He clearly differentiated his materialism from what he called 'obtuse' materialism.[9] He emphasized that German materialism has a religious origin and that his atheism is a religious atheism. Later in life he said: 'My love for man has made me into a "materialist" and "sensualist".'[10] He found his own religious materialism confirmed in Spinoza's *deus sive natura* and in Böhme's mystical philosophy of nature.

Feuerbach also had a strong affinity with his contemporary Kierkegaard, whose writings were translated into German at a much later date. Both pilloried in the same way meaningless Christianity and baseless Hegelianism. Kierkegaard's philosophy of existence and subjectivity is like Feuerbach's materialism and sensualism: a challenge to vagueness and sanctimoniousness. Both exposed the hypocrisy of the modern world, which under the cloak of affirmation actually negates Christianity. And both distinguished their philosophies from Schelling's attempt to transcend abstract thought: Feuerbach called Schelling's theories 'cosmogonic and theogonic fancies', Kierkegaard dismissed them as 'nonsense'.[11]

Feuerbach's critique of the age

Feuerbach's reversal of idealism and materialism was not the result of a theoretical reflection or historical investigation but the expression of the distressing experience of his generation, which witnessed how the great Western intellectual tradition was exhausting itself in empty phrases. His writings abound with acrid references to the hedonistic Christianity of the modern world and the intolerance and unkindness of the churches. What in the original phase of religion had been true and sacred had become in the modern age untrue and immoral.

It was Feuerbach who provided the young revolutionaries — in rejecting the faith and the culture of their elders and turning to material reality and political praxis — with the intellectual justification for their movement. The inversion of Hegelian philosophy enabled them to pursue their revolutionary goals not by destruction but by the transformation of the humanist tradition. *The Essence of Christianity* had a truly liberating effect. Even in his old age Engels was still exuberant: 'The spell was broken; the "system" was exploded and cast aside. . . . Enthusiasm was general: we all became at once Feuerbachians.'[12]

Feuerbach's influence on Marx

Marx was immediately aware of the magnitude of Feuerbach's achievement. When *The Essence of Christianity* was attacked he defended it in an article in the *Rheinische Zeitung*. He was indebted to Feuerbach for the insight that 'The concern of philosophy is not the logic of the subject-matter but the subject-matter of logic.'[13] It is therefore the task of history, 'once the other-world of truth has vanished, to establish the truth of this world'.[14]

Marx became a Feuerbachian in his pre-communist youth. Once a communist, he still acknowledged his debt to Feuerbach: 'Like Feuerbach's critique of religion, our whole aim can only be to translate religious and political problems into their self-conscious human form.'[15] This encompassed the political critique of man, who had alienated himself in the self-interested bourgeois and was to regain his true essence in communism. While for Feuerbach the head and heart were the organs of philosophy, they were for Marx the organs of political emancipation. 'The head of this emancipation is philosophy, its heart the proletariat.'[16] By 'philosophy' he meant classical political philosophy from Plato's *Republic* to Hegel's *Philosophy of Right*. He fell back on this tradition in order to clarify his ideas of communism.

Chapter seven

Marx's early communist phase: the realization of the true political community

The first standard of communism: Hegel's theory of the state

Hegel's concept of the state was the pivotal point of Marx's political thought even before he became a communist. Having turned to communism, he clarified its ideas, which did not satisfy him in their existing form, in a thorough analysis of Hegelian political philosophy. In Marx's view, Hegel's philosophy was 'the only German history which stands on an equal footing with the official modern present'; it was the 'theoretical conscience' of all nations, despite the fact that the economic and political conditions in Germany were 'anachronistic'.[1]

Hegel's political thought continued the tradition of classical Greek political philosophy. In the *polis*, the Greek city-state, a free man's life and thought were wholly devoted to public service. He was a *zoön politikon*, a political animal. This was possible because slave-labour provided for his needs, and he had therefore no economic commitments. The ethical goal of the true political community of the *polis* was adopted by medieval Christian natural law through the mediation of the Stoic tradition. When, in the sixteenth century, divine natural law was secularized (for example in More's *Utopia*), the universalism of the ideal community was not immediately questioned. It was only with Hobbes and Locke that modern natural law attempted to integrate capitalist free enterprise and the market economy into the ideal of the commonwealth.

Since Hegel's ideas were rooted in the classical political ideal of the state, it is hardly surprising that in the early writings on natural law he had considerable difficulty in making sense of the bourgeois drive for wealth and property. The bourgeois, incapable of virtue and courage, was in his terms a 'political nonentity'. He accepted the existence of the bourgeois class only in so far as it contributed to the needs of the 'first estate', i.e. the class of public servants and officers. The bourgeoisie fulfilled, in fact, the same function as the slaves in the classical city-state.[2] Thus, even though Hegel embraced the revolutionary principles of 1789, he allowed the bourgeoisie to play not more than a secondary role.

It was not until the mature *Philosophy of Right* (1821) that Hegel accepted the equality of *all* citizens. After an extensive study of the political economy of Smith and Ricardo, he also legitimated the pursuit of selfish ends and the acquisition of private property. The sphere of the self-interested drive for the satisfaction of economic needs, with all its interconnections and oppositions, was subsumed under the concept of 'civil' or bourgeois society (*bürgerliche Gesellschaft*). For Hegel, bourgeois society is the state as envisaged by the intellect (*Verstand*); it is subordinate to the political state based on reason (*Vernunft*). This view contrasts with the contemporary British view of the relationship between the economy and the state, since for the nineteenth-century British political economists the political state was merely a formal structure.

Hegel grasped more clearly than any of the German political economists the significance of the division of labour and mechanization for the modern process of production. He also described the antinomies of competitive society: the fall of 'the standard of living of a large mass of people ... below a certain subsistence level' and 'the concentration of disproportionate wealth in a few hands'.[3] He also recognized the need of capitalism to 'seek markets for the goods it has overproduced'.[4] In the essay *On the English Reform Bill* he unmasked the hypocrisy of the landlords who 'behind the pomp and display of formal freedom' appropriate the land of the peasants in order to free themselves from any obligation to look after their subsistence.[5] He saw through the class-ridden nature of parliamentary legislation, which 'remains in the hands of that class which has its interest ... in the hitherto existing law of property'.[6]

According to Hegel, bourgeois society passes into the ethical state. A connecting link between them is the 'corporation', in which the individual citizen combines his selfish private interests with the higher public interest. (Before Hegel, Montesquieu had already perceived the importance of intermediate institutions, for the intercourse between government and people.[7]) In the corporation the 'spirit of the corporation' is converted into the 'spirit of the state'.[8] The corporation and the family are the ethical roots of the state. In this way Hegel succeeded in integrating the capitalist profit motive into the concept of the ethical state, which he had failed to do in his earlier writings — just as classical political philosophy and German humanism had failed.

It was the philosophical exposition of the contradiction between individualistic bourgeois society and the ethical state which the young Marx found of interest in Hegel. In an only partly preserved manuscript, *Critique of Hegel's Doctrine of the State*, written when he retreated for a while to his studies after his resignation from the *Rheinische Zeitung*, Marx observed that 'Hegel experiences the separation of the state from civil society as a *contradiction*.'[9] He accepted Hegel's analysis of this contradiction. In addition, he accepted Hegel's characterization of the state as an 'organic unity', as the 'realization of state-citizenship', and as the 'actual incarnation of the ethical Idea'.[10] He used these Hegelian concepts in his description of what at this time he called 'the communistic entity'. Hegel's mistake lay, in Marx's eyes, in the merely theoretical solution of the contradiction. 'The mistake he makes is to rest content with the semblance of a resolution which he declares to be the real thing.'[11] The contradictions can be resolved only in reality, through communism. Marx believed that the abolition of private property would abolish individualism and instil into the people an ethical disposition to the state. He rejected notions of individual rights and intermediate institutions (neither of which, incidentally, is by definition inconsistent with communism).

Hegel's *Philosophy of Right* certainly provides points for attack, for 1 Hegel modelled the corporation on the medieval guilds, and 2 in comparison to the draft for a German constitution written about 1802, he put less emphasis on popular sovereignty and more on the political executive. But however justified Marx's objections to the anachronistic pre-capitalist form of the corporation and to the 'wretched arrogance of Prussian officialdom which, full of its own bureaucratic narrow-mindedness, regards with disdain the "self-confidence" of the "subjective opinion of the people" ', he nevertheless threw out the baby with the bathwater.[12] Primarily his use of Feuerbach's transformative method and the influence of Rousseau's ideal of the perfect democracy account for Marx's radical disavowal of Hegel at this time. In analogy to Feuerbach's method, which restored religion to man, Marx wanted to restore all political forms to the people, that is, he wanted to eliminate the political forms of individual rights, intermediate institutions and the separation of powers, and replace them with a direct democracy. The demand for the abolition of political rights was not based on an economic or any other empirical analysis but exclusively on a philosophical method of 'restoration'. Marx's flirtation with this kind of non-empirical social criticism was only a brief interlude; but from it survived the fateful conception of a social democracy without civil rights and a separation of the powers of government. Rousseau is to blame for Marx's jettison of these aspects of government from the Hegelian theory of the state.

The second standard of communism: Rousseau's general will

One cannot overestimate the influence of Rousseau on Marx. Even before Rousseau the philosophy of the Enlightenment had replaced the original sin of the Christian tradition and the canonical natural law with the natural freedom and innocence of man and secular natural law. But Rousseau was the first to provide a strong and emotional expression to the idea of the naturally free and good man. His work stood at the beginning of a movement which inspired the French Revolution, the political philosophies of Kant and Hegel, the poetry of Goethe and Schiller (especially in their storm and stress period), the choral finale of Beethoven's ninth symphony, and, somewhat later, the novels of Tolstoy and D.H. Lawrence.

Man, as Rousseau postulated in the celebrated *Social Contract*, is by nature good and free. But he has been corrupted by modern civilization. 'Man is born free and everywhere he is in chains.'[13] His original goodness has been transformed by commerce and luxury into self-love and self-interest; only business and money concern him. Now enslaved and egocentric, man can once again create a legitimate political order by changing the condition of 'aggregation', in which the people live in conflict with themselves and with others, into a form of 'association'.

To effect the imperative change, the individuals join forces in a social compact and so form an association. This will be a new identity, the 'general will', which as such excludes the possibility of a second social contract. The general will is more than the sum of the wills of all: it is an organic indivisible unity. The contract is not merely a legal relationship, but a 'total alienation of each associate, together with his rights, to the whole community', an alienation 'without ... reserve', a total surrender of one's own will to the general will.[14] (For Rousseau, *aliéné* and *aliénation* did not have the same specific meaning of 'alienation' or 'estrangement' which the terms later acquired in Hegel and Marx. *Aliéné* still had the original meaning of 'removed from oneself' – in French it also means 'deranged' or 'insane'. In this context it denotes both the degeneration of natural man into the depraved civilized man and the latter's transformation into the associate.)

The association represents a moral transformation of man; the new collectivity is a 'moral being'.[15] The association or *cité* (city-state or state) is identical to the *polis* of classical times, and its members carry the honourable title of 'citizens'. They are conscientious and virtuous citizens, quite the opposite of the self-interested bourgeois of the aggregation. In this new moral order the general will is 'indestructible', 'always constant', 'unalterable and pure' and 'always upright': it is, in short, *infallible*.[16]

Rousseau's description of the transformation of the aggregation into the association adheres to modern natural law, particularly Hobbes; but in the addition of the element of infallibility to the concept of the general will it deviated from this tradition. In classical Greek democracy the community was, as in Rousseau's state, more than the sum of its individual citizens. The democracy of the *polis* was not infallible, however: its citizens debated the common good in the popular assembly.

The postulate of the infallibility of the general will has certain consequences, fully developed by Rousseau himself. Thus, when an individual's particular will does not conform to the general will, he should voluntarily submit himself to it because he is mistaken. If he refuses, he should be compelled to obey. 'This means nothing less than that he will be forced to be free.'[17] Lest the citizens regress into self-love and pursue their particular interests in opposition to the common cause, they will not be granted any special rights or allowed to organize themselves in political parties. Furthermore, since love for his country is the citizen's only virtue — for Rousseau as for Machiavelli the concept of virtue is synonymous with patriotism — all private interests and all non-political public interests (the arts and sciences, and particularly religion) are proscribed. In view of human weakness, conformism is necessary, for 'private interest always tends to privileges, while the common interest always tends to equality'.[18] For this reason censorship must be introduced to preserve unity and morality, to prevent 'opinion from growing corrupt'.[19] Moreover, the citizens must be further protected from decadence by means of a special profession of faith. The declaration, the 'dogmas of civil religion', affirms only the love for the laws. The dogmas are not religious dogmas but an expression of a feeling of solidarity (*sentiments de sociabilité*). No one can be compelled to believe in the dogmas of the civil religion, but those who do not profess them may be banished from the state. This applies equally to the clergy, since 'theological intolerance' thwarts the secular authority. He who has recognized the dogmas yet behaves as if he does not believe them will be punished by death: 'He has committed the worst of all crimes, that of lying before the law.'[20]

Rousseau's dogmas of the civil religion correspond to those in Spinoza's *Tractatus Theologico-politicus*. But whereas Spinoza called for freedom of thought, Rousseau insisted on conformism and censorship. How could the passionate prophet of freedom have made the intolerant demands that opened the way to future totalitarian systems?

Rousseau grew up in Calvinist Geneva. Although he later rejected Calvinism, his religious background had left its mark. Once relieved of the burden borne by every Calvinist — the question whether according to God's unknowable decree he is destined for salvation or eternal damnation — Rousseau was overwhelmed by the experience of man's innocence. He expressed his new faith in the recovery of the natural goodness of man in the *cité* with the same zeal as the orthodox Christian proclaims his faith. He also transferred many of the characteristics of the true Christian community on to the secular community of the *cité*. So it happened that Rousseau's perfect state had more in common with Calvin's theocracy than with Plato's republic.

After the experiences of totalitarianism historians began to notice the seeds of the suppression of freedom in Rousseau's democracy. Rousseau himself saw no opposition between the freedom of the virtuous citizen and the coercive measures of the state, since man is virtuous 'when his particular will is in all things conformable to the general will'.[21] In the novel *Émile*, written in the same period as *The Social Contract*, he recounted the education of a young child. At the beginning of the book he presented the citizen of Sparta as his ideal, and in an earlier discourse he had also represented Spartan education as exemplary. But education is, for Rousseau, far from Spartan or even totalitarian in the sense of indoctrination. The question is whether man, enslaved by self-love and greed, can be purged of his vices and once again be in harmony with his true nature, his true goodness. This will happen when he learns to listen to the voice of his conscience; his conscience will never deceive him. Natural religion differs from the intolerant churches in that man follows his inner voice and not external force. So we hear in *Émile*: 'I am only aware of will through the consciousness of my own will'; and further on the Savoyard priest implores Émile 'to preach humanity to the intolerant'.[22]

The reader of *Émile* may be carried along with Rousseau's enthusiasm for the natural religion of conscience and the free development of man to such an extent that he might see an opposition between this religion and the omnipotent state of *The Social Contract*. Indeed, many critics find it difficult to reconcile *Émile* and *The Social Contract*. But in the first sentences of *Émile* Rousseau stated unequivocally that he intended to deal with the education of the citizen. This point can easily escape one's notice because he did not discuss the relationship of man and the state anywhere else in the book.

From the standpoint of *Émile* the state coercion described in *The Social Contract* appears in a very different light. Rousseau stressed the *voluntary* formation of the *cité*, and he contended that, contrary to other philosophers who posit the political community based on force or the will of God, the *cité* is founded on a 'free commitment'. This he considered his great achievement.[23] The voluntary identification of the individual will with the general will distinguishes the democratic republic from tyranny. Only in a tyranny could an innocent man be sacrificed to the majority. The maxim of tyranny — that 'one should perish for all' — is 'one of the most execrable rules . . . ever invented, . . . a direct contradiction of the fundamental laws of society'.[24] In the free state, on the other hand, the citizens are committed to each other, and 'the welfare of the individual citizen is as much the common cause as the welfare of the community as a whole'.[25] Even so, it is obvious from these remarks that voluntary commitment remains the basis of the state only as long as its members remain good citizens. It was precisely because he wanted to prevent the displacement of the voluntary union by the force of tyranny that Rousseau argued for a conformist civil religion and the abolition of all personal privileges. The tragedy is that these very measures aimed to safeguard freedom were suited to help the tyrants to establish their totalitarian rule.

Rousseau himself doubted whether a perfect democracy was possible; he recognized the discrepancy between the ideal of democracy and 'men being taken as they are'.[26] People would have to change morally before they could sign the contract. A legislator of unusual wisdom, who only rarely comes forward in history, would have to educate selfish men to virtue and patriotism before they could unite in the association. The success of the legislator depends on the particular geographical, political and economic situation of every nation (as he suggested in reference to Montesquieu).[27] The new state must be self-sufficient and small, it should not be too poor nor too rich, and its morals should not be too corrupted. Because of these restrictions there have been very few true communities: examples are Sparta and a number of small nations in the moral elevation after liberation from foreign rule, such as the tribes of Israel, republican Rome, Switzerland, and Holland. In the present it can be expected only in Corsica.

If according to Rousseau direct democracy is practicable only in small states, one may ask whether a system of parliamentary representation could not be appropriate for the larger states? But Rousseau rejected the formation of political parties, which sustain parliamentary democracy, because he thought they would encourage the selfishness of man and disturb the mystical unity of the general will. Thus the doctrinaire mysticism of his democratic conception prevented him from considering the only political form practicable in the modern nation-state. From his pessimistic assessment of the present he concluded, rather conservatively, that one should pay respect to the 'old laws', otherwise 'the State dies'.[28]

The question arises here whether there really has ever existed a true democracy, in Sparta or Geneva or anywhere else, in which men of conscience have surrendered themselves completely to the omnipotent state without losing their freedom? How misguided was the conception of a democratic Sparta, where the helots were kept as slaves. Should one not go further and ask whether a democracy in which the conscience of the individual is identical to the interest of the state is possible at all? Are there not even in small communities, such as the

Israeli kibbutzim, endless conflicts and splits even though all are united in a common outlook? We can find the answers to these questions in Kant.

Kant's endorsement of and objections to Rousseau

Kant confessed that before he read Rousseau he had been studying in an ivory tower, far away from the rabble that he despised; but 'Rousseau put me right, . . . I learned to value mankind.'[29] Yet his admiration for Rousseau did not blind him to the unrealistic dogmatic form of Rousseau's democracy. He knew that the perfect republic described by Rousseau had never existed in reality and could never do so.

Since the idea of a free state concerns everyone, Kant was not content to deal with a sublime theory of ideas which only scholars could understand. He therefore wrote a number of special essays which made complicated subject-matters accessible to common sense. In one of these popular essays, entitled *Idea for a Universal History*, published five years before the outbreak of the French Revolution, he wrote: 'The highest task which nature has set for mankind must . . . be that of establishing . . . a perfectly just civil constitution.' This is the most difficult of tasks and a perfect solution is impossible, he continued, because the difficulty is that man lives among other men, 'he is an animal who needs a master'. That man is an animal had been pointed out by Machiavelli and Hobbes; the idea that an animal must be tamed by its master had come from Hobbes. 'But this master will also be an animal who needs a master.' The assumption that civilization has made man an animal and that he can be re-educated to his original goodness must be rejected on the grounds that 'Nothing straight can be constructed from such warped wood as that which man is made of.'[30]

It is evident that the prerequisite for Rousseau's ideal democracy falls away if man is not by nature good but made of 'warped wood'. As there can be no perfect democracy in which the individual will invariably concurs with the public good, Kant, unlike Rousseau, called for a constitution which would guarantee the freedom of the individual. Kant here followed the Anglo-Saxon tradition. The British and Americans, sceptical of abstract doctrines, established their free institutions in political struggles for self-government. It is no coincidence that before he encountered Rousseau, Kant had been roused from his 'dogmatic slumber' by Hume's scepticism. He recognized the unrealistic dogmatism inherent in Rousseau's political ideas. To this extent he, like Montesquieu, differed from other political philosophers of the European continent who, denied any political responsibility themselves, could only advocate their views in debating clubs and often lapsed into anciful dreams of a perfect democracy. Schiller, who had studied both Rousseau and Kant, came to the same conclusion as Kant. He therefore modelled his true democracy not on Sparta but on Athens. What he found unacceptable in Sparta was that patriotism was practised as the only virtue to the neglect of all others. That Schiller's criticism of Sparta was directed against Rousseau can be inferred from their opposite views on the Spartan mother who rushes to the temple to thank the gods for the death of her son in battle: in *Émile* Rousseau had admired her as a virtuous woman, but Schiller described her as an 'heroic hybrid ... who denies her natural feelings in order to satisfy an artificial duty'.[31]

In this era of democracy, when Rousseau is particularly relevant, every edition of *The Social Contract* should have Kant's appreciation of Rousseau appended. Disaster will strike when politicians are blind to the irrationality of man and the world!

Rousseau's influence on the revolutionary movement

The Jacobins brushed aside Kant's scruples — if indeed they had any at all — and also took no notice of Rousseau's objections to the introduction of a democratic form of government in nation-states. They were not educated in a parliamentary tradition or any other free political praxis; they knew only abstract political ideas. Consequently they did not hesitate to take Rousseau's perfectionist ideal at face value. The revolutionaries venerated Rousseau's noble soul and character. Intoxicated by his ideas, they embraced the cause of liberty and equality and set out to reach for ' "the reign of that eternal justice" and "virtue", the general principle of the republic', as Robespierre put it.[32] The fact that Rousseau's general principle was not supposed to apply to the nation-state they did not care or know about. (There are strong parallels with the Hegelians, who saw the realization of Hegel's concept of the state in the foundation of the German Empire; or with Lenin, who hoped that the October Revolution would realize Marx's classless society.) They all worshipped Rousseau as the father of the revolution and solemnly placed him in the revolutionary pantheon. A metaphor by Heine captures the essence of the Jacobin tradition: 'Robespierre was no more than the hand of Jean-Jacques Rousseau, the bloody hand which delivered from the womb of time the body whose soul Rousseau had created.'[33]

Even more disastrously, the Jacobins seized on the absolute in Rousseau, the idea of the unified 'moral being' of the infallible general will, while ignoring the realistic restrictions Rousseau had put on it. The uncompromising drive for the absolute in a relative world combined with the lack of political experience inevitably produced a situation where those who disagreed or appeared to disagree with them were persecuted as enemies of the people. The 'terror of virtue' and the one-party system were the result. The Jacobins' doctrinaire and impractical methods seduced them into maintaining the old administrative centralization, and even increasing it, once they had ousted the king and supposedly handed over the administration to the sovereign people. This went so far that in the name of liberty they continued the Bourbon practice of unauthorized arrests (just as subsequently the Bolsheviks would continue oppressive tsarist practices).

It is not surprising, then, that contemporary historians of totalitarianism believe they have found its roots in Rousseau's surrender of individual rights to society or the state.[34] And although such arguments carry much weight, it should be remembered in Rousseau's defence that 1 he posited the establishment of democracy as a *voluntary* act, and 2 there exists a radical difference between the Jacobin terror of *virtue* and the modern rule of *barbarism*. The next section will attempt to throw some light upon the origin of this difference.

The combination of the general will and 'true' philosophy

Buonarotti's book on Babeuf, published in 1828, revived the Jacobin enthusiasm for direct democracy and influenced the revolutionary movement in France. Marx succumbed to this Jacobin tradition and he reshaped Hegel's concept of the state to accord with the Jacobin interpretation of Rousseau.

Rousseau's name appears not once in Marx's first communist manuscript, *Critique of Hegel's Doctrine of the State*. But it is evident from his next communist essay that Rousseau's *Social Contract*, together with Hegel's *Philosophy of Right*, served as a standard of communist society: in *On the Jewish Question* he quoted from *The Social Contract*, as we shall see below. It seems that he did not name Rousseau because, having been educated in Hegelian rational philosophy, he could not identify with Rousseau's exuberance. So he translated Rousseau's ideas expressed in emotional language into the philosophical language of Hegel.

For Hegel, the state of freedom is not, as it is for Kant, a normative idea that man should attempt to approach but an idea 'actualizing' (*verwirklichen*) itself according to dialectical and necessary laws. Marx adopted the same approach in his formulation of communism. The realization of communist democracy does not, therefore, require the education of the corrupted bourgeoisie, as Rousseau had assumed, but rather the scientific apprehension of the dialectical movement culminating in communism. Marx thus replaced Rousseau's moral transformation with Hegel's scientific dialectic. He affirmed the scientific character of his brand of socialism even before he began the empirical investigations of capitalist economy and society. The claim of scientific socialism was in the early communist phase grounded in the Hegelian dialectic and not in empirical science.

Fichte, turning Kantian philosophy into its opposite (at least in this respect), first made the arrogant claim 'to have discovered the way by which philosophy can advance to an evidential science'.[35] The same insistence on the only 'true' philosophical science and the same contempt for Kantian notions of humility and modesty reappeared in Hegel. It now appears in Marx, and it will reappear in his disciples, from Lenin to Lukács, Adorno and Marcuse. For the great philosophers from Plato to Kant philosophy was the way towards truth through *dialektike*, debate or discussion; for the post-Kantian idealists it was the full possession of the truth in a closed scientific system, the 'system of totality' (Hegel). The consequence of this claim to the knowledge of the exclusive truth — and this is the crucial point in this context — is *intolerance*. A great opportunity was lost when the Germans in their first venture from dreamy contemplativeness towards political activity ignored the realism and tolerance of Kant and instead emulated the dogmatism and intolerance of Hegel.

As Marx was reinterpreting Rousseau's democracy into Hegelian concepts, the following happened: from the peculiarly Rousseauian identification of individual conscience with the infallible general will, intolerance survived and conscience disappeared. For Rousseau the infallibility of the general will depends on the goodness of man, for Marx it depends on the infallibility of science. Rousseau presupposed the moral transformation of man before the general will could operate, Marx presupposed the dialectical law of development. According to Rousseau, the individual becomes a better citizen of the state the more he listens to the voice of his conscience; according to Marx, the individual becomes a better revolutionary the more he follows the objectively identifiable law of development and the less he follows his conscience. It may be said that the roots of totalitarian communism can be found in this combination of (certain elements in) Rousseau and Hegel.

The other totalitarian system besides communism, fascism, also has its roots in the association of Rousseau's perfect general will and the anti-Kantian claim to the absolute truth. Where Marx saw the realization of the general will in the 'true' democracy, Fichte saw it in the 'true' German nation. Fichte was in fact the first to declare the state as 'absolute' and the social contract as a 'contract of submission' in which 'all as individuals are sacrificed to the species'.[36] Fichte stood at the beginning of what Grillparzer prophetically called 'the road from humanity through nationality to bestiality'.[37]

In no way are the origins of the two totalitarian systems explained here. For one thing, neither Hegel nor Marx advocated at any point totalitarian political rule. Despite the principle of the *a priori* deduction of the totality of reality, Hegel possessed a human simplicity and lots of common sense. When reality proved him wrong, he altered what, until then, he had taught dogmatically. He never sacrificed the individual conscience to the state – quite the opposite: he justified 'conscientious objection', that is, the refusal by Christian sects to take the oath and perform military service.[38] The roots of the totalitarian system are more clearly evident in Marx than in Hegel, because he was guided by Rousseau's concept of democracy, which encouraged him to eject the notions of rights of the individual and the separation of powers from Hegel's political philosophy. But, as we shall see later, Marx gradually broke out of the Hegelian dialectical construction in which he was entangled in his early communist phase, and he learned to see actual conditions with open eyes. Only his orthodox disciples would subsequently erect the system called Marxism, which was put into political practice as a totalitarian system.

It is irritating for the historian tracing the history of Marxism back to its source that Marx adopted from each one of his intellectual fathers – Rousseau and Hegel – two contradictory intellectual forces: the political idea of freedom and the intolerant dogmatism. Those critics who attribute the unscientific dogmatism simply to the Hegelian dialectic do no justice to its role in the work of Marx. They ignore the broad historical scope of his work, for which he is also indebted to the dialectical method. And Marx adopted from Rousseau both the idea of the originally free man and the idea of the people's democracy without individual rights.

The social revolution

After an examination of the communist ideas within the framework of the political philosophies of Rousseau and Hegel, Marx commented on them in two essays published in the *Deutsch-Französische Jahrbücher* of 1843-44: *On the Jewish Question*, a review of a book by Bruno Bauer, a former Young Hegelian friend; and a *Critique of Hegel's Philosophy of Right*. In these two essays he showed that the declaration of the rights of man in the American and French revolutions concealed the opposition between bourgeois society and the political state. These declarations include two fundamentally different rights: firstly, the political rights of freedom of thought and freedom of religion, which relate to the participation of the *citoyen* in the political state; and secondly, the rights of the *bourgeois* to equality, liberty, and security of property, which detach the bourgeois society of egoistic and atomized man from the political state. How was it possible, Marx asked, that the French Revolution, which emancipated man and established a new political community, at the same time solemnly proclaimed the rights of self-interested man set apart from the state? There is a straightforward solution, he claimed. In the old society, feudal property rights and the manorial system defined the relation of the individual to the state. Feudal society had a directly political character. The political revolutions of the eighteenth century carried by the aspiring bourgeoisie overthrew this rule and gained by force the freedom of the *citoyen*, that is, responsibility for the political state, but also the freedom of the *bourgeois*, that is, the recognition of self-interest isolated from political activity.[39]

Inspired by Hegel's and Rousseau's political philosophy, Marx saw the task of the communist revolution — the abolition of private property — as the transformation of the selfish bourgeois pursuing his own interests into the ethical citizen working for the public good. Even though he was impressed by the political elevation of man in the new American democracy, he did not follow the American example, as de Tocqueville did, but instead applied Rousseau's mystical and abstract theory of the general will. The following passage encapsulates Marx's solution and summarizes the creed of his school:[40]

> Only when real, individual man resumes the abstract citizen
> into himself and as an individual man has become a species-
> being in his empirical life . . . , only when man has recognized
> and organized his *forces propres* as social forces so that social
> force is no longer separated from him in the form of political
> force, only then will human emancipation be completed.

'*Forces propres*', 'own forces', is a phrase from *The Social Contract*. This reference to Rousseau in Marx's solution is of course not coincidental.

Marx hoped to find the new world in a critique of the old. However, the 'weapon of criticism' cannot replace the 'criticism of weapons', he warned.[41] The German petty bourgeoisie was incapable of taking up arms. To expect the emancipation of man from the aspiring bourgeoisie, as the followers of Owen, St Simon and Fourier thought, was a utopian dream. A proletariat was almost non-existent in Germany. So when 'practical life is as devoid of intellect as intellectual life is of practical activity', where does the possibility of emancipation lie?[42]

> This is our answer. In the formation of a class with radical chains,
> a class of civil society which is not a class of civil society, a class

which is the dissolution of all classes, a sphere which has a universal character because of its universal suffering, which lays claim to no particular right because the wrong it suffers is not a particular wrong but *wrong in general*; . . . and finally a sphere which cannot emancipate itself without emancipating itself from — and thereby emancipating — all the other spheres of society, which is, in a word, the *total loss* of humanity which can therefore redeem itself only through the total redemption of *humanity*. The dissolution of society as a particular class is the *proletariat*.

As industrial development spreads to Germany, the proletariat will grow in number and in importance. It will demand the negation of private property and thus realize the idea of the true community. With the satisfaction of its own needs the proletariat will effect the emancipation of the whole nation. 'Philosophy cannot realize itself without the transcendence of the proletariat, and the proletariat cannot transcend itself without the realization of philosophy.'[43]

At this point, three years after completing his doctoral dissertation, in which he contended that philosophy should turn to the external world and in which he compared himself to the pioneering Prometheus stealing fire from heaven, Marx appointed the proletariat as the executor of philosophy and political emancipation. 'The head of this emancipation is philosophy, its heart is the proletariat.'[44]

Revolutionary romanticism

In the early communist essays the author of the *Communist Manifesto* is hardly visible. Initially Marx was as oblivious to economic needs as the other German communists, whom a few years later he would deride as would-be philosophers and *beaux esprits*. The arguments and concepts with which he justified the material necessity of the revolution were without exception philosophical, not economic. He articulated the revolutionary task of the proletariat from the standpoint of Plato's *Republic*, Hegel's philosophy of history, and Rousseau's *Social Contract* — not from the standpoint of actual existing conditions.

The communist ideas were justified on philosophical grounds. In this period he had so little interest in economic problems that he did not even notice Hegel's economic arguments in the *Philosophy of Right*. He had not the faintest notion of the real interests of capitalism and the real needs of the proletariat. He idealized the proletariat and vilified capitalism. Because he failed to recognize the fateful force of capitalism he reacted in the same way as the German romantics who could not cope with harsh reality: he attributed capitalist development to dark and evil forces. And so he could write:[45]

> The Jew has emancipated himself in a Jewish way not only by acquiring financial power but also because through him and apart from him *money* has become a world power and the practical Jewish spirit has become the practical spirit of the Christian peoples.

In his early communist phase Marx had less in common with contemporary revolutionary communists than with the contemporary reactionary romantic on the throne, his king, Friedrich Wilhelm IV, who wrote to a friend: 'The contemptible Jewish clique strikes daily by word and example at the root of the German character.'[46]

At the time when Marx published his essays in the *Deutsch-Französische Jahrbücher*, Engels presented him with his draft of *Outlines of a Critique of Political Economy*. This essay induced him to begin a study of political economy. He soon realized that the anatomy of bourgeois society must be sought in its economics. The study of theoretical political economy and the existing economic realities brought about a turning-point in Marx's thought. Until then he had proclaimed that 'it is ... the philosopher in whose brain the revolution begins'.[47] It now dawned on him that philosophy starts in material production. The classical ideal of the true community remained his standard. Yet from this point on he no longer sought the true community in the realm of philosophical fantasy, but in reality.

Part two

Marx's thought

Chapter eight

The birth of historical materialism

Engels's critique of political economy

In his youth, Engels also experienced the overwhelming influence of Feuerbach. While Marx exposed the alienation of the bourgeois in the state, Engels exposed alienation in the economic sphere. He alone among the German communists had any kind of practical experience. His father, a prosperous factory-owner from the German Rhineland, had sent him to school in England, and there he acquainted himself with the realities of the modern capitalist economy.

In the essay *Outlines of a Critique of Political Economy* of 1844 Engels proceeded from the principle of political economy that labour is the main factor of production and determines the value of a product. But, according to Engels, in the society of private property the price of labour is abstracted from the real value and made dependent on the exchange value. 'Thus everything in economics stands on its head. Value, the primary factor, the source of price, is made dependent on price, its own product.'[1] This inversion is the essence of abstraction, as Feuerbach has shown. The product of labour is opposed to labour itself. In this way political economy legitimates the exploitation of the worker. The 'immorality' of this situation can only be overcome through socialism.[2]

Engels's critique was only a rough sketch, but Marx later praised it as a 'brilliant essay'.[3] Through it Marx encountered the concepts of economic theory for the first time; and from it he obtained the insight that material needs, about which he had merely speculated until then, could be explained by the science of economics.

Marx and Engels had met fleetingly in Cologne, but they became closer friends during a ten-day meeting in Paris in September 1844. They discovered a complementarity of their ideas. Marx learned from Engels about the concepts of economics, and Engels learned from Marx about the wider horizons of history. They began to collaborate in intellectual and political matters. The relationship was not an equal one, though. Engels was fascinated by Marx's superior intellect; later he admitted that 'What Marx accomplished, I could never have achieved. Marx stood higher, saw further, and took a wider and quicker view than all the rest of us. Marx was a genius, we others were at best talented.'[4] When Marx lost his livelihood after the suppression of the newspapers to which he had contributed, Engels gave up his own scientific work and returned to the sordid commercialism of his father's firm so that he could support his friend during his studies.

The turning point in Marx's thought

After he had met Engels and the French and Russian revolutionaries in Paris and learned of the concepts of economic theory, a whole new world opened itself to Marx. He threw himself into work, studying the works of Smith, Say, and Ricardo. The romantic revolutionary became a scientist investigating the economic conditions for the revolution. One can follow the progress of Marx's thought exactly in the *Economic and Philosophical Manuscripts* (written soon after his meeting with Engels), in which he discussed fundamental economic categories; then in *The Holy Family* and *The German Ideology* (written in 1844-6, partly in co-operation with Engels), in which he disavowed the ideological speculations of the German communists; and finally in *The Poverty of Philosophy* (1847), in which he elaborated his interpretation of communism in contradistinction to that of Proudhon, at that time the most widely known French communist. He recognized capitalism as the fate of the age and described alienation in its *economic* form and origin. The excessively acrimonious polemic in these essays against former communist friends must be seen as an attempt to put his own past behind him. 'It has not occurred to any of these philosophers to inquire into the connection of German philosophy with German reality, the connection of their criticism with their own material surroundings.'[5] Only Feuerbach escaped his wrath. Many years later he wrote: 'Compared with Hegel, Feuerbach is extremely poor. All the same he was epoch-making *after* Hegel.'[6]

The truth is of course that he owed much to both Hegel and Feuerbach. He was indebted to Hegel for the idea that labour is not only the satisfaction of basic economic needs but also the expression of human powers and historical processes:[7]

> The importance of Hegel's *Phenomenology* and its final result —
> the dialectic of negativity as the moving and producing principle
> — lies in the fact that Hegel conceives the self-creation of man as a
> process, objectification as loss of object [*Entgegenständlichung*],

as alienation and as supersession of this alienation; that he
therefore grasps the nature of labour and conceives objective
man — true, because real man — as the result of his own labour.

Marx inherited from Feuerbach the inversion of the dialectic from
idealism into materialism. He also accepted Feuerbach's idea that man
finds his true essence in the community. But, significantly, he did not
adopt Feuerbach's concept of love, which leads the individual to the
other in the community. The exclusion of the dialogue of love partly
explains why Marx regressed into idle speculation during the initial
phase of his materialist philosophy. The concrete concept of labour
derived from Hegel allowed him to find his way back from speculation
to real concerns.

Not idealism, only naturalism 'is capable of comprehending the
process of world history', Marx decided.[8] His materialist conception of
history was born! 'We know only a single science, the science of history' — true science demarcated from unhistorical classical economics
and idealist Hegelian philosophy.[9]

Empirical science of history

Marx had criticized Hegel's idealism from the standpoint of materialism
even before the move to Paris. But this materialist critique had been
philosophical, not empirical. In fact, it had contained fewer observations about material reality, about the true interests of capital and the
proletariat, than Hegel's philosophy. To indicate the change in his
approach, he took pains to stress in the preface to the *Economic and
Philosophical Manuscripts* that 'I arrived at my conclusions through an
entirely empirical analysis.'[10] Only now did he bring not only philosophical materialist arguments against Hegel but also empirical materialist
arguments:[11]

> History does nothing, it 'possesses no immense wealth', it 'wages
> no battles'. It is man, real, living man who does all that, who
> possesses and fights; 'history' is not, as it were, a person apart,
> using man as a means to achieve its own aims; history is
> nothing but the activity of man pursuing its aims.

Henceforward he would deal only with the empirically verifiable
life processes.

The other great historian of the period, Leopold von Ranke, also
wanted to show 'how it really happened' (*wie es wirklich gewesen*). He
set apart his science of history from that of Hegel using almost the same
words as Marx: because 'only the Idea would have an independent life'

in Hegel's world, men became means: 'all men would be mere shadows'.[12]
But Marx's empirical approach also differed from that of Ranke. For
although he accepted that men make their own history, he also contended that they do so 'not of their free will; not under circumstances
they themselves have chosen but under the given and inherited circumstances with which they are directly confronted'.[13] A change in the
material conditions, such as the technological advance from the hand-
mill to the steam-mill, sets man in a historical context. As he later
wrote in *Capital*, the historical development is to be demonstrated in
'free scientific inquiry', which[14]

> has to appropriate the material in detail, to analyse its different
> forms of development and to track down their inner connection.
> Only after this work has been done can the real movement be
> appropriately presented. If this is done successfully, if the life of
> the subject-matter is not reflected back in the ideas, then it may
> appear as if we have before us an *a priori* construction.

This methodological clarity guided him throughout his scientific
work.

The dialectic

Marx, then, conceived the dialectic as an empirical historical method.
Because this view is not generally accepted — the controversy over the
status of the dialectic has raged ever since Marx's death — it will be
necessary to substantiate the view that *in Marx's own mind* the dialectic
was an empirical method and not a rigid doctrine.

The economists of the eighteenth century, profoundly affected by
the great discoveries made at the time in the field of natural science,
began to search for scientific correlations in the free interplay of
economic forces. François Quesnay was the first to observe a unifying
scientific pattern in the economy in the flow of goods, which he
compared to the newly discovered circulation of the blood. Smith's
successors began to speak of economic 'laws'. Hegel acknowledged the
discovery of economic laws as a great scientific achievement: the
science of political economy 'is a credit to thought because it finds
laws for a mass of accidents'.[15] Marx, while adopting the economic laws
of classical economics, questioned their eternal truth:[16]

> The selfish misconception that induces you to transform into
> eternal laws of nature and reason the social forms springing
> from your present mode of production and form of property,
> . . . this misconception you share with every ruling class.

Unlike his predecessors, he saw through the historicity of economic laws.

Like no other of his time Marx was aware of the special character of historical laws. He realized that they were neither *a priori* laws, as in Hegel's philosophy, nor deterministic laws analogous to those of natural science, as in the fallacious theory of the political economists: rather, 'the economists' material is the active, energetic life of man'.[17] A Russian reviewer of *Capital*, I.I. Kaufman, wrote that according to Marx

> abstract laws do not exist. . . . On the contrary, in his opinion, every historical period possesses its own laws. . . . The old economists misunderstood the nature of economic laws when they likened them to the laws of physics and chemistry.

These words were quoted by Marx in the postface to the second edition of *Capital*, and he commented that they depict 'in a striking . . . way' the character of his historical dialectical laws.[18] He accepted Vico's contention that human history differs from natural history in that 'we have made the former, but not the latter'. In the same passage, which is remarkable because it sounds like a jibe at his orthodox followers, he also dealt with crude materialism:[19]

> The weakness of the abstract materialism of natural science, a materialism which excludes the historical process, is immediately evident from the abstract and ideological conceptions expressed by its spokesmen whenever they venture beyond the bounds of their own speciality.

When Marx referred to historical laws as 'natural laws' or 'laws of nature' (in German this distinction is syntactically clumsy and generally not made), he was contrasting them, in concurrence with common usage at the time, with divine laws. 'Natural laws' in this sense comprises historical laws *and* laws of natural science. In German philosophy the concept of nature was restricted to physics and biology and differentiated from human history only at the end of the nineteenth century; only since then has 'natural law' meant unequivocally a law of natural science.

But, one may interject, did Marx not argue in *Capital* that the economic laws apply 'with the inexorability of a natural process'?; that 'It is a question of these laws themselves, of these tendencies winning their way through and working themselves out with iron necessity'?; and that society 'can neither leap over the natural phases of its development nor remove them by decree'?[20] He did indeed. However, Marx's historical necessity does *not* mean the *logical* necessity for two twos to make four nor the immutability of the laws of natural science, but rather the necessity of historical development in the sense of *inevitability*.[21]* Goethe had the same in mind when he described the impending industrialization of Germany as having 'taken its course'.[22] Both Goethe and Marx perceived the inevitability of mechanization and industrialization.

Marx left no doubt about his view of the method by which the whole of history is brought under 'a single great natural law': this is, he said ironically, 'a very impressive method — for swaggering, sham-scientific, bombastic ignorance and intellectual laziness'.[23] And he went further than this. Because economic and historical laws are not deterministic like physical laws, they can show 'infinite variations and gradations in appearance, which can be ascertained only by analysis of the empirically given circumstances'.[24] But, as he wrote in the *Grundrisse*, the variations in appearance or 'coincidences' do not in the end invalidate the laws of inherent development.[25] Shortly before his death he responded to a question, put to him by Russian revolutionaries, on the expropriation of the agricultural producer:[26]

> The 'historical inevitability' of this movement is expressly
> limited to the countries of Western Europe. . . . In this western
> movement the point in question is therefore the transformation
> of one form of private property into another form of private
> property. With the Russian peasants one would on the contrary
> have to transform their common property into private property.

The passages quoted in this section show indisputably that Marx conceived the dialectical law purely on an historical plane, a law which is to be 'tracked down' in empirical analysis. But, it must be pointed out, despite Marx's methodological clarity about the empirical character of the dialectical laws, the Hegelian *a priori* view of the dialectic crept into his thought — and this, as we shall see, gave rise to the contradictions in his work.

---

*This point is illustrated, with reference to the Marxian law of accumulation, in note 21, p. 191.

Chapter nine

Economic base and ideological superstructure

Base and superstructure in Marx

In the great turning-point of his thought Marx grasped that labour, in which man creates himself, is not the intellectual activity of consciousness, as Hegel had supposed, but rather the concrete economic labour in which man provides for his needs. To investigate it, he picked up the threads of political economy. He subscribed to Smith's conception of labour as an eternal nature-imposed necessity; but he found that Smith had been ignorant of the self-realizing aspect in labour. Instead of the denial of man in classical economics, which regarded labour only as 'Jehovah's curse on Adam', Marx saw in the history of the industry 'the open book of the essential powers of man'.[1] He thus linked the external relationships of economic utility to the Hegelian conception of the self-creation of man through labour. Both aspects are illustrated in the famous comparison between the bee and man:[2]

> A bee would put many a human architect to shame by the construction of its honeycomb cells. But what distinguishes the worst architect from the best of bees is that the architect builds the cell in his mind before he constructs it in wax.

Every social form, Marx discovered, is always related to a specific mode of production. When the relations of production change, the relations of distribution alter accordingly. As manual labour gave way to machine production, greater capital and labour resources were required than could be supplied by the feudal and guild society. So the fetters of the old social conditions had to be burst asunder, and they were. The hand-mill produced a society with the feudal lord, the steam-mill produces a society with the industrial capitalist. The conditions of production reveal 'the innermost secret, the hidden basis of the entire social structure, and with it the political form of the relations of sovereignty and dependence, in short, the corresponding specific form of the state'.[3]

Every society has its specific ideas. In the age of aristocratic land-ownership the ideas of honour and loyalty predominated, while in the age of the capitalist bourgeoisie the ideas of freedom and equality prevail. They function as the standard of life for the oppressed class, 'partly as an embellishment or recognition of domination, partly as a moral means for this domination'.[4] The 'heroism, self-sacrifice, terror, civil war' which had brought capitalist society into the world was certainly impressive. But no sooner had the bourgeoisie seized power than it discarded the ideas of freedom and equality and put itself under the protection of a dictator (Napoleon III, for example) so that it can pursue its private business affairs.[5] The market appears as 'a very Eden of the innate rights of man'.[6] But because this is a mere appearance, the ideas that dominate society are called 'false consciousness'.

Marx's view of the relationship between the economic base and the ideological superstructure is summarized in the famous passage in the preface to the *Critique of Political Economy*:[7]

> My inquiry led me to the conclusion that neither legal relations nor political forms could be comprehended whether by themselves or on the basis of a so-called general development of the human mind, but that on the contrary they originate in the material conditions of life, the totality of which Hegel, following the example of English and French thinkers of the eighteenth century, embraces with the term 'civil society'; that the anatomy of this civil society, however, has to be sought in political economy. . . . In the social production of their existence, men inevitably enter into definite relations, which are independent of their will, namely the relations of production appropriate to a given stage in the development of their material forces of production. The totality of these relations of production constitutes the economic structure of society, the real foundation, on which arises a legal and political superstructure and to which correspond definite forms of social consciousness. The mode of production of material life conditions the general process of social, political and intellectual life. It is not the consciousness of men that determines their existence, but their social existence that determines their consciousness.

Never have morality and ideals been so debased and material life so glorified as in these words. But Marx's materialism actually articulates much more than crude materialism; it is an expression of the indignation at the disregard for morality in practical life. In 1842 he passionately urged the bourgeoisie to read St Augustine's *City of God* and study the fathers of the church and the spirit of Christianity — 'and then come back and tell us whether the state or the church is the "Christian state"! Or does not every moment of your practical life brand your theory as a lie?.[8] This criticism has its source in the experience, shared by Marx, Feuerbach and Kierkegaard, of contemporary morality; Nietzsche would later describe this morality as 'a Christianity depraved by hypocrisy and mediocrity allowing itself to be used as a buttress for this society and its property'.[9] The discrepancy between the spiritual tradition and practical life induced Marx (and Feuerbach and Kierkegaard, and Nietzsche in the next generation) to turn away from 'consciousness' towards material (or existential) 'being'. When one hears Marx's own words on the relationship of being and consciousness, it becomes painfully obvious how little of his spirit has been preserved in the doctrinaire theories of his school.

It was Feuerbach who had said 'Thought is out of being, but being is not out of thought.'[10] Marx took up this proposition but argued that Feuerbach had not seen being in its social and historical context. The 'religious sentiment' to which Feuerbach had traced consciousness is itself a product of society. Marx therefore amended Feuerbach by showing that it is *social* being which determines consciousness. For Marx, only an analysis of social conditions could confirm Feuerbach's materialism. As he said in another context (the hypocrisy of the privileged classes), 'It was, of course, only possible to discover all this when it became possible to criticise the conditions of production and intercourse in the hitherto existing world. . . . That shattered the basis of all morality.'[11]

Base and superstructure in Marx's contemporaries

Ranke also explored the nature of the driving force, the 'active essence', in history and concluded that it exists in political power. He also saw through the illusory character of moral ideas in practical life. Ranke perceived the potent factor in history in political terms, Marx in social terms. 'Parties do not merely defend opinions, they are forces in themselves, opposing each other', Ranke said, and Marx could also have said.[12] Ranke made the whole man into a political being, Marx made him into a social being. Individual existence, which until then had been at the centre of German thought, receded into the background.

After the Germans had lived in a fool's paradise for centuries, this generation became aware of the inefficacy of ideas and the importance of worldly forces in real life. Marx certainly did not claim to have discovered the significance of material forces. He drew attention to the French historians (e.g. Guizot and Thierry) and the British economists who had discerned the ideological character of the superstructure.

'Long before me bourgeois historians had described the historical development of this class struggle and bourgeois economists the economic anatomy of the classes.'[13] He also referred to Destutt de Tracy, who first defined ideology as a dependent idea.

But the intellectuals and politicians of this generation differed from their successors in that for them the substance of the Western spiritual tradition still carried weight. When they descended from heaven to earth, they still attempted to interpret the worldly powers within a framework of universal ideas. Marx deemed the idea of a free competitive society too simplistic and posited against it the idea of the free society. Ranke the historian and Bismarck the champion of *Realpolitik* proclaimed the primacy of political power, but to them it seemed integrated into the balance of power in Europe. Ranke maintained that 'a collection of natural histories . . . would not yet constitute a world history'; it is the task of the science of world history 'to recognize the interrelations and to show the course of the Great Events which unite and rule all peoples'.[14] Bismarck still possessed the moderation that his unsophisticated successors and admirers lost. The disciples learned from their master only the ruthless justification of power politics or (in the case of the Marxists) class interests and the contempt for morality.

While German humanism was admired in many countries and embraced by von Staël in France, Carlyle in Britain, the transcendentalists in America, the Westernized elite in Russia, and the educated Jews in the ghettos, it lost its formative force in its country of origin and was superseded by the anti-intellectual theories that helped to open the door to disaster.

Ideology and truth

Marx assumed that in a communist society the products of the mind would no longer be the untrue ideological superstructure of the economic base but would become the adequate expression of human essence. This must be anticipated here in the dicussion in order to ask whether ideas can have intrinsic value in an alienated society. Marx tackled this subject in the introduction to the *Grundrisse*, the posthumously published draft of the *Critique of Political Economy*:[15]

> The difficulty lies not in understanding that the Greek arts and epic are bound up with certain forms of social development. The difficulty is that they still afford us artistic pleasure and that in a certain respect they count as a norm and as an unattainable model. . . .
> Why should not the historic childhood of humanity, its most

beautiful unfolding, as a stage never to return, exercise an eternal charm? . . . The charm of their [the Greeks'] art is not in contradiction to the undeveloped stage of society on which it grew.

But even if, as Marx suggested, the norm and eternal charm are not in contradiction to the stage of society from which they arise, they certainly contravene the character of false consciousness which Marx attributed to all forms of consciousness — including art. There lies a difficulty here, as Marx saw: either the forms of consciousness are considered as a norm, or they are without exception untrue palliatives of economic interests.

As Marx raised the question whether art possesses an intrinsic value independent of its historical conditions, so Ranke asked whether the individual epochs of history could be seen as valid in themselves. He affirmed this on the grounds that 'Every epoch is immediate to God'; and 'Because of this the historian's study acquires a unique charm [the very word used by Marx!], since every epoch must be seen as something valid in itself.'[16] Did Marx attribute intrinsic value to art as Ranke attributed intrinsic value to the epochs of history? If his words could be interpreted in this sense, then the pitfall of the relativity of all values, to which German historicism until Dilthey and the social Darwinism of Spencer succumbed, could have been avoided.

It must be stressed that Marx *might* be interpreted in this way, for after all he restricted the validity of the norm and the eternal charm of art with the qualification 'in a certain respect'. Continuing his reflection on this problem, he maintained:[17]

A man cannot become a child again, or he becomes childish. But does he not find joy in the child's naïveté, and must he himself not strive to reproduce its truth at a higher stage?

The qualifying addition 'in a certain respect' and the rhetorical form of the above question betray that Marx, whose writing was always clear and unequivocal, had not mastered the 'difficulty' at hand. It is therefore no coincidence that he discarded the introduction and published only the preface of the *Critique of Political Economy*, in which he explained, as we saw, intellectual life as conditioned by the mode of production.

In the preface Marx also gave the reason for the omission of the introduction: 'It seems to me confusing to anticipate results which still have to be substantiated.'[18] He knew he was in a quandary, and, as he wrote to Engels, he wanted to come back to the problems of the philosophy of history once he had finished with 'the whole of the economic shit'.[19] But the laborious, time-consuming preparation of his economic works never allowed him to carry out his intention. As he did not take time to work out the materialist conception of history, it is not surprising that apart from the inconsistency discussed above, a number of other contradictory formulations appear in his writings. Thus we read at one point that language 'only arises from the need, the necessity, of intercourse with other men'; or 'Milton produced *Paradise Lost* for the same reason that the silk worm produces silk.'[20] But elsewhere he suggested that 'really free working' is exemplified in 'composing' and the 'semi-artistic worker of the Middle Ages'.[21]

It is interesting to note that in the French edition of the *Critique of Political Economy* Marx insisted that the word *bedingt*, literally 'conditions' or 'determines', which defines the relationship between the base and the superstructure, be translated as *domine* rather than *détermine* or *conditione*. (In the new Penguin translation of the preface the sentence reads: 'The mode of production of material life *conditions* the general process of social, political and intellectual life'.) The word *domine* is not a literal translation of *bedingt* but an interpretation: it allows more than *bedingt* a degree of autonomy to the superstructure. Sadly, this translation supervised by Marx went unnoticed until Rubel first pointed it out in 1971 in his biography of Marx.[22] The words of the preface were adopted in their 'strong' and rigid sense by Marx's disciples, who made them into *the* dogma of Marxism.

At any rate, Marx cared little for realistic art with a tendency, and he ridiculed Lasalle's political drama *Franz von Sickingen*. Contrary to the impression given by the simple formula of the preface to the *Critique of Political Economy*, Marx was definitely moved by the eternal charm of art. He read Aeschylus in the original and Shakespeare. When in his later years he taught himself Russian in order to study the Russian economy, he viewed the chance to read Gogol and Pushkin in the original as compensation for the drudgery of study.[23] He obtained the norm with which he judged his age from Aeschylus and Shakespeare, Kant and Hegel, Goethe and Pushkin.

Chapter ten

Historical sociology

The historical process of alienation

For Marx, there exist two sides of economic alienation in modern society. The labour process exhibits two characteristic phenomena: firstly, the worker works under the control of the capitalist; and secondly, the product of the worker's labour belongs not to himself but to the capitalist. The product of the labour process belongs to the capitalist just as much as 'the wine which is the product of the process of fermentation going on in his cellar'.[1] But these two sides of alienation did not begin with the capitalist mode of production; they are rooted in the origin of civilization itself. Every primitive has his own cave, hut or tent; he is 'a hunter, a fisherman, a shepherd, . . . and must remain so if he does not want to lose his means of livelihood'.[2] With the first form of private property (according to Marx pure private property was differentiated from communal tribal property only at a later date) and with the division of labour the product begins to dominate man. The division of labour impoverishes individual activity, and contradictions arise between the individuals and the community, and eventually between the classes within the community. The division of labour spreads from the economic sphere to permeate the whole of life.

Marx, like Nietzsche, deplored this segmentation of man. 'We make a nation of Helots, and have no free citizens', he quoted from Ferguson.[3] At times he pondered on a 'natural state' in which man was not yet dominated by his products. In the unpublished *Grundrisse* he spoke of the 'beauty and greatness of . . . this spontaneous interconnection' existing before the division of labour.[4] He deleted this passage in the published text of the *Critique of Political Economy*, presumably because he did not want it to be misconstrued as a romantic yearning for a past golden age. Elsewhere he explicitly rejected the idea that 'the childish world of antiquity appears . . . as loftier', and emphasized that 'the most odious exploitation' still took place in the pre-industrial stage of society.[5]

Strongly opposed to any romantic contemplation of the past, Marx showed that it is in fact the negation of the natural state which 'produces man in all the richness of his being, the rich man who is profoundly and abundantly endowed with all the senses'.[6] The ascent of man occurs in the dialectic of, on the one hand, the impoverishment of his individual activity through alienation and, on the other hand, the differentiation of talents and occupation through the division of labour.[7]

Historical progress through conflict

Marx argued that the acquisition of new means of production and the correlated changes in the mode of production will lead to collisions with the existing social conditions. Already in the 1840s he maintained that the growing contradictions must necessarily come to a head in a revolution; and in *Capital* he analysed how the contradictions mature in the advancing process of production.

Marx's work was concerned with the history of the European economy, especially the contemporary economy, because he wanted to 'reveal the economic law of motion of modern society'.[8] Influenced by Hegel, he originally assumed that the whole of history is governed by the single dialectical movement from the classical slave economy to the feudal and capitalist economy, and from these to the socialist economy. But he soon realized that in Asia, for instance, the same mode of production had existed for centuries. It had not been set in motion by an internal dialectic but only by the intrusion of European colonial powers. He therefore classified the Asian mode of production as a particular mode besides the classical, feudal, and capitalist modes.[9]

The last conflict of 'prehistory'

In Marx's view, the process of alienation reaches its greatest intensity in capitalist society. Products are no longer produced for consumption but for exchange. They form a separate world outside of the individuals — a world that assumes for them 'the fantastic form of a relation between things'. This inversion of all relations is called 'fetishism', which consists[10]

> in the fact that the commodity reflects the social characteristics of men's own labour as objective characteristics of the products of labour themselves, as the socio-natural properties of these things.

Alienation inherent in economic activity is comparable to the religious alienation uncovered by Feuerbach. 'Just as man is governed, in religion, by the products of his own brain, so, in capitalist production, he is governed by the products of his own hand.'[11]

Human relationships are replaced by exchange relationships. 'The motive of those engaged in exchange is not humanity but egoism.'[12] Only self-interest brings people together: 'Money is the universal whore, the universal pimp of men and peoples.'[13] People serve each other only as means: the worker serves the capitalist as a means to production, the capitalist serves the worker as a means to subsistence. The worker is a commodity like any other, bought for a price which only just allows him to stay alive and be in a condition to propagate his race. He can barely provide for his most basic needs with the price he receives for his labour. Political economy, which calls itself the 'science of wealth', gives as a standard the worst possible state of privation that life can know. The people have lost their free humanity. The capitalist is 'the ascetic but rapacious skinflint' and the worker is 'the ascetic but productive slave'.[14] When 'humanitarian' authors reproach economics for its cynical language, they fail to realize that the cynicism 'is in the facts and not in the words which express the facts'.[15] The science of economics exposes economic relations in all their crudity.

The emancipation of the peasants and artisans, which initiated the development of capitalism, was merely a change in the form of servitude, a change from feudal to capitalist exploitation. The antagonism between the occupations at the beginning of civilization was intensified in feudal society into the opposition between the estates, and comes to a head in the opposition between the two classes, the bourgeoisie and the proletariat. 'The history of all hitherto existing society is the history of class struggles.'[16] The proletarian revolution will be a total revolution that will abolish all classes. 'The prehistory of human society accordingly closes with this social formation.'[17]

Chapter eleven

Political economy

Marx believed that the anatomy of bourgeois society must be sought in political economy. He therefore devoted himself mainly to the study of economics after the great turning-point in his life. An adequate exposition of his economic theories would require a separate book. For the purposes of this study they will be outlined only to the extent necessary for an understanding of Marx's conception of socialism.

The labour theory of value

Political economy begins with the analysis of the commodity, because the value-form of the commodity is the cell of bourgeois society. In capitalist production the factory-owner produces commodities not for his own consumption but for others, for exchange, thereby satisfying his needs indirectly. The product of labour is in all social epochs a use-value; but only in an exchange economy does it acquire an 'objectivity' (*Gegenständlichkeit*), the fetishism of the commodity, which differs qualitatively from the natural form and is quantitatively exchangeable. The product of labour is transformed into a commodity. Only the exchange proves the utility of the commodity for others, proves that it has a use-value for others. As at other times in history, the conversion of the product into a commodity constitutes an enrichment of the productive forces of society, for the production of commodities creates not only use-values but also use-values for others, 'social use-values'.[1]

When the value of the commodity exists not in its use but in its exchange, what then is the common factor that makes this exchange possible? The common denominator cannot be a characteristic of the commodity itself, since exchange is independent of its use-value as, say, wool or iron. What remains as the common factor after the abstraction from use-value is the *labour* contained in the product – this Smith and Ricardo had already established. The magnitude of the value is measured by 'the quantity of the "value-forming substance", the labour, contained in the article'; or to put it more precisely: since the quantum of labour required for the production of a commodity varies according to the state of technology, value is measured by 'the labour-time which is necessary on an average, or in other words is socially necessary' to produce a commodity.[2] 'As exchange-values, all commodities are merely definite quantities of *congealed labour-time*'.[3]

The commodity of labour-power is measured like any other commodity by the quantum of labour necessary for its production, in this case by the quantity of foodstuffs, clothing, and so on, required for the reproduction of the worker's labour-power. This labour-time is not only necessary for the reproduction of the worker; it is also necessary for the factory-owner and his world, 'because the continued existence of the worker is the basis of that world'.[4] Every value is measured as a quantum of labour-time. The labour-time socially necessary for the production of commodities is a 'law of nature' regulating the contingent and constantly vacillating conditions of exchange.[5]

Originally in history, a social act of agreement made a specific commodity such as cattle or wheat into the general equivalent relating the different commodities to each other as values. The commodity that serves the present age as the equivalent of exchange is money. The money that buys commodities for exchange, and not for the needs of the money-owner, is called 'capital'.

Surplus-value, the 'secret' of capitalist production

How is it possible that the capitalist, who buys commodities at their value and sells them at their value, still manages to extract more value — a profit — than he has invested? The answer, which reveals the 'secret' of capitalist production, is that there is only one commodity which is a source of surplus-value: labour-power. When the worker sells his labour to the capitalist as a commodity on the free market, he gives to his contractor not only the quantum of labour which the latter pays him as the value of his commodity — the value necessary for its reproduction — but in addition a quantum of unpaid labour. This generates surplus-value, which for the capitalist 'has all the charms of something created out of nothing'.[6] The worker allows himself to be cheated out of this difference because the threat of starvation compels him to sell his labour-power on the market.

Unpaid surplus labour has existed in all social formations. In the ancient slave economy all labour appeared to be unpaid, in the free enterprise economy unpaid labour appears to be paid. It is the illusory legal relationships obtaining in society that conceal the reality behind the appearances: where they formerly concealed the labour of the slave working for himself, they now conceal the free worker's working for nothing. Thus, surplus-value in bourgeois society does not appear as theft or exploitation but as property.

The law of accumulation of capital

There are two components of capital: the constant part, which is turned into instruments of labour and raw materials; and the variable part, which is turned into labour-power. Constant capital does not undergo an alteration of value in the process of production; variable capital, however, reproduces and increases its value. A small part of the surplus-value, which has been extracted from labour in excess of its actual value, is consumed by the capitalist, but the larger part is transformed into capital. Accumulation is made possible with the variable part of capital. In other words, the creation of surplus-value ensures the continuation of the capitalist process of production because it allows the reproduction and accumulation of capital. 'The production of surplus-value, or the making of profits, is the absolute law of this mode of production.'[7]

The accumulation of capital occurred initially by the expropriation of the means of production. This is called 'primitive accumulation'. It is 'the history of economic original sin' which tells us how it came to pass that the owners of capital accumulated wealth and the producers had nothing to sell but their own skins.

> And from this original sin dates the poverty of the great
> majority who, despite all their labour, have up to now nothing
> to sell but themselves, and the wealth of the few that increases
> constantly, although they have long ceased to work.[8]

The constant appropriation by the capitalist, without equivalent, of a portion of the labour of others which has already been 'objectified' (i.e. turned into means of production) is transformed into a second, additional capital.[9] Accumulation, then, occurs on a progressively increasing scale. 'Accumulate, accumulate! That is Moses and the prophets!'[10]

The bourgeoisie attempts to justify the capitalist drive and the profit motive by renouncing all worldly pleasures. 'Industry furnishes the material which saving accumulates' (a quote from Smith).[11] In so far as the capitalist's actions are a mere function of capital, his own private consumption 'counts as robbery committed against the accumulation of his capital'.[12] But with increasing prosperity the bourgeois no longer needs to forgo the pleasures of life. The continual exploitation of the workers enables him to indulge in any luxury. He loses the last remnant of shame and conscience. The ascetic skinflint begins to enjoy leisure. The worker, however, suffers increasing degradation and almost becomes part of the machine, intellectually and physically crippled.

The introduction of modern machinery reduces the price of commodities. Competition forces the entrepreneur to purchase newer and better machines; in this way capitalist production revolutionizes all social conditions. No previous epoch has experienced this kind of revolutionary dynamic. The old crafts are destroyed, both in the home market and abroad; production requires an ever-expanding market and so creates a world market. The bourgeoisie compels all nations 'to introduce what it calls civilization in their midst, i.e. to become bourgeois themselves.'[13] The net of the world market devours all peoples. The big capitalists ruin the small capitalists. Competition together with credit eventually lead to the point where capitals are concentrated in fewer and fewer hands.

Marx's historical and dialectical approach enabled him to see the negativity of the ruthless exploitation of the worker as the motive and creative principle of progress. He recognized that the conditions of production based on exploitation are conducive to the development of the means of production and the growth of social wealth. Marx admired the achievements of capitalism. 'The bourgeoisie, during its rule of scarce one hundred years, has created more massive and more colossal productive forces than have all preceding generations together'; 'It has accomplished wonders far surpassing Egyptian pyramids, Roman aqueducts, and Gothic cathedrals.'[14] In a study of the dissolution of the old stagnant Indian economy by British capital, he rebuked the British because their desire to cause a social revolution in India 'was actuated only by the vilest interests.' But in the same breath he all but justified Britain's actions: 'whatever may have been the crimes of England she was the unconscious tool of history in bringing about that revolution'.[15] Marx accepted the view of the classical political economists who asserted that because of its accumulation capitalism possesses 'historical value' and a 'right of historical existence'.[16]

The theory of crisis

The contradictions within capitalist production mature in the development of the process of production. Labour-saving requirements decrease as labour-saving machines are introduced, and a surplus population of labour is created. At the same time over production precipitates economic crises (which had been described – and feared – by economists before Marx). Crises occur in cycles. The sudden expansion of the economy causes a sudden contraction, and then the latter once again leads to the former.

On the one hand, the surplus population of workers constitutes a disposable human material, 'the industrial reserve army'.[17] Wages are regulated solely by the expansion and contraction of the reserve army of labour. 'The movement of the law of supply and demand of labour on this basis completes the despotism of capital.'[18] This law, which bourgeois economists treat as eternal and sacred, has a corollary:[19]

> The more extensive . . . the pauperized sections of the working class and the industrial reserve army, the greater is official pauperism. This is the absolute general law of capitalist accumulation.

On the other hand, the despotism of capital turns against itself as it grows. The constant part of capital, which is converted into machinery, increases; and the variable capital, which is converted into labour, decreases in relation to constant capital. And because only variable capital generates surplus-value, its relative reduction will reduce the relative quantity of surplus-value: the rate of profit will fall.[20] The falling rate of profit can be explained in terms of the internal contradictions of capitalist production.

> The real barrier of capitalist production is capital itself. . . . The means — unconditional development of the productive forces of society — comes continually into conflict with the limited purpose, the self-expansion [*Selbstverwertung*, 'self-valorization'] of the existing capital.[21]

Capitalist production will come to an end because it is self-contradictory.

The historically transitory character of capitalism becomes evident at this point. The unity of capitalist production, which classical economists regarded as a harmonious interplay, is exposed as chaotic. The contradiction between unemployed capital and unemployed workers leads to the bursting asunder of the chains of capitalism and the formation of a new mode of production through the action of the immanent laws of capitalist production itself.

As a young communist Marx had argued against the utopian socialists that 'Communism is for us not a state of affairs which is to be established, an ideal to which reality will have to adjust itself. We call communism the *real* movement which abolishes the present state of things.'[22] His mature scientific work showed the scientific laws of this movement — Q.E.D.

The process of socialization

The elements of the new society, which emerge at the same time as those of the old are disintegrating, are formed from elements in the two classes of the old society: from the concentration of capital within the capitalist class and from the co-operation within the proletarian class. On the one hand the means of production are transformed into 'social production capacities', for the means of production are not produced by individual capitalists but by the co-operation of the whole society.[23] On the other hand the combined co-operation in the division of labour creates 'the co-operative forms of the labour process'.[24]

Modern competitive society began with the expropriation of the producers' private property by the capitalists. Competition continued the process of expropriation. It allowed the big capitalists to expropriate the smaller capitalists, until (as Marx observed in 1848) 'in your existing society, private property is already done away with for nine tenths of the population'.[25] Those few who survive in the competitive struggle will meet the same fate in the end.

The history of capitalism can be summarized as follows: 'Capitalism begets, with the inexorability of a natural process, its own negation. This is the negation of the negation.'[26] The negation of private property makes possible for the first time in this world a social organization in which the producers are no longer dominated by the productive forces; the producers regulate them rationally and co-operatively. The 'pre-history' of human society comes to an end, a new epoch begins.

The importance and shortcomings of Marx's economics

Marx continued the tradition of classical economics. He acknowledged that to have destroyed the prevalent mystified view of the capitalist mode of production was the great merit of classical British political economy. And he admired the intellectual honesty of Ricardo, who in cases where his analysis opposed the interests of the bourgeoisie would be 'just as ruthless towards it' as he was at times towards the proletariat and the aristocracy.[27] There is a reason for this praise: since Marx wanted to derive socialism objectively from a critique of existing society, he could use the labour theory of value, as well as the dialectic, as the foundation of scientific socialism.

However, there exists a fundamental ambiguity in the economic concept of value. Classical economics, like the political philosophy of the same period, was still steeped in the tradition of natural law, according to which specific norms are naturally just and therefore binding. The norms correspond in each case to the conceptual system of the age. The natural law of medieval Christianity recognized as natural, i.e. legitimate, the guarantee of subsistence and the just price. Modern secular natural law, in contrast, proceeded from the assumption that man is good and free by nature. Natural and binding was the free market and the price determined by market forces in the economic sphere, as was the state founded on the contract of free individuals in the political sphere. Conversely, intervention in the free market by means of price and wage controls and any restrictions on political freedom were considered unnatural and hence inadmissible. Partly consciously, partly unconsciously, the axioms of natural law entered into the price theories of classical economics.

Only later economists became aware of the natural law presuppositions in their price theories. As far as I am aware, Eugen von Böhm-Bawerk was the first to state clearly that economic value is only a means to a specific end, namely the satisfaction of wants, and that it has nothing to do with value in the sense of intrinsic value.[28] Weber avoided the concept of value altogether, so as to preclude any ambiguity. A number of critics (e.g. Myrdal and Arendt) have since contended that the concept of 'absolute' value does not belong in economic theory.

A more comprehensive objection to the labour theory of value must also be mentioned here: the marginal utility theory of the Austrian school of economists. Menger, Wieser, Böhm-Bawerk and others also continued the work of Ricardo. Their refutation of the labour theory of value is beyond the scope of this study. Suffice it to say that it is argued as follows: if, as Marx said, profits can only be made from the variable part of capital, the part that is converted into labour, how then does the labour theory of value explain the phenomenon of capitalists buying labour-saving machines, for which the variable capital is minimal, in order to *increase* their profits? The Marxian theory is reduced to absurdity.

But even if Marx's labour theory of value and, by extension, the theory of surplus-value (let alone the law of pauperization) are not scientifically tenable, his political economy does not collapse. Its significance lies not in these theories but in something quite different. Precisely because he acknowledged the historical achievement of the capitalist bourgeoisie − the creation of the greatest mass of productive forces ever − he set himself the task of exposing the dark side of capitalist production. Both the capitalist, 'the ascetic but rapacious skinflint', and the worker, 'the ascetic but productive slave', are forced into the service of the process of production and become dominated by objects.[29] In establishing the laws which ostensibly govern the happiness of the majority of the people (Ricardo's point), no one considered the cost of this 'happiness'. The workers are formally free, but they have no security. Their freedom consists only of being able to sell their labour-power on the free market. So even when the theory of exploitation through extraction of surplus-value is wrong, Marx's conclusion that the continued existence of the worker is necessary for capitalism because it is the basis of that world is not invalidated. To have diagnosed the subjugation of the worker under the entrepreneur as the precondition of modern industrial society is one of Marx's great scientific achievements. Furthermore, in a period when the mechanism of the free market was functioning properly, Marx foresaw 'the centralization of the means of production' in a few capitalist hands — multi-national corporations, as they are called today — and 'the socialization of labour' (though admittedly he may not have imagined the organization of labour in powerful trade unions).[30] Marx recognized that both developments interfered with the free interplay of market forces and would give rise to a new organization of production.

Chapter twelve

Towards the new society

The tasks of the self-conscious proletariat

With the discovery of the dialectical and historical economic laws Marx
had succeeded in the goal he had set himself from the moment he
became a communist: to discover the new world in a critique of the
old, rather than construct utopias like other socialists. Socialism was
put on a scientific basis.

Marx was convinced that the development from feudalism to
capitalism had been 'an incomparably more protracted, violent and
difficult process' than the development from capitalism to socialism
would be, because in the latter case only a few usurpers are opposing
the people.[1] The proletariat possesses one element of success: numbers.
But, he noted, 'numbers weigh only in the balance, if united by a
combination and led by knowledge'.[2] The proletariat could learn from
the bourgeois revolutions in England and France. The organization of
great numbers does not guarantee success; heroism and self-sacrifice are
as essential. It is however in *knowledge* that the proletarian revolution
is ahead of the bourgeois revolutions. Cromwell and Robespierre
thought they were fighting for the rights of man, but in fact they set
free the market economy of the bourgeoisie. Their ideals made them
blind to the material forces that decided the outcome of their revolutions. Scientific socialism, in contrast, makes the working class conscious
of the goal of the imminent revolution. Consequently, 'The working
class ... have no ideals to realize, but to set free the elements of the
new society.'[3] The revolutionary praxis to achieve the goal of the new
society will require 'the strictest centralization of power in the hands
of the state authority'.[4] The syndicalism of Proudhon and Bakunin
must therefore be rejected. Although the goal of the revolution is
scientifically predetermined, the political struggle to achieve the goal
will depend 'everywhere and at all times, on the historical conditions
for the time existing'.[5] The process of transformation is in progress.
It can take a form more brutal or more human, society can 'shorten

and lessen the birth pangs'.[6]

The clarity of Marx's ideas on the economic development towards the new society contrasts markedly with his vacillating assessment of how the birth of the new society will proceed. In the preface to the new German edition of the *Communist Manifesto* (1872) he admitted openly that the revolutionary measures suggested twenty-five years previously were outdated.[7] At times he modelled the dictatorship of the proletariat on the Jacobin dictatorship, but, influenced by democratic advances such as the second electoral reform of 1867 in Britain, he also thought it possible that workers may attain their goal by peaceful means in democratic countries.[8] The Paris commune of 1871 provided him with an example of heroism and greatness at the time, but ten years later he criticized its lack of common sense.[9] Yet though he wavered on matters of tactics, taking into account the historical constellation, his strategic goal — the establishment of the new free society — never changed.

The early vision of the new society: the supersession of alienation

Economics can go no further than reveal the economic laws operating in modern society. This was the ultimate aim of *Capital*. To go beyond this and describe the new society would be, in Marx's view, utopian. Not only the struggle for a socialist society but also its future organization will depend on specific circumstances. That is why there are no more than a few indications of the practical organization of communist society in *Capital* (or anywhere else, for that matter).

But can science not give indirect hints of the positive new aspect of the future social order, in the same way that negative theology, by avoiding direct statements about God, makes indirect statements about him? Such indirect indications of the supersession of alienation are indeed scattered in the works of Marx. Alienation embraces, for him, the two aspects of 'real life' (i.e. economic life) and 'consciousness' (i.e. political and spiritual ideas).[10] About the emancipation of economic life from alienation, he wrote in *The German Ideology*:[11]

> Communism differs from all previous movements in that it overturns the basis of all earlier relationships of production and intercourse, and for the first time consciously treats all naturally evolved premises as the creation of hitherto existing men, strips them of their natural character and subjugates them to the power of the united individuals. Its organisation is, therefore, essentially economic.

Moreover, the development of productive forces is an absolute premise

for the socialist organization of production, because 'without it privation, *want*, is merely made general, and with want the struggle for
necessities would begin again, and all the old filthy business would
necessarily be restored'.[12] This sentence is noteworthy in view of the
modern objection to consumer society. Marx would never have indulged
in the romantic reflections of Mill, his contemporary and also successor
to Smith and Ricardo, who preferred the 'stationary state' of capital
and wealth to the 'struggling to get on, trampling, crushing, elbowing
and treading on each other's heels'.[13] He confirmed the insight of
classical economics into the dynamic character of the modern economy,
whether it be capitalist or socialist. He disapproved of a crude and
'unthinking' communism, which would be tantamount to the 'return
to the unnatural simplicity of the poor, unrefined man who has no
needs'.[14]

In the early writings Marx argued that socialist society differs from
capitalism because it subjects production to the power of the united
individuals, production is put in the service of human needs. Society
becomes a true co-operative community caring for its members. The
coercive aspect of the division of labour is eliminated. 'Only at this
stage does self-activity coincide with material life.'[15] When society
regulates production, it will be possible for everyone to do one thing
today and another tomorrow, 'to hunt in the morning, to fish in the
afternoon, rear cattle in the evening, criticise after dinner . . . without
ever becoming a hunter, fisherman, shepherd or critic'.[16] (Evidently
Marx had in mind the medieval artisan who was completely absorbed
in his work. He expected the industrial worker to regain the same
relationship to his work as the medieval artisan had enjoyed, though
without the aspect of servitude.)

As alienation is overcome in the economic form of production, so it
will be overcome in the intellectual sphere, in the political forms, and
the forms of consciousness. In the 'prehistory' of human society
political power is only an extension of the ruling class; in the classless
society there 'will be no more political power properly so called'.[17]
Individualistic society is superseded by the 'human society', the atom-
ization of man is superseded by the 'real community'.[18] Communist
society is 'the only society in which the genuine free development of
individuals ceases to be a mere phrase'.[19] 'Our productions would be
as many mirrors from which our natures would shine forth.'[20]

Anticipating man's redemption from the fate of alienation, Marx
burst out in jubilation:[21]

> Communism is the possible supersession of private property as
> human self-estrangement, and hence the true appropriation of
> the human essence through and for man. . . . This communism,

as fully developed naturalism, equals humanism, and a fully developed humanism equals naturalism; it is the genuine resolution of the conflict between man and nature, and between man and man, the true resolution of the conflict between existence and being, between objectification and self-affirmation, between freedom and necessity, between individual and species. It is the solution of the riddle of history and knows itself to be the solution. . . .

Society is therefore the perfected unity in essence of man and nature, the true resurrection of nature, the realized naturalism of man and realized humanism of nature.

By asserting the identity of naturalism and humanism Marx in fact asserted the identity of necessary labour for the satisfaction of needs and the free development of man's essence. The above excerpts from the *Economic and Philosophical Manuscripts* reaffirm European humanism, which the bourgeoisie had degraded to non-committal phraseology and hypocrisy.

The later vision of the new society: does alienation remain?

In the course of his economic studies Marx had to admit that a future communist society could not come into existence in the form he had envisaged and outlined in the early works. There are at least five areas in which he either changed the emphasis of the argument during the course of his work (from the *Grundrisse* of 1857-8 to the unfinished third volume of *Capital*), or failed to resolve a problem and so became entangled in a mesh of contradictions.

1 Already in the *Grundrisse* Marx realized that labour could not become 'play' in the communist society but must remain 'discipline'. Free time, which is both 'idle' time and time for the 'higher activity' of the individuals' artistic and scientific development, is only possible *outside* the labour process.[22] He had moved away from his earlier view that humanism, labour as self-creation, would coincide with necessity, labour as a means to satisfy basic needs.

2 In the first volume of *Capital* Marx assumed that production and distribution in a socialist society would be regulated, in accordance with a definite plan, by an 'association of free men'. Social planning is in this case reconcilable with individual freedom, he maintained, because the people themselves organize in 'self-awareness' both the common labour and the distribution of the total product according to the measure of individual labour-time. Domination by the blind market forces is overcome, the social relations of the producers are 'transparent

in their simplicity', in production as well as distribution.[23] But in
volume two he recognized that, contrary to the transparent and simple
model of social production, it is necessary to control the processes of
the economy through 'book-keeping'. Moreover, book-keeping, as the
supervision of the process of production, becomes even more necessary
when production takes place on a social scale. It is 'more necessary in
communal production than in capitalist production'.[24] He reiterated
this view in volume three: 'distribution of social labour among the
various production groups, ultimately the book-keeping encompassing
all this, become ever more essential than ever'.[25] Indeed! But is it not
possible that this kind of comprehensive accountancy will oppress the
people and render their relations unfathomable, even Kafkaesque?

3   Marx had no doubt that, 'with the inevitable conquest of
political power by the working class, technological education, both
theoretical and practical, will take its proper place in the schools of the
workers'.[26] Leaving aside the question as to whether technological
education could not be provided within the existing social organization
(as has in fact happened since Marx wrote these words), it must be
asked whether technological education can be the way to the supersession of the division of labour? Is the technically educated worker,
even when he takes up different modes of activity in turn, the totally
developed individual of the earlier essays?

4   As an example for the communist mode of production Marx
proposed the co-operative societies, in which the owner of capital is
replaced by an 'industrial manager'. A separation of factory management and ownership has also occurred in the limited company; but the
co-operative factory is distinctive because the manager is paid by the
workers. Thus the antagonistic nature of supervision disappears, and the
workers and management establish a harmonious relationship in the
same way that the members of an orchestra relate to the conductor.[27]
But is this comparison of social labour to an orchestra not facile and
illusory?

5   The real barrier of capitalist production is for Marx the fact that
'production is only production for capital and not vice versa, the means
of production are not mere means for a constant expansion of the living
process of the society of producers'.[28] Because capital appears as the
motive and purpose of production, the capitalist is forced to accumulate. But, as Marx argued in volume three of *Capital*, lest the old struggle
for necessities begin again the productive forces must be constantly
developed – and this applies as much to socialism as to capitalism.[29] Does
this not imply that communist production, just like capitalist production, is subject to the law of accumulation? This question must be
asked despite the obvious differences between the two modes of
production.

The issues raised here lead to the core of Marx's work and the contradictions within it. Their implications will be discussed in the next chapter.

Chapter thirteen

Contradictions in Marx

Reconciliation or conflict between the realm of necessity and the true realm of freedom?

As we saw in chapter 12, Marx stipulated in volume three of *Capital* a number of requirements for social production, namely 1 disciplined work; 2 comprehensive control of production through book-keeping; 3 professional training; 4 managers; and 5 accumulation. But it is precisely these requirements that are characteristic of 'the formal independence of . . . conditions of labour in relation to labour' — that independence which he called 'reification' (*Verdinglichung*), because the conditions of labour oppose the worker as objects and dominate him.[1] Reification describes, in other words, man's alienation from production. Are we to conclude from this that alienation is not only inherent in capitalist production but in all industrial production, including social production? Marx himself admitted that freedom in social production could consist only in the freedom of the associated producers to regulate their interchange with nature on a rational basis, instead of being ruled by nature's blind forces. He also admitted that social production must remain a realm of necessity. 'Just as the savage must wrestle with Nature . . . to maintain and reproduce life, so must civilised man.' To this he added the unequivocal comment that 'he must do so under all possible modes of production'.[2] But the real goal of socialization — the human society, true humanism — would then not be achieved at all! The monumental study of society, for which he had made so many sacrifices, would then have resulted in the refutation of his vision of a society emancipated from alienation.

It is a tribute to Marx's scientific integrity and human greatness that he did not close his mind to this unexpected discovery. He had certainly not given up the ideal of the restitution of humanity; but he did realize that the supersession of alienation could not include both sides of life, the economic base and consciousness, as he had assumed until then.

Man, he wrote, will always be compelled to work hard for his daily bread, and therefore the sphere of production will remain a realm of necessity. But the realm of freedom has not become an impossibility: it begins 'only where labour which is determined by necessity and mundane considerations ceases'. But this, the 'true' realm of freedom, lies 'in the very nature' of things beyond the sphere of material production.[3]

Already in the *Grundrisse* of 1857-8 Marx had made a distinction between the artistic and scientific development of the individuals in their free time and the productive labour in their working hours. Free time would naturally transform its possessor into 'a different subject'.[4] He also raised an objection to Fourier's hope that labour could become pure amusement and play. This almost sounds like an oblique criticism of his own earlier view of communist society as a near-paradise in which the individuals could do as they pleased.

The distinction between higher leisure activity and toilsome industrial labour suggests a resignation from the vision of the *Economic and Philosophical Manuscripts*, in which communism achieves the true resolution of the conflict between freedom and necessity. It suggests, therefore, a second turning-point in Marx's thought. Initially, in the *Grundrisse* he tried to present the 'abstract antithesis', as he called it, between economic labour and higher activity as beneficial for the free development of the individuals, because the latter would redound upon the former.[5] Presumably Marx thought that the working masses, who under capitalism struggled to provide for the needs of society, would in communist society be able to participate in cultural activities which had previously been the domain of a small elite. In the *Theories of Surplus-Value*, written a few years after the *Grundrisse*, he also demanded a reduction in working hours and the abolition of the social conflict between 'master and men'. A man's labour would then acquire 'a quite different, a free character', and it would be 'of a much higher quality than that of a beast of burden'.[6]

But as he continued his investigations of modern industrial society, Marx observed a divergence rather than a convergence between necessary economic labour and free higher activity. He found that even when the capitalist no longer appropriates the free time of the worker and the worker enjoys the fruits of his own labour, man still has to work to make a living. Artistic creativity may have been reconcilable with the labour of the medieval craftsmen, but it is not reconcilable with disciplined work at the machine.[7] Besides, social production requires comprehensive book-keeping and control, which the workers themselves cannot carry out. They will remain subject to the demands of production even in a socialist society.

Eventually Marx struggled through to the realization that the distinction between a free development of human energy and necessary economic labour is not 'abstract' (as he had assumed in the *Grundrisse*); rather, the two activities are 'in the very nature of things' different and are performed in different realms. He died before he could draw the conclusions from this insight.

The preparatory drafts of *Capital* leave no doubt that in his later economic works Marx was still very much concerned with more than an economic goal. This non-economic goal is the free development of individuals and their participation in the life of the community — the advance to higher activity; and it includes the worker's option to squander his money (on drink, for instance), for he will be free and 'responsible to himself for the way he spends his wages'.[8] Marx investigated the economic conditions of the emancipation of man. But his goal is not achieved with the abolition of class society: what is necessary is the transformation of the 'beast of burden' into a new man. This goal inspired him in his youth and in his old age. Not in the goal can inconsistencies be observed, only in the road towards it. In the *Economic and Philosophical Manuscripts* he expected the emancipation from social labour itself, then in the *Grundrisse* in the free time reacting back upon production, and finally in volume three of *Capital* in a sphere of life that arises out of and moves away from the sphere of production.

Once he had distinguished the freedom of human development from the necessity of hard economic labour, Marx hesitated to admit that there are indeed separate spheres of human life involved. Why? He was obviously troubled by the thought that the true realm of freedom is detached from the organization of production. The political praxis prescribed to the working class — to 'have no ideals to realize, but to set free the elements of the new society'[9] — would realize a new organization of production but clearly not the realm of freedom he strove for! Even worse: this praxis could prevent the realization of freedom because the proletariat could become accustomed to a life without ideals and a life of passivity, when instead it should be preparing itself for its cultural and political tasks. Marx was faced with a dilemma: either he had to change his politics (because they were wrong), or he had to eliminate the contradiction between higher activity and necessary labour.

He did the latter. He believed he could overcome the discrepancy between the two realms by explaining that the realm of freedom could 'blossom forth only with this realm of necessity as its basis'.[10] But does this provide concrete proof, as Marx wanted it to, that in present capitalist society the material conditions have been created which 'enable and compel' the worker to break the curse of capitalism?[11] No. It only proves that the material conditions *enable* the worker to change and establish the realm of freedom, not that it *compels* him to do so.

The inexorability of the dialectical and historical laws that 'compel' mankind applies only to the development of the economic base and not to the development of man. Marx was never clear about the fact that this development is only a potential.

So there appears a striking contradiction in the thought of Marx: on the one hand he predicted that the antithesis between intellectual and physical labour would disappear in a truly communist society (this prediction was suggestively formulated by Engels as 'humanity's leap from the realm of necessity into the realm of freedom'[12]); on the other hand, he noted dispassionately that the realm of necessity will always remain, and that the development of human energy will begin only beyond this sphere of labour. The contradiction is all the more staggering considering that these two mutually exclusive assertions were made more or less at the same time, the first in the *Critique of the Gotha Programme*, the second in volume three of *Capital*.[13]

It is a sign of strength that Marx did not ignore awkward facts when they did not correspond to his own convictions. The contradiction attests to the existence of a conflict where he attempted a reconciliation. He did not modify his political praxis because he was not aware of the existence of a conflict here. For the same reason his disciples did not modify the political praxis either. Indeed, the orthodox school has failed even to perceive the opposition between economy and humanity, which Marx at least attempted to reconcile. It has ignored the views of those Marxist theoreticians (notably Adorno, Marcuse and Mandel[14]) who have explicated Marx's separation of the two realms, and still teaches today that 'Labour will no longer be merely a means of existence, it will be transformed into true creativity into a source of joy.'[15] The consequences of this intellectual failing of orthodox Marxist theory are obvious: whereas the social revolutions established a new organization of production, they did not inaugurate the true realm of freedom.

It should be mentioned at this point that dissenting Marxists have at times made very dubious evaluations of the complex problem of necessity and freedom. In their confrontation with intolerant Soviet orthodoxy they have relied heavily on Marx's anticipation, set out in the early *Economic and Philosophical Manuscripts*, of the emancipation from alienation and the full achievement of humanism through communism.[16] In his refutation of this interpretation Althusser rightly stressed the ideologically pre-Marxist character of Marx's early communism.[17] Yet he was clearly wrong when he denied the humanist standpoint of the later economic studies and when he found in Marx 'strictly speaking an a-humanism and a-historicism'.[18] The antihumanist view of Marx is as one-sided and false as the purely humanist perspective.

The subjugation of man to the necessity of labour, which the later

Marx recognized theoretically, has been experienced practically in the Israeli kibbutzim. The founding fathers of the collective settlements hoped to achieve a regeneration of man and his relationship with nature by renouncing urban professions in favour of working on the land. Former academics and shopkeepers alternately drained swamps, planted trees, and performed kitchen duties. They found a new meaning of life through physical labour. Marx's vision of a society of free producers emancipated from alienated labour seemed to have been realized. Everyone worked according to his or her abilities, performed a certain task one day and another task the next. The fulfilled individual replaced the atomized and insignificant cog in the great wheel. But as the children grew up and the economy of the commune diversified, a more rigid allocation of tasks proved inescapable. Some took charge of the children, some concentrated on the various production units, some negotiated with the merchants in the cities or became active in politics, and some had to do the menial jobs. The rotation of labour was on the whole abolished and a division of labour emerged: the harmonious equality of the kibbutz had been disturbed. In many kibbutzim the second generation no longer regards labour as the primary requirement of life, more as a necessary means towards the satisfaction of needs. The older and younger generations are unhappy in this situation, but they cannot change it. In the kibbutzim the relationship to labour changed from the generation of the fathers to the generation of the sons in the same way as it had changed in Marx from the *Economic and Philosophical Manuscripts* to volume three of *Capital*.

Tendencies against the collapse of capitalism

Apart from the striking contradiction in the concept of labour, other contradictions can be found in Marx's work. In the *Communist Manifesto* he celebrated the British social reforms of the early 1840s as a victory for the working class because they had been wrested from the government by the Chartist movement. Yet the reforms of 1867 took him by surprise. In this period the working class was politically weak and unorganized. He wondered how a government which is no more than an extension of the ruling class could adopt 'in principle, such extraordinary and extensive measures against the excesses of capitalist exploitation'.[19] These measures were not only irreconcilable with his view of the impotence of ideas but also with the economic theory of pauperization. (John Stuart Mill also found himself in an impasse. As a bourgeois economist, he believed that the law of production determines the price of labour as the minimum required for the maintenance and reproduction of the worker; but he also believed that the lot of the workers should be improved. Holding both views, however, amounts to trying to reconcile the irreconcilable.)

The social and political reforms of 1867 raised the working class from a state of pauperization and admitted it to the political community — they represented, in other words, the first steps towards the welfare state. They were 'extraordinary' because their adoption occurred in defiance of the interests of the ruling class. This Marx did not grasp fully (nor did Mill), which explains why he took an ambivalent view of them. He admitted that parliament had intervened impartially against the interests of the ruling bourgeoisie, but he also denigrated the significance of the reforms by criticizing the hesitation with which the measures were actually put into practice.[20] Of course Marx assumed correctly that the capitalist mentality still prevailed in the industrialized countries. In Germany, for instance, bourgeois university professors pleading for social reforms (Brentano, Schmoller and Gneist — the so-called 'armchair socialists') could not publish their articles in any Berlin newspapers until the middle 1870s, and even then they were bitterly attacked in the bourgeois press. After the adoption of social legislation Bismarck conceded that 'If there were no Social Democratic Party, and if not so many had feared it, then the moderate progress in social reform achieved so far would not yet exist.'[21] In the United States economists and politicians rejected state intervention as unnatural until the New Deal of the early 1930s.

In volume three of *Capital* Marx discussed another phenomenon that contradicted his view of economic development. The rise of the stock company, in which 'the active capitalist becomes a mere manager, and the owner of capital a mere money-owner', leads to a situation where profit assumes the pure form of interest. This is 'economically important' because it is one of the factors *stemming* the fall of the rate of profit. The large stock companies have a high ratio of constant capital to variable capital, and therefore they 'do not necessarily enter into the equalisation of the general rate of profit'.[22] But he had established the real barrier of capitalist production precisely in the falling rate of profit. Once again he was confronted with a tendency in capitalism that seemed to contradict the theory of its self-destruction.[23]

The revolution of 1848 in Britain: theory and reality

In the postface to the second edition of *Capital*, Marx wrote:[24]

> In France and England the bourgeoisie had conquered political power. From that time on, the class struggle took on more and more explicit and threatening forms. . . . The Continental revolution of 1848 also had its reaction in England.

Today, more than a century after these words were written, it is quite easy to contend that Marx overestimated the conflicts that were supposed to lead to the downfall of capitalism and underestimated the tendency towards its stabilization. But did the events of 1848 not show already at the time that the class struggle in Britain had abated after the social reforms of the early 1840s, and that because of them the continental revolutions of 1848 did not have major repercussions in Britain?

Marx did not seem to realize that the material of parliamentary inquiries and the statistics from the first half of the century, which he used to deduce the process of pauperization and the collapse of capitalism, were already out of date when the first volume of *Capital* was published. The analysis of the dissolution of human dignity in the exchange-value was certainly correct when he and Engels wrote the *Communist Manifesto*. But these years also saw the rise of the counter-movement against the self-interested *homo oeconomicus*. It began in the 1820s and 1830s with the laws on the protection of working children and the Factory Act of 1833, subsequently prompted the social reforms of 1867, and eventually achieved its goal in the modern welfare state.

The source of the contradictions

By the end of his scientific studies Marx perceived that 1 socialization will always remain within the realm of necessity, and the true realm of freedom can blossom only beyond it; 2 ideas can influence tendencies of development; 3 the fall in the rate of profit and the self-destruction of capitalism can be checked. How could such a conscientious and thorough scientist as Marx ignore the fact that these insights into the anatomy of capitalism clearly invalidate his main theories? His conception of the dialectic provides the answer:[25]

> In its rational form [the dialectic] is a scandal and an
> abomination to the bourgeoisie and its doctrinaire spokesmen,
> because it includes in its positive understanding of what exists
> a simultaneous recognition of its negation, its inevitable
> destruction.

The words chosen here are revealing. The phrase 'a scandal and an abomination' is a quote from the New Testament: 'We preach Christ crucified — to the Jews a scandal and to the Greeks an abomination.'[26] Is what is expressed in this passage not more a confession of faith than a scientific law? (Are we to conclude, by analogy, that 'we preach the dialectic'?) Is this faith in the inevitable destruction of capitalism not the source of the conflict between his theories and his observations of empirical reality?

Indeed, the merit of the Marxian dialectical approach supposedly lies in its undogmatic representation to the world. And it is undoubtedly scientifically fruitful when it is employed to 'track down' the emergence of the new society in empirical investigations. To this extent it does include in its positive understanding of what exists a recognition of its negation. But the assumption that this negation includes a positing of the negation of the negation, that is, the supersession of all previous alienation, is no longer a scientific law based on empirical analysis but a dialectical construction grounded in personal faith. Did not, for instance, Marx's later observations on the role of managers and book-keepers in social production indicate that alienation, inherent in capitalist production, will actually increase in social production?

Engels once remarked that in his economic studies Marx grasped fully 'what he had hitherto deduced half *a priori* from fragmentary source material'.[27] Engels's observation gives a clue to the mixture of empirical research and dogmatic faith in Marx. In his economic studies he indeed grasped the economic movement towards the socialization of production. But already in his early romantic communist phase, before he began his scientific studies, he had decided that the economic process of socialization would 'include' the supersession of alienation. He had arrived at this conclusion not half *a priori* from scanty material but purely *a priori* without any empirical evidence. Because he approached his scientific studies with an *a priori* construction of man's redemption, he could not correctly judge the significance of the developments which his analyses brought to light. Although he recognized more and more that in socialist society the forces of production must continue to expand in order to satisfy increasing needs, and that supervisory book-keeping and industrial management will be necessary (even more necessary than in capitalist society) for the regulation of the complicated process of production and distribution, he glossed over the rational and bureaucratic character, the *alienated* character, of this organization of labour by comparing it to an orchestra. This unrealistic and absurd comparison betrays the continued influence of Marx's implicit faith in the supersession of alienation through a dialectical development — a faith so deeply rooted that it could not be shaken by any analysis.

Adoption of the Hegelian hypostatization

Marx had inherited from Hegel the conception of human history as a dialectical development through alienation to restitution. With the inversion of the Hegelian philosophy of history from the sphere of spirit into material reality he intended to avoid Hegel's mystifying *a priori* construction. Concrete science of history was to replace the metaphysical speculation of history. In empirical research Marx succeeded in showing the dialectical development of the conditions of production, in contrast with Hegel's *a priori* deduction of the development of spirit. How then could he still regress into an *a priori* construction? There is evidently only one answer to this question: the inversion of the Hegelian philosophy of history did not eliminate the distortion caused by the one-sidedness of an explanation of history from a single factor.

Marx accepted without question the Hegelian notion of the negation of the negation as the only positive act. But where Hegel merely discovered the abstract and speculative expression of the movement of history, Marx claimed to have discovered the key to an understanding of the 'real' history of man:[28]

> For Hegel, the process of thinking, which he even transforms into an independent subject, under the name of 'the Idea', is the creator of the real world, and the real world is only the external appearance of the idea. With me the reverse is true: the ideal is nothing but the material world reflected in the mind of man, and translated into forms of thought.

As this passage shows, Marx posited the material world in place of the Hegelian idea. Just as Hegel had hypostatized the creative force of the 'idea', so Marx hypostatized the material world. While Hegel relegated the material world to the impotence of nature, Marx relegated the idea to the ideological superstructure. Both hypostatized in the same way the concept of labour: the labour of consciousness for Hegel, the labour of economics for Marx. In this hypostatization lies the source of the contradiction in the Marxian concept of labour, since it arose because he failed to distinguish between higher activity and labour as a means of providing the necessities of life (even though he described this distinction empirically).

The hypostatization in Marx becomes apparent when his materialism is compared with that of Feuerbach. At first both seem to say the same thing — that consciousness does not determine being, but that being determines consciousness. But there exists a profound difference behind this superficial similarity. For Feuerbach, man becomes man 'by no means through himself, his own power, his will; but through that complete synthesis of hidden and evident determinations of things which . . . we ascribe to the power of "chance" '.[29] Being, the finite being of the man of flesh and blood, is for him essentially unfathomable, mysterious. For Marx, however, being was as comprehensible as consciousness was for Hegel. When Feuerbach inverted the Hegelian dialectic he rediscovered the mystery of life which had also baffled the young Hegel; when Marx inverted the dialectic he continued the attempt of the mature Hegel to resolve the mystery and comprehend the totality of history.

But can man comprehend the flow of history in which he is swimming? Marx, like Hegel, took little notice of Kant's admonition not to transgress the limits of knowledge. Despite the critique of Hegel's mystifying metaphysics of history and despite the correct empirical analyses, he committed the very error he accused Hegel of: combining correct science of history with a mystificatory construction of history. Because, according to Marx, there exists no unresolvable mysteries of history, 'Mankind . . . inevitably sets itself only such tasks as it is able to solve.'[30] This assumption links Marx to the optimistic and rationalistic attitudes of the Enlightenment philosophers from Leibniz to Smith and Hegel. He did not accept their optimistic contention that the world is rational; but he did contend that it could be organized on a rational basis.

Marx ridiculed Hegel's philosophy of history. In Hegel's world 'the whole body of materialistic elements has been eliminated from history', for they are not part of the hypostatized consciousness, 'and now full rein can be given to the speculative steed'.[31] Yet Marx did exactly the same, only in reverse. He removed the important ideological superstructure and then gave full rein to *his* speculative steed, to let it gallop along the road of dialectical economic development towards the society emancipated from alienation. It was precisely his empirical investigations that led him astray and tempted him to go too far. He was influenced by studies showing the overwhelming dominance of material interests in politics and by Hegel's monocausal explanation of history. Consequently, the material basis of production is for Marx not merely an important factor determining the course of history, but the *only* factor. He once said 'Nature takes revenge on Hegel for the contempt he has shown her.'[32] About Marx one can equally say that the spirit takes revenge on him for the contempt shown her.

Because he considered his materialist interpretation of history an empirical method of research and not a dogmatic theory of history, Marx recorded unworriedly what he observed in empirical investigations. It did not occur to him that he might be lapsing into a metaphysical hypostatization. Marx saying 'I am not a Marxist' was not mere phraseology but meant in earnest. In opposition to the common view that he proceeded in a dogmatic fashion, it cannot be emphasized too often that his intentions, contrary to those of his disciples, were anything but dogmatic. When he none the less fell prey to dogmatism, he was unaware of it. But his inability to see through the dogmatism inherent in his view of history had dangerous consequences for his science and even more dangerous consequences for his doctrinaire disciples. In this mixture of scientific concern for empirical research and unconscious hypostatizing dogmatism lies the source of the contradictions in which he became entangled.

Contradictions and character

A letter from his father might explain why Marx adhered so stubbornly to dogmatism despite taking great pains to be truly scientific. Heinrich Marx asked his son, who was then a student:[33]

> Is your heart in accord with your head, your talents? Has it room for the earthly, but gentler sentiments? . . . And since that heart is obviously animated and governed by a demon not granted to all men, is that demon heavenly or Faustian?

Was his father right, was he ruled by a demon? Goethe, who had the opportunity to observe demonic people both from nearby and from afar, realized that the more clear-headed part of man can do nothing against it, and that the demonic 'is that which is not to be solved by means of the understanding and reason'.[34] Such people, he noted in a different context, 'rarely recommend themselves by their kindheartedness . . .; but an enormous energy emanates from them, they exercise an incredible power over all creatures'.[35] Marx's thought and actions seemed to correspond to Goethe's description of the demonic. Evidently his reason could not cope with the demonic side of his character. Even after he had discovered that spiritual liberation is possible only beyond and outside of the economic sphere of production, his demonic obsession prevented him from discarding the deadlocked dogmatism of the materialist conception of history.

Accounts by friends and opponents who met him may be instanced as evidence of Marx's demonic side and his incredible power over people. Moses Hess, his editorial colleague at the *Rheinische Zeitung* and his socialist teacher, was overwhelmed by his intellect:[36]

> Dr Marx, that is the name of my idol, is still a very young man, about twenty-four, who is about to give the final blow to medieval theology. He combines profound philosophical commitment with most biting wit. Imagine Rousseau, Voltaire, Lessing, Heine and Hegel united in one person — I say united, not simply thrown together — then you have Dr Marx.

Engels, a communist thinker in his own right, was throughout his life under the spell of Marx's personality. And a member of the *Doktorklub* was so impressed by Marx (who was ten years his junior) that he dedicated his first book to him. But others were repelled by his personal magnetism. Carl Schurz, who for a while embraced Marx's revolutionary ideas, wrote after a meeting: 'Marx's utterances were indeed full of meaning, logical and clear, but I have never seen a man whose bearing was so provoking and intolerable. . . . Everyone who contradicted him he treated with abject contempt.'[37] Ruge and Bakunin commented in a similar vein. Although Bakunin valued his intellect, he found Marx 'intolerant and absolute like Jehovah, the god of his ancestors, and like him vindictive to the point of madness'.[38] Even Hess, who had once respected him so much, considered it 'a pity, a great pity, that the ego of this man, who is unquestionably the party's most brilliant member, is not satisfied with the tribute paid by all who know his work but seems to demand a personal submission'.[39]

Violent demonism appeared already in a letter he wrote to his father when he was still studying in Berlin. In it he spoke of the 'rugged . . . emotions' of his soul, and of the attempts to force them into a system (something he quickly abandoned but then tried time and again).[40] Because he lacked the sensual and gentle feelings, he had no real friends. Even his relationship with Engels was characterized more by scientific co-operation and the common political struggle than by personal warmth. One may infer from the fact that Marx's daughter Laura Lafargue destroyed her father's letters about Engels — presumably to avoid hurting the latter's feelings — that Marx must have been rather scathing about him in his intimate correspondence. His heartlessness also determined his politics. Franz Rosenzweig once said that 'The tyrants of the kingdom of heaven, far from hastening the advent of the kingdom, only delay it', because they fail to love their fellow men and instead reach for those beyond.[41] In a comment which is revealing in its naïvety, Marx's disciple Ignaz Auer confirmed this near hate for his fellow men: 'We would preserve the people if we loved them. But we want to transcend them, with the violent means of a new social order: so we hate them.'[42] Marx was obsessed with this kind of misanthropy, which appears to have been the expression of the demonic in him.

References to the opinions of his father and his contemporaries cannot of course explain Marx's character; they only illustrate the real mystery of how, despite his clear and methodical mind and painstaking empirical research, he could not free himself from an unscientific construction.

Chapter fourteen

Consequences of the contradictions

The ambivalence in Marx's historical dialectic

Because Marx incorporated the Hegelian metaphysics of history into his empirical historiography, the same ambivalence we found in Hegel permeates Marx's work. 1 On the one hand Marx distinguished rigorously between human history and natural history on the grounds that the former is made by man and the latter is not. On the other hand he saw history as a deterministic process independent of human will: the proletariat need not translate any ideals into reality, it need only set free the elements of the new society. 2 Even though he inverted the Hegelian consciousness, he still hypostatized a single factor, material production, and devalued everything else to an ideological superstructure. Yet he also acknowledged Greek art as a 'norm'. 3 He investigated in empirical studies the development from the capitalist to the socialist mode of production. But under the influence of Hegel's three-tiered dialectical method he explained this development *a priori*, without providing any empirical evidence, as the development towards the supersession of alienation. 4 Although he strove for empirical science, he claimed to have solved the riddle of history. This claim is unscientific and has, as in Hegel's philosophy, totalitarian consequences.

It was suggested in the chapter on Hegel that the dual character of the Hegelian philosophy of history – as empirical investigation and unscientific dogmatism – reappears in Marx. But there is a fundamental difference in so far as Marx, in contrast to Hegel, recognized that the dialectical movement occurs only in history and can be discovered only through empirical investigation. Marx was not aware of the dogmatism that entered into his work. This was not the case with Engels. For him the dialectic was a general law that 'holds good in the animal and plant kingdom, in geology, in mathematics, in history and in philosophy'.[1]

In the postface to the second edition of *Capital* Marx noted that his presentation might appear as an *a priori* construction once the study of the inner dialectical connections had been successfully completed.[2]

Engels is to be blamed for the fact that the exposition did not appear as such but has been understood as if it actually had been an *a priori* construction. His *Anti-Dühring* was received as an authentic reproduction of Marxian theory, for it was known that Marx had assisted in its writing. Marx and Engels had worked together before on *The German Ideology* and the *Communist Manifesto*. But Marx contributed to *Anti-Dühring* for a specific personal reason. Dühring's polemic against Marx was interwoven with anti-semitic insults. And although the allusions to his Jewish origins clearly distressed him, Marx refused to reciprocate in kind. It is probable that he assisted Engels with the polemical section dismissing Dühring's theories; but it is unlikely that he was at all involved with the section on the development of the dialectic of nature. This he discussed only once in a letter, and that only as a token of his interest in Engels's work.[3] What he really thought about the dialectic of nature can be inferred from a comment in *Capital*, where he criticized the 'weaknesses' of the abstract materialism of natural science which cannot distinguish between human history and natural history.[4]

In order to appreciate what happened subsequently in the Marxist school, we must keep in mind the divergence betwen Marx's and Engels's respective conceptions of history. It is a divergence no less significant than that between Marx and Hegel. Engels's writings, aimed at a wider public, were read more than the difficult studies published by Marx. It should be mentioned at this point that Lenin followed Engels when he posited the dialectic as a law of nature, and that he outdid him when he rejected scientific objectivity as eclectic and unprincipled. With Lenin the true dialectic of history disappeared altogether. Marx himself, however, turned away from the dogmatic aspect of the dialectic in his later years.

As a result of this complexity, judgments on Marx's scientific work have often been diametrically opposed. The economist Joseph Schumpeter, for instance, wrote approvingly:[5]

> He liked to testify to his Hegelianism and to use Hegelian phraseology. But this is all. Nowhere did he betray positive science to metaphysics. His argument everywhere rests on social fact.

But Böhm-Bawerk judged differently:[6]

> Marx has not deduced from facts the fundamental principles of his system, either by means of a sound empiricism or a solid economico-psychological basis; he founds it on no firmer ground than on a formal dialectic. This is the great radical fault of the Marxian system at its birth; from it all the rest necessarily springs.

But neither Schumpeter, who acknowledged the truly scientific character of Marx's work, nor Böhm-Bawerk, who denied it, saw the whole Marx; they saw only one side and missed the interlacing of 'metaphysics' with 'sound empiricism'.

The dialectic and morality

The blending of science and dogma had fateful consequences for Marx's politics. Already in his pre-communist phase he had justified liberalism not as a moral duty but as a dialectical necessity. As a communist he retained this attitude to politics. He ridiculed the moral zeal of the socialists as 'fantastic emotionalism' and 'childish pomposity' in the same way that he had ridiculed the ignorance of his liberal friends who viewed freedom as a moral idea rather than as an historical necessity.[7] He showed a singular contempt for those who wanted to give socialism a moral foundation.

So dialectical necessity renders ideals superfluous in politics! This explains why he thought that the working class need not realize any ideals but need only set free the elements of the new society; 'no exertion of mind or will can free them from this fate'.[8] Right 'is but the will of your class made into a law for all, a will whose essential character and direction are determined by the economical conditions of your class', he called out to the working class.[9] The proletariat's appeals to ideals and rights serve only as a 'means of making them take shape as "they", as a revolutionary, united mass'.[10] Marx's amoral dialectic comes precariously close to Darwin's struggle for survival, for which he in fact had some sympathies.[11] (Engels even compared Marx's discovery of the dialectical economic laws to Darwin's discovery of the law of evolution.[12])

Marx said ironically against Proudhon: 'There is no longer any dialectics but only, at the most, absolutely pure morality'; and against Bakunin: 'The *will*, and not the economic conditions, is the foundation of his social revolution.'[13] Because Proudhon's thought was undialectical, Marx ranked him far beneath both political economists and philosophers:[14]

> Beneath the economists, since, as a philosopher who has at his
> elbows a magic formula, he thought he could dispense with
> going into purely economic details; beneath the socialists, because
> he has neither the courage nor insight enough to rise, be it even
> speculatively, above the bourgeois horizon.

There can be no doubt that Marx had a far superior knowledge of economic detail than Proudhon. But he too had a 'magic formula' at hand: the magic formula of the dialectic had him spellbound until the end. That is why he could write callously, with reference to the assassination of Tsar Alexander II, that the terrorists' method of action is an 'historically inevitable method about which there is no more reason to moralise — for or against — than there is about the earthquake in Chios' (which had occurred a few days before the assassination).[15]

Today, after the Russian Revolution, we know the inevitable consequences of the justification of terror in the name of historical necessity. Lenin at least had some scruples over the introduction of terror as an element in the construction of the communist society.[16] But what about those intellectuals who witnessed the terror and expressed no objections whatsoever? Even years after Stalin's death, Lukács wrote about the show trials of the 1930s: 'From the beginning I was sceptical of their legitimacy . . .; I agreed to their historical necessity, without laying great stress upon the question of legitimacy.'[17] He, who went forth to proclaim Dostoyevsky's gospel of love and compassion, was tempted by the dialectic to do precisely that which had so infuriated Dostoyevsky: to sacrifice love and conscience to necessity. Brecht did the same. After the bloody suppression of the workers' riots in East Berlin in June 1953, he confided to his diary that in certain circumstances the historical tasks of socialism are to be carried out against the opposition of the workers.[18]

The establishment of the Marxist school

Engels's interpretation of the dialectic as a deterministic law applying in history as in natural science and mathematics transformed the materialist science of history into a materialist world-view. Marx did not want to be known as a Marxist; but Engels did exactly that, he made his science into what is called Marxism. The Marxist programme of the Social Democratic Party of Germany, drafted by Engels and Kautsky in 1891, became the model for all continental socialist parties, and its tenets were soon embraced as a comprehensive world-view. The party programme acquired the character of a confession of faith; it united the various parties in the Marxist church. Only the pragmatic spirit of the Anglo-Saxon countries rejected the 'panacea' against all social evils, as the Fabians called the German party programme.

But it had such an unprecedented influence and conquered half the world precisely because it seemed to be a panacea. It restored a degree of self-confidence to the declassed proletariat and assigned a specific task to the intellectuals who had disowned the bourgeoisie. By anticipating the abolition of the class structure, the communist society seemed to reaffirm the prophetic promise of fraternity. Set free the elements of the new society, which are formed in the womb of the old, and you will be freed from your chains! The socialists gained a sense of historical mission from the formulation of the prophecy in terms of a dialectical historical law effective with iron necessity.

Which of Marx's predictions have come true?

Some fifty years after the publication of *Capital* the new society emerged in Russia. Yet the once revolutionary demands of the *Communist Manifesto* have been more or less put into practice in the so-called capitalist countries as well: for instance, progressive income tax and death duty; state control of credit, the railways, and the arms industry; state education; efficient cultivation of agricultural lands; reduction of working hours. In addition, both the people's democracies and the capitalist welfare states provide services that Marx could not have dreamed of: a guaranteed minimum wage, and insurance schemes for health, old age, and unemployment.

It is often argued against Marx that economic development has followed a very different course than the one he had outlined. In the eyes of these critics, Marx was wrong on at least three counts: 1 he had assumed an intensification of class divisions, to the extent that 90 per cent of society would become proletarianized and pauperized, which would culminate in open revolution; 2 he had predicted the communist revolution in the advanced capitalist economies; 3 he had made no allowances for national differences. However, these objections ignore the fact that Marx viewed the economic law of movement of modern society, which he attempted to present in *Capital*, not deterministically but historically. As such the laws may show infinite variations in appearance, and these can be ascertained only by empirical analysis. One of the variations is the network of social reforms with which the ruling bourgeoisie hoped to protect the workers. The prediction of the movement towards a new organization of society is not refuted; it merely shows that the form of the transition may vary.

In accordance with the altered empirical circumstances, Marx himself had come to the conclusion that a peaceful road to socialism was possible in some countries and that in Russia one might expect a different development than in Western Europe. In the later works he certainly appreciated the significance of special national problems.

According to Marx, the criterion that distinguishes the new society from the old is the mastery over the process of production by means of a rational regulation and common control. He never discussed how this regulation was supposed to operate, for, in his eyes, a description of the new organization of production would be utopian. The significant fact today is that in all developed industrial countries production is in some way controlled or regulated by the state. The continued use of the old concepts 'capitalism' and 'socialism' is responsible for the hitherto inadequate recognition of what the two systems have in common, at least in the sphere of production. In those countries where private capital has been preserved, production is more or less subject to some kind of planning or other controls. The large corporations are no less dependent on government plans than on market forces. And apart from such indirect control there are in many countries co-operative societies and companies owned by trade unions and the state. In communist countries, small-scale private enterprise has been allowed and is sometimes even encouraged. The convergence in the *economic* sphere between capitalism and communism is undeniable, but it has been recognized only gradually.[19]

Which of Marx's predictions have not come true?

But contrary to Marx's expectations, socialization (or nationalization) has not eliminated the master-slave relationship. In the place of the rule of the capitalist bourgeoisie another dominance appeared: the rule of the bureaucracy. The citizens possess, at least in principle, equal rights and can move up the social ladder in the spheres of politics and economics. To this extent modern society may be described as classless. But this equality had already been achieved in America before the advent of socialization, and it has not prevented the formation of bureaucratic power.

As he gave up the original vision of socialist society, Marx realized in the later volumes of *Capital* that the united producers themselves are not capable of organizing and taking charge of the complicated process of production. This task falls to 'managers' and 'book-keepers', as he called them, who are equivalent to the functionaries running the government administration and the judicial system of the modern state. But he spoiled this valuable insight by imagining that the opposition between management and workers would disappear when the management is paid by the workers. This would, in Marx's view, ensure the kind of harmonious co-operation found in an orchestra. Such an accord may exist in small co-operatives, but never in the extensive organization of collective production. He failed to recognize book-keeping for what it is: the bureaucracy he so detested. The dialectical doctrine that the negation of the negation yields a 'position' — a doctrine he never doubted — gave him the certainty of the positive new society and blinded him to its actual character. It is ironic that Marx, who throughout his life despised and condemned centralized bureaucracies wherever he found them (in Prussia, in France under Napoleon III, and in China), gave his fiat to the establishment of a bureaucracy in social production.

The crucial difference between the two social systems lies in the role of the bureaucracy. Some months before the outbreak of the Russian Revolution, Weber predicted with uncanny clarity that where private capital is abolished 'the private and public bureaucracies, who now work alongside each other (and so at least hold each other in check) would be fused in a single hierarchy'.[20] (Socialist opponents of Marxist, or Leninist, centralism — Proudhon and Bakunin, and later Kropotkin, Landauer and Luxemburg — also warned of this danger.) While in capitalist countries the state bureaucracy is subject to parliamentary control, in communist countries a privileged caste comes into being, the 'new class' (Djilas), known colloquially as the 'chevroletariat'. In the Soviet Union, the Soviets elected by the workers retained only a nominal importance after their bloody suppression by Lenin, who stripped them of all political power.

Thus, despite far-reaching similarities in the form of social organization, there exists a profound opposition between Western and Eastern societies. It is the old opposition between the free structure of society in the West and the autocratic structure in the East, which de Tocqueville had already noticed and is evident in the views of the Russian dissidents (Solzhenitsyn, in particular) who misinterpret Western tolerance as weakness.

The growth of bureaucracy goes hand in hand with the transformation of man into another subject — not into a humanly fulfilled subject, as Marx had hoped, but rather into an intellectually and spiritually even more vacuous subject. Illustrative of this are the concepts and phrases used in analyses of twentieth-century society: 'suppression in the name of function' (Simone Weil); 'the atrophy of the individuals amid consumption and life expectancy' (Horkheimer and Adorno); 'the triumph of the regressive and retarding forces' which reduces the full man to the *One-Dimensional Man* (Herbert Marcuse); *The Lonely Crowd* (David Riesman); *The Organization Man* (William Whyte); *The Status Seekers* (Vance Packard); 'the language of mystification' (Karl Jaspers); 'the subordination of individual personality to the needs of the organization' (J.K. Galbraith); a society of 'job-holders', 'which does no longer know of those other higher and more meaningful activities for the sake of which this freedom [the liberation of the workers] could be won' (Hannah Arendt); the 'boredom' against which the *'flâneur'* protests (Walter Benjamin); 'the great "Ennui" ' (George Steiner); 'In America and Russia — in differing ways but often with frightening convergence — we now witness the rise of the cheerful robot, the technological idiot, the crackpot realist, . . . a common method: rationality without reason' (C. Wright Mills); 'The more power [man] has over machines the more powerless he becomes as a human being' (Erich Fromm).[21] In no other age have authors such as Kafka, Camus, Beckett, Ionesco, Dürrenmatt, and others depicted the loneliness and desperation of their heroes, or to be more exact, their anti-heroes.

The situation is no different in the communist countries of Europe. It is true that scientific papers or works of fiction expressing criticism of society cannot be published. But suffice it to mention the poet Vladimir Mayakovsky, who as early as the 1920s exposed the pervasive quasi-bourgeois philistinism that had killed off the enthusiasm of the October Revolution.

Nevertheless, some critics of modern society forget too easily that spiritually free and fulfilled people have at all times been a minority. 'People in a large town ... live in a constant whirl of getting and spending' — these words were not written by a sociologist analysing the acquisition and consumption processes of consumer society, but by Goethe.[22] Even though we sense the distance between the present and the heyday of the pre-capitalist bourgeoisie, Goethe's letter should be a warning against seeing in his age only fulfilled humanity and in our age only one-dimensional uniformity.

In any case, the qualification of the critique of modern society should not detract from the fact that Marx's expectation of the supersession of alienation in socialism was simply illusory. Even intellectuals in communist countries have asked whether the end of capitalism means the end of alienation, and Adam Schaff, for instance, has asked further whether private property is really the basis of all alienation.[23]

Part three

Marx's influence

Chapter fifteen

Weber's lifelong dialogue with Marx

Weber's encounter with Marx and Nietzsche

Max Weber was the first to praise Marx as a 'great thinker' and regard his work as a 'scientific achievement of the first order'.[1] At the same time he freed Marx's work from the dogmatic Procrustean bed that constrained it. As Albert Salomon has said, Weber was engaged in a 'lifelong dialogue' with Marx. He belonged to the few of his generation who attacked Bismarck's opportunistic *Realpolitik* and the philistinism of the politically ignorant German middle class. He welcomed the unification of Germany but regretted the relative insignificance of the parliament in the new political structure as well as the denial of political rights to the working class. History, he said in his inaugural lecture, had bestowed on his generation a curse, namely 'the harsh fate of following the period of political greatness'.[2]

Weber discovered an affinity with Marx and Nietzsche in their respective critiques of modern society. 'The sincerity of a contemporary scholar, and above all of a contemporary philosopher, can be estimated by his attitude to Nietzsche and Marx', he said shortly before his death.[3] His proximity to Marx and Nietzsche also brought him into contact with their followers. Students, academics and politicians from the *Jugendbewegung* influenced by Nietzsche; the circle around the novelist Stefan George; and the socialist movement gathered in his house. But as much as he accepted wholeheartedly their diagnosis of society and the need for its renewal, he differed radically from these groups in the proposed therapy. He saw Nietzsche's aloofness from the rational technological civilization as a sign of weakness, and his contempt for the masses infuriated him. Nietzsche was, in this respect, 'a German philistine'.[4] He valued Marx all the more because he had recognized capitalism as the fateful force of the present. A relative who grew up in his house remembered: 'Weber could . . . cry out against all literature, from Kant to Kierkegaard, from Goethe to Nietzsche: "Away with this trash!" – with one exception: Marx.'[5] Yet he knew the Marxian hope to be illusory. He perceived socialization not as the road to the free society but as the road towards 'the house of new bondage'.[6]

The fate of rationalization

Already in his youth Weber was disturbed by the threat to freedom posed by the process of bureaucratization. In his work he showed that the bureaucracy, which originated towards the end of the Roman Empire (the causes cannot be examined here), stifled economic and political freedom. The decline of trade entailed the decline of the cities and the culture which owed its existence to them. He concluded one of his early investigations with the following reminder:[7]

> The choking-off of private economic initiative by the bureaucracy
> is not in any way peculiar to the ancient world. Every
> bureaucracy tends to arrive by expansion at the same result. This
> is no less true of our own.

According to Weber, the modern bureaucracy is distinguished from the classical and Chinese bureaucracies by its rational professional training and the specialization of its officials. The Chinese mandarin was not an expert, as is his modern counterpart, but a gentleman educated in the literary arts. The rational spirit is specific to the West. The concept of experimental science, the notion of musical harmony, the linear perspective in painting, and a written constitution exist only here. Moreover, in the West the 'most important functions of everyday life and society have come to be in the hands of technically, commercially, and above all legally trained government officials'.[8]

The primary sources of the process of rationalization lie in the demystification or 'disenchantment' (*Entzauberung*) of the world, that is, in the elimination of magic by Jewish prophecy and Greek philosophy. The great sectarian movements of ascetic puritanism heightened the rational way of life to a universal explorative and exploitative activity. The puritan work ethic encouraged the development of modern capitalism.

Once its original religious sources had been exhausted, the process of rationalization continued independently. But rational action now acquires a radically different character. It is no longer meaningful in an ethical or religious sense, 'value-rational' (*wertrational*), or motivated from a belief in an intrinsic unconditional value and therefore a value for its own sake irrespective of the consequences; it has become purely 'purpose-rational' (*zweckrational*): 'A person acts rationally in the "means-end" sense when his action is guided by considerations of ends, means and secondary consequences.'⁹ Purpose-rational action is in this sense *ethically* irrational. There is no return from this rationality deprived of meaning (*Sinn*), for — whether we like it or not — modern mass society cannot be supported and administered without it. 'The Puritan wanted to work in a calling; we are forced to do so.'¹⁰

Through rational specialization the modern bureaucracy gains a particular efficiency which the classical and Chinese bureaucracies lacked. This applies especially to the German bureaucracy, which is admired for its efficiency even by Lenin, who had in mind the German postal service as a model for the future socialization.

However, there is an obverse to the coin of rationalization, namely the power which the bureaucracy acquires over people precisely because of its rational performance. The living machine is 'coagulated spirit', like the dead machine. 'Because it is this, it gains power to coerce people into its service.'¹¹ (Weber thus showed the same alienation in the bureaucracy which Marx had exposed in economic production: the domination of man by his product.)

Rationalization, which occurs in society as bureaucracy, appears in intellectual life as intellectualization. The discovery of the notion of rationality by the Greek philosophers seemed to show the path to eternal truth. Today, however, the kind of intellectualism associated with scientific progress is often hated 'as the worst devil'.¹² The claim of science to possess the answer to the meaning of life has proved to be a fanciful illusion. But this in no way permits a glorification of the irrational 'experience'. Quite the contrary. Science conveys technical expertise, refines the methods of thought, and helps man to achieve clarity. This intellectual achievement of science cannot and should not be renounced. Nevertheless, it is indisputable that as a consequence of the progressive process of disenchantment and intellectualization over a period of almost 2,000 years, the sublime imperative of the religious ethic no longer determines the actions of everyday life, and the various spheres of life — the economic, political, scientific, erotic, etc. — are in unresolved struggle with each other. This is the fate of intellectualization: while religious revelation is no longer taken seriously in life, science cannot replace it.

What did Weber mean by 'the fate of rationalization'? Does it mean that man is at the mercy of tendencies working themselves out with iron necessity, as Marx thought, but rather in reverse, that man is at the mercy of trends towards political oppression and intellectual paralysis? On the whole, interpretations of Weber follow this line of argument. The numerous references to the inescapability of bureaucratization and the inevitable dissipation of the religious ethic in public life seem to confirm this interpretation. But such a view could not be further from the truth. As much as Weber was conscious of the power of this 'devil', he also knew its limitations. He urged all 'to swim against the stream' of material developments; but he also warned that time is pressing: 'We must work while it is still day.'[13] The realization that people could still be active in the face of this power was to clarify fundamentally his methodological analysis of historical processes.

Methodology

Ever since its beginnings, political economy was plagued by a methodological confusion. Its founders discovered the interconnections of economic processes and subsumed them under general laws. Moved by the overwhelming impression of the great discoveries in astronomy and biology, they came to view the economic laws as analogous to the deterministic laws of natural science. The problem raised by this doubtful interpretation of the status of economic laws went unnoticed for a long time. Marx was the first to grasp the difference between historical and natural laws. He saw the uniqueness of the historical law in the dialectic, which is to be analysed in empirical investigations. Despite Marx's own clarity about the nature of the dialectical historical laws, in the wake of Hegel's philosophy of history it was interpreted as if it were effective *a priori*. In both cases, whether the economic and historical laws are treated as deterministic in the sense of natural science or as *a priori* in the sense of Hegelian logic, human freedom is eliminated.

In opposition to natural science and the Hegelian school, the historicist economic school of Schlosser, Roscher and Knies stressed the fact that economic history deals with the mystery of the personality, which is irrational. Historical events cannot be explained but only understood. This complacent satisfaction with mere understanding seemed to Weber no less crippling to freedom, because it accustomed man to a 'relativistic resignation' to the *status quo*.[14]

So all three economic schools — the classical, the Marxist, and the historicist — enfeebled the very factor which mattered most for Weber: human action. To obviate this danger, he took upon himself the task of re-examining the methodology of economics. He did so very reluctantly. Methodology was for him only a tool for concrete research, i.e. historical sociological research, and therefore he wanted to complete the methodological clarification as quickly as possible. As a consequence of this impatience, the methodological essays, when compared to the clear organization and the precise and graphic presentation of the sociological studies, suffer from provisional formulation and inelegant style, as Weber admitted himself.

Weber's approach to the social sciences is summarized in a letter written shortly before his death:[15]

> I became a sociologist . . . essentially to put an end to a practice which continues to haunt the discipline, namely the use of collective concepts. In other words, sociology too can be pursued only when it proceeds from the actions of a single individual or a number of individuals — it is thus strictly 'individualistic' in its methodology.

To proceed from the individuals means to understand them. The personality is not a 'riddle', Weber argued; it is, on the contrary, 'the only possible object of interpretive "understanding" ' (*deutendes Verstehen*).[16] The sciences of man, the historical and economic sciences, must rest on this *interpretive* understanding. In 'understanding' we re-experience the meaning or sense which other people attach to their actions or non-actions, and we then interpret it in analogy to our own being. This meaning cannot be found in the material itself but only in a selection of the elements relevant to us. It does not suffice to establish facts and test them; they must be related to our own standards, to 'values'. This 'value-orientation' (*Wertbeziehung*) is for Weber an achievement of historical philosophy.[17]

A historical concept is thus not defined according to a simple taxonomic formula, but in the classificatory combination of individual aspects of reality into an intellectual construct illustrating the historical phenomenon. This construct is called an 'ideal type' because it is a logically 'adequate' type. By this method the meaning of an individual instance can be understood, and, in addition, the meaning of a relationship such as the market economy. When classical economists explained the market economy in terms of an interplay of individuals striving for their self-interest, they assumed unwittingly that human beings act rationally according to economic considerations. But the human being motivated exclusively by economic maxims, *homo oeconomicus*, does not exist. Invariably other, non-economic considerations play a part, and they distort the law of supply and demand. Or to quote another example, Marx's observation that the hand-mill produces a society with feudal lords and the steam-mill produces a society of industrial capitalists explains only that the passage from feudalism to capitalism will occur *when* the owners of capital begin to invest their capital in machinery and new factories. It does not explain *why* they do so. Capital was accumulated as much in Spain as in England; but it was the ascetic and enterprising Puritans, and not the Spanish grandees, who were prepared to forgo luxury and instead invest their money into their businesses. Hence capitalism first developed in England and not in Spain. This example illustrates graphically that economic laws apply only when people act economically rationally.

The above examples also illustrate the true nature of economic laws as distinct from the laws of natural science. Economic and historical laws[18]

> are observationally verified statements of the probability with which a certain outcome can be *expected* from social action if certain conditions are realized, and they are understandable in terms of the typical motives and typical intended meaning of the agent in question.

To this extent every rational interpretation of a concrete historical process, including economic laws, 'obviously and necessarily *presupposes* the existence of "freedom of the will" '.[19] (To differentiate both types of patterned relationships, Weber often wrote the term 'economic law' in inverted commas or qualified it with a phrase like 'what one usually calls a law'.)

Since the historian or sociologist tries not only to show the existence of a phenomenon but goes further and tries to understand it by referring it to his own set of values, there is a danger of allowing personal opinions to enter, perhaps involuntarily, into the scientific presentation. A surreptitious incorporation of personal value judgments into the presentation can be found in Treitschke's lectures (which Weber heard as a student). It is an 'elementary duty of scientific self-control and the only way to avoid serious and foolish blunders' that the scholar become aware of his own value judgments and rigorously keep them out of the scientific analysis.[20] The hermeneutical social sciences require therefore both value-orientation and value-freedom. The common objection that value-freedom is synonymous with relativism or even lack of principle is entirely spurious.

Chapter sixteen

Marx in the light of Weber's clarification of method

Positive critique of the materialist conception of history

Weber's logical elaboration of historical concepts evinced the possibility 'to work while it is still day'. But action is restricted by the historical conditions, especially economic factors, as revealed by Marx's materialist interpretation of history. Weber accepted the analysis of history with special reference to economic conditions as 'a scientific principle of creative fruitfulness'.[1] But he rejected as unscientific dogmatism the hypostatization of the economic base into the sole factor determining the course of history.[2] Weber of course was not familiar with Marx's early writings (they were published in the 1930s, after his death), in which he had accused Hegel of 'mystification', because in his philosophy of history the Idea is active 'behind the scenes'; he reasserted that 'History does nothing. . . . It is man . . . who does all.'[3] Here Marx, no less than Weber, confronted the spectre of collective concepts — 'mystification' — and expressed his intention to proceed from the individuals. None the less, the spectre survived in Marx in a materialist guise, because in the inversion of Hegelian philosophy the monocausal explanation of history is retained. It is therefore no exaggeration to say that Weber's transformation of economic historical dogmatism into an economic interpretation of history realized Marx's original aim, which he himself failed to achieve.

Once the materialist interpretation of history is detached from its dogmatic hypostatization, the statement that the mode of production conditions the general process of social, political, and intellectual life acquires a new meaning. The dependence then refers to the restriction of the independence of political and intellectual life by the conditions of production, but *not* to the exclusion of a certain autonomy. Economic interests undoubtedly govern everyday life. Nevertheless, Weber argued, extraordinary and revolutionary intellectual forces — he called them 'charismatic' — can direct the course of history into new channels. Let us recall the historical examples mentioned in the previous chapter:

the origin of the process of rationalization in the West from Jewish prophecy and Greek philosophy, and the origin of the capitalist work ethic from the Calvinist faith. Here material base and political and intellectual superstructure influence each other. There exists a constant conflict between economic interests and individual charisma. If one reads Marx's famous dictum that 'men make their own history' (even if not under circumstances they have chosen themselves but under given and inherited circumstances) from Weber's standpoint, then Weber's critique is without a doubt a positive contribution to the critique of the materialist conception of history.

In this positive critique the contradictions in Marx's work are resolved. Marx had been irritated by the fact that art can count as a norm and an unattainable model even though it is conditioned by the mode of production. This difficulty is overcome when art and the forms of consciousness are not seen as untruthful embellishments of economic interests but are accepted as having intrinsic value. Further-more, the contradiction between the permanent realm of necessity and the goal of the realm of freedom disappears when the conditions of production are not considered to be the cause of human actions but a limiting condition. Marx wanted to show that the material conditions which 'enable and compel' the worker to break his fetters exist in contemporary capitalist society. His proof is valid in so far as certain material conditions *enable* the worker to act in such and such a way; but the 'proof' that material conditions *compel* the worker to act in a certain way is a regression into the mystification and the spectre of collective concepts of which Marx had accused the Hegelian philosophy of history. Since political praxis depends on whether the material conditions enable and compel men to act (as Marx assumed), or whether they merely enable but do not compel them (as Weber showed), the problem may be clarified further once again with the examples from the previous chapter. The invention of the steam-engine produced the material conditions that enabled society to progress from feudalism to capitalism. However, the new conditions of production did not compel the social transformation, for capitalism did not develop in Spain, as accordingly should have happened, but in England, where the charis-matic force of Calvinism, which provided a strong psychological incen-tive for rational capitalist action (i.e. saving and investing), comple-mented the material conditions. Similarly, the development of capitalist production created the material conditions enabling the workers to become involved in 'higher activity', which hitherto had been the prerogative of a small ruling class. But have these conditions in any way compelled the workers? While Marx answered this question in the affirmative on principle, his empirical analysis in the third volume of *Capital* suggests the opposite.

By exposing and eliminating the spectre of a history that does everything and compels man, Weber indicated the possibility of independent action.

Against the stream!

Because of the increasing complexity of the economy and government administration, action becomes more important as bureaucratization progresses. Therefore Weber urged everyone not to rely on developments but to swim against the stream. Although bureaucratization is inescapable and as such the fate of our age, it can be and must be prevented from becoming absolute, as it had once been in Egypt and China.

Weber emphasized the importance of the private entrepreneur as a counterbalance to the bureaucracy. Yet he also knew that it was 'ridiculous to suppose' that advanced capitalism has 'an elective affinity with "democracy" or indeed with "freedom" (in any sense of these words)'.[4] Weber agreed with Marx that the domination by entrepreneurs is 'a further element of substantive irrationality in the modern economic order'.[5] But in contrast to Marx he said clearly that an organization of society on a socialist basis, no matter how well thought out, could not eliminate the exploitation of man; it could only be reduced.[6] In the modern welfare state, which looks after the material welfare of the workers, this aspect is particularly relevant. Weber imagined a future organization of society, in fundamental opposition to a nationalization of production, as a kind of consumer socialism which did not exclude private enterprise.[7] In 1907 he wrote to his friend Robert Michels, a syndicalist, that 'Political democratization is the only thing which is attainable in any foreseeable future, and this is not as little as it seems.'[8]

Against the incompetent German party cliques Weber advocated a democratic constitution allowing for the selection of charismatic leaders. In the context of Marx this need not be pursued further.

Political action in an irrational world

A more profound opposition between Marx and Weber is concealed behind the differences on the matters of democratization and the form of socialist society. In the same letter to Michels, Weber suggested that he (Michels) had not thought through his revolutionary aspirations. Not only had he ignored that a socialist society could not eliminate the exploitation of man, but also that every action must invariably confront evil. Life is eternal struggle for power, Weber reminded him. 'The man who receives even a penny of rent', he wrote elsewhere, 'or who consumes a product made with another man's sweat, keeps himself and even profits in the hard and pitiless struggle for survival.'[9] Herein lies the 'tragic element with which all action ... is, in fact, intertwined'.[10] Goethe too had said that the active man has no conscience, and admitted that he 'would rather do a wrong than endure disorder'.[11] But unlike Goethe, Weber preferred disorder to injustice.

According to Weber, the sense of tragedy is intensified in the political arena, where the active man necessarily deals with the means of power, behind which stands force. Every politician is therefore involved with 'diabolical forces', whether he likes it or not. This does not trouble the devotee of power politics, who worships power for its own sake. He has no commitment to an issue. But without a cause a politician must bow to 'the curse of futility to which all finite creatures are subject, even in what may seem from the outside to be his greatest success'.[12] The impotence concealed behind the ostentatious 'but totally empty posturing' of prominent politicians in Wilhelmine Germany is so despicable for this very reason.[13]

In Marx and Marxism Weber found a cause. He saw the revolutionary Russian intelligentsia as the champions of the 'last great' faith — a religious faith in the socialist eschatology; and he noted that in Western Europe the syndicalists showed a commitment equivalent to a religious faith.[14] He was fascinated by these intellectual movements which, with their strong religious overtones, could flourish in a godless world. He became so friendly with the Russian revolutionaries who had come to Heidelberg after the collapse of the uprising in 1905 that they invited him, the bourgeois professor, to deliver a speech at the opening of the Russian library.

Yet the religious and revolutionary 'warriors of faith' or 'crusaders' (*Glaubenskämpfer*), as Weber called them, are only rarely aware of the diabolical forces at play, precisely because they aspire to a noble end. How often have such crusaders, motivated by the noblest intentions, created havoc in history! Weber feared this especially from the Marxists, who as disciples of Hegel denied the irrationality of the world. In the letter to Michels mentioned above he expressed his intention to write something on this subject. Some ten years later, after the Russian Revolution and the collapse of Germany, he took up the matter in a lecture entitled 'Politics as a Vocation', delivered in January 1919. The address is an appeal to the 'proponents of an ethic of absolute ends' — those 'crusaders' motivated by moral sentiments — to consider fully the consequences of the actions which they have not thought through to the end.

In 'Politics as a Vocation' Weber went on to argue that the dilemma of the political use of the ethically dangerous medium of power to achieve an ethical end cannot be resolved logically. For the ethically oriented politician there remains only the choice between the 'ethic of intention' or 'conscience' (*Gesinnungsethik*) and the 'ethic of responsibility' (*Verantwortungsethik*). Invariably the ethical politician will be confronted with the impossibility of reconciling both ethics. 'The genius, or demon, of politics lies in a state of inner tension with the God of love.' Certainly, 'The great virtuosi of other-worldly love of mankind and saintliness, whether from Nazareth or Assisi or the castles of Indian kings, have not employed the instruments of politics. Their kingdom was "not of this world".' But whoever wants to be politically active in *this* world cannot avoid violence. Ethical politics seems to have run aground. However, now that the tensions and paradoxes have been brought to the level of consciousness, we must not resign, but rather say 'But still!', in spite of all! Every one of us who is not inwardly dead, who feels a responsibility for the consequences of his conduct with heart and soul, must be able to say at some point: 'Here I stand; I can do no other, ethically I cannot reconcile this with my conscience.' To this extent, the ethic or intention and the ethic of responsibility are not diametrically opposed 'but complementary: together they make the true man, the man who can have the "vocation of politics" '.[15]

The audience must have been so shocked or confused by the dramatic intensification of the opposition between the ethic of intention and the ethic of responsibility that they took in only the aspect of inevitable futility and not the 'But still!', especially since the pessimistic prediction of the 'polar night of icy darkness and severity' lying ahead of us seemed to confirm the futility of political activity.[16] Until today only this aspect of the lecture is remembered. Hence it is almost without exception misinterpreted as an indirect justification of unethical power politics.[17] Weber is still maligned for failing to understand the significance of revolutionary movements, and he is sometimes caricatured as a parochial bourgeois German. Only a few have grasped Weber's intention. Isaiah Berlin, for instance, noted: 'The right policy cannot arrive in mechanical or deductive fashion. . . . The classical − and still . . . the best − exposition of this state of mind is to be found in Max Weber's distinction between the ethic of conscience and the ethic of responsibility in "Politics as a Vocation".'[18]

What appears in Weber as narrow-minded is actually the inner strength to admit, free of any illusions, the hopelessness of eliminating all injustice and oppression, while still preserving the revolutionary and passionate will to fight for the possible. 'For the problem . . . is simply how both passion and cool judgment can be made to combine within the same personality.'[19] This combination of hot passion and cool judgment set Weber apart from both the revolutionary fanatics who knew only hot passion and the reactionary conservatives who possessed only cool judgment. The former thought it necessary to employ terror in a transitional phase in order to force the realm of freedom; the latter regarded the people as too stupid to be capable of freedom. Weber replied to both extremes in a remark which expresses succinctly the nature of his political commitment:[20]

> We thank the 'Principles of 1789' — even though we smile at
> their childish innocence and protest against their rape of reality;
> they are things without which life would not be bearable.

Shortly after the Russian Revolution Weber met Schumpeter. Like so many intellectuals, Schumpeter enthused about the great experiment and said that the communist revolution would be a 'laboratory' — to which Weber replied dismayed 'but a laboratory with piles of corpses!'.[21] Weber's indignation at Marx's (or Lenin's) justification of violence in the name of the classless society reveals what ultimately Marx and Weber shared and where they differed. Both were 'warriors of faith'. But Marx and his loyal disciples (particularly Lenin and Trotsky) were convinced that the goal they were striving for could only be achieved through a terror whose morality or immorality was beyond argument. They had no eye for reality as it is and they lacked the ethic of responsibility. Weber warned in vain against the consequences of their actions.

'An ever-disappointed, but tenacious hope'

Western scholars have generally acknowledged the importance of Weber's sociological investigations and his methodological foundation of the social sciences. The scope and bulk of the studies undertaken in the short span of his life is remarkable (even more so considering that his research was interrupted for a number of years owing to illness and political activity). His observations are as relevant today as they were then. But almost without exception critics have found in his work and his passion for politics a hidden relativism, or even nihilism, albeit, in the words of Leo Strauss, a 'noble nihilism'.[22] Even Karl Jaspers, who revered Weber as the greatest intellectual of our age, wondered whether 'his titanic efforts come to anything' and whether 'he lacked "the One" '.[23] Because in this study the interpretation of Weber deviates from the common view, it is necessary at this point to digress from the main argument, in which his work has been examined only in direct relation to Marx.

At a first glance, Weber's speeches and essays indeed convey a dismal picture. He concluded that 'culture, that is . . . the most precious thing in this world for the inner man, seems so utterly meaningless when measured by its own standards'.[24] Formerly the experience of futility provided the impetus for further development of religion by the prophets. But it is the fate of our intellectualized world today that there is no prophet, or if there is, 'his message is no longer believed in'.[25] And science cannot be an adequate substitute. The last great religious faith, the socialist eschatology, he believed to be falsified by an almost superstitious scientific foundation, and he foresaw its disastrous results. He dismissed as 'plain humbug or self-deception' the attempt of the romantics to replace religion, which they simply 'do not possess', with surrogates.[26]

But often it is not realized why Weber wished to present the fate of our epoch in its forceful significance. He did so in order to rouse his audience from a world of illusions and confront it with its task:[27]

> The fate of an epoch which has eaten of the tree of knowledge is that it must know that we cannot learn the *meaning* of the world from the results of its analysis, be it ever so perfect; it must rather be in a position to create the meaning itself.

The phrase 'to create the meaning' (*den Sinn schaffen*) is certainly equivocal. It cannot be read literally, for that would yield a fraudulent surrogate. What then did Weber mean by it? The appreciation of Weber's work depends on the answer to this question.

A direct answer is not to be found, however. Only in personal letters did he state that he was 'neither anti-religious nor unreligious', and in private conversations he admitted that 'it could be that I am a mystic'.[28] In this context it should be noted that in the sociology of religion he distinguished between the intellectual religious systems and a more genuine faith. He showed how the intellectual character of religiosity fades as soon as it becomes an ethic of intention: 'every genuinely devout religious faith . . . stresses, here as everywhere, the inadequacy of the individual's intellectual powers when he confronts the exalted state of the divinity'.[29] Could not the inadequacy of the intellectual powers of science to explain the world show the way towards faith even today? And would then faith enable us 'to create the meaning'? Further on in the letter quoted above Weber called himself a 'cripple' as far as religion is concerned, 'a stump which now and then is able to break into leaf . . . but does not want to pose as a fully grown tree'.[30] Thus there can be no doubt as to what he meant by the enigmatic 'to create the meaning'; he did not explain the phrase because he did not want to pose as a 'fully grown tree'.

An objective reason also stopped him from speaking openly about his faith. Since genuine piety has no intellectual character, he feared that those who teach something about it 'are apt to make the belief that there is such a thing as the "meaning" of the universe die out at its roots'.[31] Yet he did write, once again only in a letter, that there exists a mode of thought which is not bound by the limitations of science, i.e. the limitations of logical concepts; but, he added, it 'should not masquerade as science'.[32] The mode of thought not constrained by the limitations of concepts is more natural than the mode that accepts modern philosophy from Descartes to Kant as scientific. Unaware of the implications of his reflection, he anticipated the insights of many philosophers who came forward in the decade after his death: Wittgenstein, Rosenzweig, Jaspers, Heidegger, Benjamin, and others. Despite the differences among themselves and between them and Weber, they all sensed man's inability to explain the factuality of the world and his confrontation with seemingly meaningless culture.

For these thinkers, as for Weber, pointing out the futility of existence is only the first step. In the second step, the divine, which gives meaning to existence, 'reveals itself' (Wittgenstein, Heidegger), or each in his own way makes a 'leap' towards it (Rosenzweig, Jaspers, following Kierkegaard). The source of the ray of truth that falls on a transient and dark world is not accessible to conceptual thought but only to that mode of thought which Weber knew was not bound by the limitations of conceptual science. For this reason he did not mention it in his work. Whoever has taken the second step views the world '*sub specie aeterni*' (Wittgenstein), experiences it as a 'miracle' (Rosenzweig), sees it in 'ciphers' (Jaspers), experiences being in the existing (Heidegger); or as Walter Benjamin put it very enigmatically:[33]

> The order of the profane is to take heart from the idea of
> happiness. The reference of this order to the messianic is one of
> the essential parables of the philosophy of history.

What Weber concealed can still be found in his scientific studies at points where, to name but a few examples, he emphasized experience of faith as the driving force in the development of religion, or when he showed that the apparent sense of futility evident in the novels of Tolstoy and Dostoyevsky in fact hints at a faith 'in which human relationships form the path towards a recognition of the meaning of the world, towards a mystical relationship with God'.[34] Occasionally he expressed in footnotes and asides what he was holding back, that 'the direction of his personal beliefs, the refraction of values in the prism of his mind', gives direction to the work of the scientist; or that to judge the values which gave meaning to historical events is a 'matter of faith'.[35]

So the provocative formulation 'to create the meaning' sprang from a dilemma: on the one hand Weber advocated a kind of political activity inspired by faith, so that one is not burdened by the 'curse of futility'; on the other hand he did not wish to discuss in public something which in his view was scientifically indefensible. Certainly the above formulations could be regarded as relativistic, and this interpretation has indeed predominated.

Since Weber never used meaningless phrases, the words he chose to circumscribe what he did not want to express openly are significant in themselves. They mean, first of all, that ultimately any scientifically unverifiable viewpoint must be reduced to the extreme case of the concrete problem, and then tried out individually, decided individually, and to this extent created individually, in a combination of the ethic of intention and the ethic of responsibility. But the words also mean something more. The political ethic of ultimate ends presupposes the belief in a mission in the world. This secular faith originated in the Jewish prophecies, and the West is indebted to it for the Faustian striving. 'To create the meaning' means in this context *re-creating* the faith in the meaning of history, which today people either pay lip-service to or have lost altogether. We are in a position to achieve this, because, as Weber hinted in a veiled passage, even today[36]

> in *pianissimo*, something is pulsating that corresponds to the prophetic *pneuma*, which in former times swept through the great communities like a firebrand, welding them together.

This 'something' is also the hidden force that inspired Weber's titanic efforts.

In the following chapter we will examine the intellectual struggles within Marxism. Before and after the Russian Revolution they were and are controversies over the correct version of the dogma. After the great disappointment after 1917 many jumped out of the magic circle of dogmatism. Of those ex-communists only a few still professed the faith after their resignation from the 'church'. One of them was Ignazio Silone, who recounted his political experiences in the story of the medieval hermit-pope Celestin V. He discussed the tensions between the ethic of intention and the ethic of responsibility without using these terms and possibly without knowing of Weber's lecture. In the introduction to the tale Silone explained what remains in a post-Marxist world: 'an ever-disappointed, but tenacious hope'.[37] Weber's outlook can also best be described with these words.

Chapter seventeen

The controversy over the dialectic

Because we are concerned mainly with tracing, from their sources, the consequences of the contradictions between true science and dogmatic construction that have forced a split in the Marxist school, this chapter will not so much deal with the history of the Marxist parties in the different countries but will concentrate on the principal phases of the intellectual confrontation since Marx's death. For this reason the debate between Lenin and Bernstein will be examined in some detail, because it highlights conflicts of principle. Particular scientific achievements of individual Marxist scholars do not belong in this context. (That I have, perhaps paradoxically, drawn extensively from Weber, who is not a member of the school, must be justified by the analysis itself.)

The main argument about the status of the dialectic

Against the prediction of Marx's general law of capitalist accumulation, the progressive pauperization and intensification of class conflict that were supposed to trigger the proletarian revolution did not occur. In the preface to the second English edition of the *Condition of the Working Class in England*, written in 1892, Engels conceded that in the fifty years since the publication of the first edition a permanent improvement in the material and moral condition of the working class had come about.[1] Because Engels and the Marxist school insisted that the economic laws were deterministic laws, they were confronted with the dilemma arising out of the contradiction between the law of pauperization and the reality of the economic advance of the working class.

Eduard Bernstein, a friend of Engels, observed only a few years after the latter's death that the working class could count on a gradual improvement of its lot and a more equitable distribution of production. He drew the conclusion from this insight and called for a reformist policy to replace the revolutionary party programme. Moreover, he tried to locate the error in Marx's evaluation of the historical tendency of capitalist accumulation, and found it in 'a dualism which runs through the whole monumental work of Marx ... – a dualism which consists in this, that the work aims at being a scientific inquiry and also at proving a theory laid down long before its drafting ... it appears that this great scientific spirit was, in the end, a slave to a doctrine'.[2] Although a number of reformist German Marxists (Schönlank, von Vollmar, David) had previously criticized Marxian theories, only Bernstein dared to discredit Marx so openly.

Bernstein's 'revisionism' (as his deviation from orthodoxy came to be called) caused an uproar in the whole school. The latent conflict came to the fore at the 1899 party congress in Hanover, but a tenuous compromise was struck. The German social democrats were finally pledged to a revolutionary programme at the Jena congress held six years later. But the decisive answer to revisionism was not provided by these party congresses but by a young Russian revolutionary, Lenin, who published the essay *What Is To Be Done?* after his release from a Siberian prison in 1902. He intervened in the debate with the angry words 'don't besmirch the grand word of freedom!'.[3] Only the revolution can bring freedom; without revolutionary theory, which is founded on the dialectic, there can be no revolutionary government, he argued.[4] In *Materialism and Empirio-Criticism*, his main theoretical work, he laid down four principles as 'epistemological premises': 1 the recognition of the laws of external nature; 2 the primacy of nature over the human will and mind; 3 the existence of 'blind necessity', a necessity unknown to man; and 4 the leap from theory to practice.[5] The dialectic, which guarantees scientifically the unity of theory and practice, is for Lenin the epistemological theory of Hegel and Marx. In the formulation of the four principles he took his bearing from Engels, but he believed (erroneously) that they could equally be developed from Marx. In an unpublished manuscript he wrote: 'One cannot fully comprehend Marx's *Capital* and especially its first chapter unless one has studied and comprehended Hegel's logic.'[6] He interpreted Marxism as a purely deterministic system based on Hegelian logic. In the dialectic he saw 'the algebra of the revolution' (Herzen).

Rosa Luxemburg and others in the orthodox camp had countered Bernstein with similar arguments already before Lenin's attack. She called the dialectic 'the cornerstone of scientific socialism'; in rejecting it 'Bernstein also rejects the whole doctrine of socialism'.[7] Even though she detected a theoretical stagnation in the movement, she was convinced that it had its source in the fact that 'Marx's theoretical achievement is in advance of us as a practical militant party'.[8] But in the realization that the collapse of the capitalist economy was not imminent she was free of narrow-minded dogmatism. She considered a re-examination of Marx's economic laws overdue and published *The Accumulation of Capital* in 1912. It is, apart from Robert Hilferding's *Das Finanzkapital*, the only significant study produced by the Marxist school until the work of Ernest Mandel. Luxemburg did not doubt the dialectical contradiction in capitalism and the historical barrier to the movement of accumulation (i.e. the end of capitalist production). But, she argued, Marx had tackled the problem 'from the wrong approach'.[9] He had considered accumulation only in the internal market of a capitalist country and not in the 'external market', which includes both the non-capitalist countries and the non-capitalist sections in a capitalist country such as the peasants, the learned professions, and the civil servants. Only after the conquest of this external market will capitalist production collapse under its internal contradictions. Luxemburg's empirical re-examination of the dialectical economic laws was undoubtedly consistent with her own view of Marxism, but clearly not with Lenin's view, who recognized the alternative interpretation of the dialectical law and condemned it. But the school failed to grasp the differences between Luxemburg and Lenin and claimed her work for the Marxist orthodoxy as defined by Lenin.

Basically Bernstein accepted Lenin's presentation of the dialectic as blind necessity. He rejected it for precisely that reason and warned against its pitfalls: 'Historical materialism cannot obscure the fact that it is human beings who make their history.'[10] Neither Bernstein nor Lenin knew that Marx had turned against Hegel's dialectic using almost the same words: 'History does nothing. . . . It is man, real, living man who does all.'[11]

Bernstein and Lenin fought with philosophical arguments. Bernstein appealed to Kantian arguments to refute the dialectic as science, Lenin used Hegelian arguments to justify it. Once he had disposed of the dialectic, Bernstein attempted to complement scientific socialism with an ethical code. This moral foundation of socialism met with approval among some Marxist academics (von Struve, Tugan-Baranowsky Woltmann) who were influenced by neo-Kantianism. Lenin, like Marx before him, categorically rejected the separation of science and ethics on the grounds that the dialectic also prescribes praxis (even less dogmatic Marxists have subscribed to this view). In conclusion it must be said that the level of debate did not rise above the general undistinguished philosophizing of the period. Lenin even went so far as making use of the then fashionable but vulgar — here the pejorative so popular in Marxist circles is appropriate — scientific materialism of Ernst Haeckel.

Dogma against science

To escape from persecution during Bismarck's regime, Bernstein moved to London, where through contacts with the Fabian Society he came to appreciate the pragmatic and democratic policies of the socialist movement in Britain. He was perhaps not a political leader, but he did possess something which German socialists have so often lacked, namely the courage to face uncomfortable facts and question party taboos. Not afraid to dismiss the hope of revolution as tantamount to a belief in miracles, he advocated a democratic take-over of the state.

Lenin, though, was a member of the Russian intelligentsia which had been educated to believe in the truth of Russian Christianity and then encountered the secular libertarian ideas of the West. The combination of messianic faith in the Third Rome and the politically revolutionary movements of Western Europe lit the revolutionary fire in Pushkin and Gogol, Tolstoy and Dostoyevsky, Bakunin and Herzen, Plekhanov and Lenin. They all proclaimed the mission of the Russian people to renew history against the decaying West. Herzen's words are characteristic: 'The messianic mission which is enjoined to Russia for the salvation of the world consists of making it clear to the world that salvation goes hand in hand with social revolution.'[12] (Conversely, Marx spoke maliciously of 'the rejuvenation of Europe ... by the infusion of Kalmuck blood'.[13]) The Slavophiles and 'Westerners', despite their great differences, were united in their contempt for the Western bourgeoisie and 'abstract' democracy. The eschatological consciousness that had once sustained the founders of European socialism still inspired the founders of the Bolshevik party.

With the same passion once displayed by the medieval schoolmen arguing over whether the Father and the Son were homoiousian or homoousian, of like substance or identical substance, Lenin and Bernstein were at loggerheads over the status of the dialectic as a scientific theory of knowledge. Or to put it more accurately: only Lenin fought a crusade; Bernstein was a cool man of science. Scholastic dogmatism against free science − that was the crux of Lenin's attack on Bernstein. The Russian communists of the first generation tried to find in Marxist theory the 'scientific proof' for the salvation of suffering humanity through a social revolution. For Lenin there was only one exclusive truth, an 'integral and pondered theory'; everything else was defamed as 'eclecticism and lack of principle'.[14] The phrase 'freedom of criticism' he invariably wrote only in inverted commas, and he rejected it like all orthodox Marxists.

The dichotomy between science and dogmatism, which had been uniquely evident in Marx's work, came to the surface but was not recognized as such because Lenin thought of his dogmatism as science.

Whereas Marx engaged in free scientific inquiry and also appreciated the contribution of bourgeois economists, Lenin had not the slightest sympathy for free science. Marx would never have accepted Lenin's pronouncement that 'Not one professor of political economy ... can be trusted with a single word where the general theory of political economy is concerned.'[15] Lenin often ridiculed any attempts to integrate the tradition of European philosophy and Marxism.

In this way the orthodox Marxist school acquired the character of a sect. It saw Marx and Lenin not only as party leaders but as the 'pope of communist theory' (Lasalle on Marx), and it venerated *Capital* as 'the Bible of the working class' (Engels). The communist parties fought for political power, but they also guarded orthodox dogma. Whoever deviated from it was persecuted as a renegade. That is why Lenin turned with such vehemence against Bernstein's revisionism. Individual freedom was subordinated to the needs of the party – *de facto* in all countries, but in Russia officially in a resolution of the Russian Social Democratic Party. (The sectarian struggles continue today even against exiled Russian dissidents. It would not be surprising if Western Marxists turn against exiles who have broken with communism; but it is grotesque when Mandel and other Trotskyists discredit Roy Medvedev, a fellow Marxist-Leninist and opponent of the Soviet regime.)

But what happened when reality did not correspond to the words of the Bible? In such a case the orthodox did not try to gain a better understanding of reality but were more concerned about the correct interpretation of the dogma. It was told as a joke about Hegel that in reply to an objection that a specific event in reality contradicted his theory he had said 'All the worse for reality!' – the Marxists took it quite seriously. Only in this frame of mind could faithful Marxists faced with the tragic situation of obviously innocent comrades being arrested and murdered by Stalin's secret police, study the works of Marx and Lenin to find in them an explanation for the problems of the age. The incredible thing about the confessions during the show trials is that some – certainly not all – were made not under duress but half voluntarily. In their almost schizophrenic state some of the accused admitted to crimes they had never committed, since in the face of certain death they could only thus reassure themselves that their life-long dedication to the party had not been in vain. Trotsky denied in public the suppression of Lenin's will by the central committee because, as he confided to Max Eastman, 'To a Bolshevik the party is everything.'[16] In this way he helped Stalin, his rival and eventually his murderer, to establish his rule.

Lenin himself had, despite all his anti-scientific dogmatism, a profound respect for the spirit. He appointed Anatoly Lunacharsky, with whom he had philosophical differences, as commissar for education when he took over the revolutionary government in 1917. He even reversed the dismissal from the University of Petersburg of Ivan Ilyin, a non-Marxist religious Hegelian, because he regarded non-Marxist Hegelianism as the Old Testament of Marxism.[17]

Labriola

At this time only Antonio Labriola, professor of philosophy at Rome, criticized the deterministic interpretation of the dialectic. He had come to Marxism from Hegelian philosophy, which he had first encountered in his student days in Naples. This familiarity with Hegel allowed him to perceive the distinction between historical and scientific materialism. In *Essays on the Materialist Conception of History* he elaborated his views and noted that Marx himself had been contemptuous of crude scientific materialism. Though surprisingly, in the incipient struggle between the revisionist rejection and the orthodox retention of the dialectic he endorsed the orthodox line. But what is most significant is that during the polemic between revisionism and orthodoxy the only valuable contribution to the understanding of the Marxist dialectic went unnoticed. Engels's deterministic interpretation of the dialectic gained general acceptance in the school, and when thirty years later Lukács and Korsch expressed similar ideas to those of Labriola they were dismissed as heretical.

The German Social Democratic Party (SPD)

The SPD retained throughout the orthodox view of Marxism and repeatedly rejected revisionism. But it paid only lip-service to the doctrine of revolution. All the party's activities, even during Bismarck's despicable anti-socialist law, were essentially reformist. The prevalent self-deception within the SPD is shown in Franz Mehring's official party history. He seriously thought that Marxism 'is as alive as ever among the working masses, the most conclusive proof of this being provided by the fact that revisionism never gained a foothold with them, that it never had the slightest impact on the practical movement'.[18] Lenin was right to call his German opponents 'semi-doctrinaire and semi-philistine'.[19] And Weber aptly characterized the hypocrisy of the party when he replied to a heckler who had asked why he refused to join the SPD: 'If after this lecture I meet one of its leaders in the hotel, he will carefully lock the door of his room and say "Herr Weber, you are right Marx would" — he goes towards the wardrobe to make sure no one is eavesdropping — "Marx would concede that the theory of pauperization does not work" . . .: Sir, do you understand, that church I will not enter!'[20] The revolutionary doctrine, which German socialists continued to proclaim without really believing in it, determined their political praxis. No wonder they failed so miserably when they formed the government in the Weimar Republic.

The difference between Lenin and Marx

For Lenin the leap from theory to practice was clearly marked; it required the dictatorship of the proletariat and terror. But because he thought the proletariat was as yet unprepared to carry out the revolution and regarded the trade unions as lackeys of capitalism, he assigned the task of leading the revolution to a vanguard formed out of the revolutionary intelligentsia.[21] For this purpose he held together the compact Bolshevik party — the vanguard — with iron discipline.

In *State and Revolution*, written a few months before the October Revolution, Lenin postulated the necessity of dictatorship during a transitional period in order to crush the resistance of the bourgeois and military apparatus of domination. After the initial phase of communism in which capitalist exploitation is eliminated and the administrative apparatus of the state is destroyed through terror, the revolution will bring about the higher phase of communist society. For the first time in history a democracy for the poor and for the people, a democracy 'without force, without coercion, without subordination, without the special apparatus for coercion called the state' will be founded.[22] In this phase human relationships are formed and 'the elementary rules of social intercourse that have been known for centuries and respected for thousands of years in all copy-book maxims' will be observed.[23] The communist society will be based on elected soviets, which unlike the 'pigsty' of bourgeois parliamentarianism (a term borrowed from Bismarck) will make laws and execute them. Contrary to the anarchists' aims, the people's democracy must erect a new apparatus of officials. (He could here refer to Marx's analysis in *Capital*.) The new officials will not be like the old state bureaucracy; they will be 'simply carrying out our instructions as responsible, revocable, modestly paid foremen and accountants'.[24] All officials will be elected and are subject to recall at any time.

Lenin contended that Marx's ideas had been most ignored on this point of the new officialdom. But crucially, the passages he quoted from Marx to support his argument referred to the election and removal of *judges*. As far as managers and book-keepers are concerned, Marx thought it important to put the right man in the right place.[25] In *Capital* he wrote that the officials would be more necessary for the control and distribution of production in a socialist society than in capitalist society. What did Lenin write?[26]

> Capitalist culture has created large-scale production, factories, railways, the postal service, telephones, etc., and *on this basis* the great majority of the functions of the old 'state power' have been so simplified and can be reduced to such exceedingly simple operations of registration, filing and checking, that they can be easily performed by every literate person.

In other words, since the workers would perform alternately the functions of control and supervision, Lenin was sure that the formation of a new bureaucracy could be prevented once the bourgeois apparatus of domination had been smashed.

Lenin's ideas are so naïve that they almost sound like a parody. It is inconceivable how he, having studied *Capital* and economics, could totally miss the point of what he considered one of the most striking analyses in Marx. Whereas Marx aimed for empirical research and dogmatism entered into his work surreptitiously, Lenin did not appreciate empirical science and instead presented Hegel's *a priori* dialectic as science. He followed Marx in the dogmatism of the dialectic and the mysticism of the people's democracy, but clearly not in the empirical analysis. This doctrinaire element in Lenin blinded him to reality, and it accounts for the horrific events that occurred after he seized power.

Vision and reality in Lenin

Lenin possessed the authority and the energy to lead the revolution; with ruthless terror he consolidated the rule of the party as the vanguard of the proletariat. But he was never corrupted by his absolute power. He gave up the extra-territorial rights in China and the oil concessions in Persia inherited from the tsarist government because they contradicted his notion of democracy. He on occasion pardoned political prisoners when charges could not be proved. When his secretary, Anzhelika Balabanova, took him to task for his unscrupulous policies, he replied that Russia needed brave and outspoken people like her but did not have them.[27] Although he disagreed violently with Luxemburg over his centralist policies, he always respected her intellectual integrity. Has any Marxist before or after Lenin treated an opponent in the party with such magnanimity? Despite all the brutality of his politics he exuded an aura of compassion and could inspire hope for the future.

Lenin knew that the first phase of communism could not yet provide justice and equality.[28] Only the compact group of the Bolshevik party could ensure the success of the revolution, and he therefore dissolved the coalition with other socialists after a few months and introduced a programme of rigid state centralization. In the spring of 1921 the sailors of Kronstadt, who had fought in the October Revolution with the slogan 'All power to the Soviets!', rebelled in order to secure democratic elections to the Soviets. The rebellion was put down after much bloodshed.

Yet he was not prepared for the eclipse of the professional revolutionaries and their replacement by professional bureaucrats. Actual developments ran contrary to his theory, in which in the higher phase of communism all state coercion would be dissolved in a true democracy. When he recognized the danger posed by the centrally organized bureaucracy, it was too late. In his will he demanded the dismantling of the power concentrated at the centre of the party. He died before he could carry out any decentralization.

Lenin suffered the same fate as Robespierre. His unrealistic dogmatism vitiated his efforts to establish a true democracy without force or coercion. The old tsarist administrative apparatus he had wanted to smash was replaced by an even more centralized and intolerant apparatus. Balabanova, who knew Lenin through years of political co-operation, valued his sincerity but was repelled by his corrupting and unscrupulous methods. She said of him: 'Lenin's life is an immense tragedy. In Goethe's phrase, it can be said that "he desired the good and created evil", and both in an unsurpassable measure.'[29]

Chapter eighteen

Marx's influence on the communists of the second generation

Lenin's successors

Whereas the first generation after Marx was still very much under his spell, the next generation realized that[1]

> It would be ridiculous to expect the Marxist classics to have elaborated for our benefit ready-made solutions for each and every theoretical problem that might arise in any particular country 50 or 100 years afterwards, so that we, the descendants of the Marxian classics, might calmly doze at the fireside and munch ready-made solutions.

Stalin, who wrote these words, was unlike the earlier Bolshevik leaders in that he was not familiar with the Western intellectual tradition, even though he had lived in Vienna for a while and had studied Marx. Stalin, Khrushchev and Brezhnev never seriously believed that the first phase of the communist revolution would be succeeded by a higher phase of communist society in which the basic rules of social intercourse would be put in practice. They were more concerned with the growth of material production and the consolidation of political power.

In his youth Stalin had been active in the underground, master-minding bank raids and organizing political actions for the party. He possessed neither the faith that had inspired Lenin nor the aura of compassion that had fascinated Lenin's followers. He extended the bureaucratic apparatus bequeathed to him by Lenin to a consummate instrument of power. Dialectical materialism was summarized in a rigid doctrine, the so-called 'diamat' (a portmanteau word for dialectical materialism), which was taught as the official 'ideology' of Marxism-Leninism in all schools and universities of the Soviet Union. Ideas were crudely manipulated to extend his rule — precisely what Marx had called ideology. Since Stalin had studied Marx, it is certainly conceivable that the official doctrine he introduced was termed 'ideology' not out of dogmatic narrowness but pure political cynicism. He falsified the ideas of Marx without compunction: whole sentences from Hobbes, whose materialism Marx had condemned as one-sided and misanthropic, were attributed to him; and the reference to the Asiatic mode of production (oriental despotic bureaucracy) in the preface to the *Critique of Political Economy* was suppressed because of its obvious parallels with the Soviet system. Henceforward the official economic histories of Russia (and China) taught the economic past of these countries in the concepts of Stalin and not in those of Marx.

So an inhuman monolithic block stifling all free political and intellectual expression was created in the name of Marx and Lenin, who had been committed to the humanist tradition of the West and aspired to a revival of man. To writers Stalin prescribed 'socialist realism'. As a result, literature, which had blossomed under Lenin, grew silent. Out of a society which according to Lenin wanted to realize justice plus electricity arose, as Camus commented, a society 'with electricity, minus justice'.[2] Milovan Djilas, who took part in the construction of the communist society but also experienced the emergence of the tyrannical 'new class', described the new society in the following words (for which he was imprisoned):[3]

> In the East, only a residue of formalism and dogmatism remained
> of Marx's dialectics and materialism; this was used for the
> purpose of cementing power, justifying tyranny and violating
> human conscience.

Once Stalin had secured his position on the throne of the tsars, he pursued the same foreign policy as his tsarist predecessors. Wholly undogmatically he proclaimed 'socialism in one country'. During the rise of the Nazis he confounded hopes of an alliance between communists and social democrats in Germany, either because he planned a pact with Hitler (in which he temporarily succeeded), or because he hoped to forestall the rival claims of the German Communist Party to the leadership of the Comintern. He thus achieved the destruction of the KPD, but could not prevent Hitler's invasion of Russia.

Stalin's autocratic rule precipitated splits in the communist bloc. Tito broke with him to secure his own political survival. He had to initiate a degree of liberalization of the Yugoslav economy to make it viable after it had been cut off from the Russian market; only subsequently did this become a matter of ideology. (It is not possible to discuss here the economic form of Yugoslav socialism.) And the great split with China, which admittedly occurred after Stalin's death, was nevertheless programmed in his reign.

The 'thaw' announced by Khrushchev did not go very deep. At the twentieth party congress he advocated de-Stalinization not because he opposed the Stalinist system, on whatever grounds, but because he wanted to assert himself over his political opponents. He permitted the publication of Solzhenitsyn's experiences in the Siberian prison camps, detailed in *One Day in the Life of Ivan Denisovich*, not to arouse people's consciences but to disavow his Stalinist rivals. When the liberal spirit he had allowed to flourish endangered Soviet supremacy in Hungary, it was crushed with tanks. The only thing that survived from the period of active de-Stalinization was that dissidents were no longer simply executed but in a more civilized manner sentenced to internal exile or locked up in mental hospitals. When the economy was liberalized to a certain extent, it occurred not in the spirit of political thaw but as an unavoidable correction to unsuccessful central planning. The man responsible for the programme of economic liberalization, Yevsei Liberman, explained it wholly in economic terms: 'The economic reform will not tolerate the retention of anything that is obsolete and that has failed to justify itself in our methods of management.'[4] In fact, in a memorandum Stalin himself had pointed out the disadvantages of central economic control, but he died before he could undertake any concrete steps to alleviate the problems caused by centralism.[5] (It is of course quite a different question as to what extent economic reforms can be effective in an authoritarian bureaucracy. In any case, economic issues can be discussed more openly than matters of ideology.)

Despite years of suppression, the humanist spirit of Lenin and his generation has not been suffocated altogether. Even in Stalin's reign the totalitarian regime had a different character from that of the Nazis, because the former was founded on an idea, however dogmatically constricted, whereas the latter was a criminal state without morality and justice. The intellectuals of the post-Stalin era saw in communism not merely an ideology but also a real promise. A rhetorical comment by Roman Rosdolsky, formerly employed at the Marx-Engels Institute in Moscow, typifies the attitude of his generation:[6]

> However, marxist social science has more than three decades of unparalleled degradation behind it; only half freed from the Stalinist straitjacket, it has to learn the difficult art of free thought and free speech. Is it then any surprise that it is still far from attaining the relative high point of the 1920s?

Intellectuals and managers and engineers can lead the way to a gradual break-up of the monolithic bloc, for the independent thought now expected of economic planners and scientists is a very infectious disease which cannot be contained within the factories and academic establishments. The educated know the great Russian literature and Marx's humanist vision too well to be placated with the sterile diamat. Any specialist who has achieved something in his field will in the long run not be prepared to put up with obscurantism and political irresponsibility outside of it. Indeed, in spite of the many setbacks since de-Stalinization a relative security of the individual and a relative freedom in scientific debate has prevailed. This situation would have been inconceivable before.

The extent of the unrest among intellectuals in the 1960s can be measured by the various attempts to go beyond the eradication of Stalinism and question the authority of Lenin and Marx themselves. In this way links with Western thought were once again established, though it goes without saying that these advances were carried out very cautiously. The Yugoslav philosopher Mihailo Marković observed with some irony that 'In order to break one authority (Stalin), another, greater authority (Marx) is being used. . . . However, rethinking some-one else's thoughts is a far cry from the concreteness for which a dialectician should strive'.[7] Milan Prucha from Czechoslovakia even contested the right of the people's democracies to 'raise a philosophical line to an official state philosophy'.[8] The Soviet invasion of Czechoslovakia in 1968 cut short these efforts. Subsequently, Solzhenitsyn's *The First Circle* described the dilemma of the Russian writer who must either conform and suppress his own conscience or follow his conscience and suffer for it. As early as 1951 the Polish political writer Czeslaw Milosz had described in his novel *The Captive Mind* this internal struggle and its schizophrenic consequences for the intellectual who maintains an individual moral standard. And Osip Mandelshtam distinguished between literature written with or without authorization, considering the latter 'true' and dismissing the former as trash.[9] Nadezhda Mandelshtam has aptly summarized the intellectual situation in Eastern Europe: 'The keepers of the flame hid in darkened corners, but the flame did not go out.'[10]

Since the early 1970s the monolithic bloc has been dismantled further. Yet one cannot expect that the diamat will be criticized or even openly challenged in the near future. One should compare this state of affairs to the New Left's critique of advanced capitalism to get an idea of the extent of intellectual oppression still obtaining in the Eastern bloc. There are some Soviet intellectuals who have inter-preted the diamat less dogmatically.[11] Nevertheless, it remains the official creed whose study is obligatory. To impede the formation of an internal organized opposition, the authorities force into exile those intellectuals who dare protest against the lack of freedom. This may be contrasted with the degree of criticism now possible within the Western European communist parties, when before the invasion of Czechoslovakia any dissident would have been expelled from the party.

The debate on the dialectic in the 1920s

Western Marxists were firmly rooted in the European intellectual tradition. The young Georg Lukács, who was to extricate himself from rigid Marxist dogmatism, mixed with Stefan George and his circle and frequently visited Weber's home in Heidelberg. In the university town of Heidelberg intellectuals from all disciplines and politicians of all persuasions met and exchanged ideas.

Lukács had already made a name for himself before becoming a communist with the essay *Soul and Form*, published in 1911; with the dialogue 'Von der Armut des Geistes' ('On the Poverty of Spirit'), published in a journal the following year, in which he preached a religious message of love derived from Tolstoy and Dostoyevsky; and with the book *Theory of the Novel*, written in 1915 but published some years later. In these essays he presented the history of art in the spirit of the romantics and in the dialectical categories of the Hegelian philosophy of history. He outlined the contrast between the fulfilled ages of Homer and Dante and the present 'godforsaken' world in which artistic forms have lost their connection with reality. At the same time he sensed 'intimations of a breakthrough into a new epoch' in Tolstoy and Dostoyevsky.[12]

Even before the publication of *Theory of the Novel* he experienced the fulfilment of his anticipation of a new epoch in the 'Great October' of the Russian Revolution. Now he viewed the dialectic in the spirit of Marxian materialism as 'reification' (*Verdinglichung*), the alienation of man – he borrowed this concept from Marx after the publication of the *Economic and Philosophical Manuscripts* in 1932 – and as the 'practical, actual supersession of the atrophy and dismemberment of human existence wrought by class divisions'.[13]

It is understandable that Lukács, who in his pre-Marxist phase saw the (idealist) dialectic as an historical process, would interpret the materialist dialectic in the same way. He considered the mechanical and causal dialectical materialism of Engels, Kautsky, and Lenin, to be erroneous. In his first Marxist work, *History and Class Consciousness*, he wanted to give, in good faith, 'an "orthodox" interpretation, an exposition of Marx's theory as Marx understood it'.[14] The character of the proletarian dialectic is not, according to Lukács, 'the knowledge of an opposed object', as Kautsky assumed (he avoided naming Lenin); it is, rather, the historical process which awakens in the class consciousness of the proletariat. As the proletariat recognizes reification, i.e. the fetishistic character of the exchange society, it sees its task as replacing it with a society free of alienation. As Marx had said: 'The working class ... have no ideals to realize, but to set free the elements of the new society.'[15] Thus what matters is the awakening of the proletarian masses to self-consciousness.

Karl Korsch arrived at a similar interpretation of Marx's dialectic. He published his findings in *Marxism and Philosophy*, which appeared only a few months after Lukács's book. Korsch was a professor at the University of Jena, a communist member of the Reichstag in the Weimar Republic, a minister of justice in Thüringen, and a friend of Brecht. In an afterword to the book he declared his basic agreement with Lukács on the nature of the dialectic. Admittedly some differences existed between the two, but these were insignificant compared to their joint opposition to dialectical determinism. Both conceived the dialectic as an historical movement in which man acquires consciousness. They concurred almost word for word: on the one hand, 'the consciousness is nothing but the expression of historical necessity' (Lukács), or 'the coincidence of consciousness and reality characterizes every dialectic' (Korsch); on the other hand, 'a dialectic is far from being the same thing as a mechanical, causal necessity' (Lukács), or it is not at all 'naturalistic and abstract' (Korsch).[16]

Their differences with official party doctrine were minimal. Both accepted the basic tenets that the dialectic is the core of Marxist theory and a necessary process, and that in consequence a special ethic beside the dialectic must be rejected as petty bourgeois; and both endorsed Lenin's revolutionary politics. They were nevertheless condemned as revisionists at the behest of Stalin. When Bernstein had been attacked passionately twenty years earlier, he was at least given a chance to defend his views at a party congress. Neither Lukács nor Korsch were granted a similar opportunity.

A few years later, Antonio Gramsci formulated an historical materialism comparable to that of Lukács and Korsch. He had been educated in the tradition of Labriola's Marxism and in the Hegelian philosophy of Benedetto Croce, who had distinguished what is 'living' in Hegel's philosophy, i.e. the concept of history, from what is 'dead', i.e. the philosophy of nature. Gramsci acquired from Croce the philosophical armoury to separate the living historical dialectic from dead scientific determinism. He even dared to reiterate Luxemburg's objection to the centralism of the communist parties: he called the party leaders 'little Machiavellis' and sarcastically commended them for their 'heroic attempts to imitate the French Jacobins'.[17] He demanded that the revolutionary strength of the masses be trusted. But the victory of fascism over the socialist parties in central Europe at the end of the 1920s shook his faith in the spontaneity of the masses, and later he pinned his hopes on the leadership of a revolutionary machiavellian 'modern prince' (the title of an essay written in prison). Gramsci was probably never branded a heretic because he was the general secretary of the Italian Communist Party and languished in prison while fighting fascism from 1926 until his death eleven years later; or perhaps because his writings became known outside Italy only after his death.

The Dutchman Anton Pannekoek also adopted an independent position within the orthodoxy. He was already a famous astronomer when he joined the Dutch Social Democratic Party in 1902. In Lenin's dispute with the revisionists he sided with the former, and founded with others the Communist Party of the Netherlands. After the First World War he came to the conclusion that a communist revolution no longer had any prospect of success with the increasingly affluent and quasi-bourgeois workers of the West; it would be possible only in the underdeveloped countries. He became popular after his death when the New Left began to take an interest in the third world.

The opposition between intellectuals and functionaries

In the controversy over the dialectic in the 1920s a new opposition between intellectuals and functionaries appeared in the Marxist camp. Marx and Engels, and Bernstein and Lenin, had become politically active in order to put into practice what they so passionately believed in. They had, regardless of their materialist conception of history, a profound respect for culture and the intellect. Stalin too might have been totally committed to communism when he was a novice at a theological seminary. From his communist conviction there remained only the manipulation of an ideology aimed to legitimate his brutal regime and guarantee the unity of the party. Korsch, unlike Stalin, was a politician *and* an intellectual. He was perhaps the first to realize that Stalin was not concerned with honest debate but only with political manoeuvres. So he did not comply with party dictates and was promptly expelled. He remained an ardent communist free of' party commitments, and warned in the Reichstag against the secret co-operation of the German Reichswehr with the Red Army. He observed that 'the pursuit of the revolutionary class struggle is ... different from the system of intellectual oppression established in Russia today in the name of the "dictatorship of the proletariat" '.[18] Lukács was a politically ignorant intellectual who often remained silent in the hope that Stalin might yet perceive the correctness of his orthodox Marxism.

The verdict against Lukács and Korsch was hardly noticed at the time. Rather, the prevalent view was that the liberalization of Marxism, which for too long had languished in crude economic materialism, signalled a return to the tradition of European humanism. Just as once the philosophers and poets of Europe had celebrated the French Revolution as a 'great dawn' (Hegel), intellectuals all over the world celebrated the Russian Revolution as an historical event inaugurating a new aeon. The literary elite made pilgrimages to Moscow and supported the communist side in the Spanish Civil War. Only a few doubted the integrity of Soviet policies.

Luxemburg was the first to criticize Lenin's restrictions on political expression. In 1904 she had sharply criticized Lenin's theory of the concentration of power in the party — 'ultra-centralism', as she called it — and warned that it endangered the positive and creative spirit of the revolutionary movement.[19] Later she implored him to permit free political discussion because it is 'the life element, the very air' of the proletarian revolution without which it could not succeed.[20] Some months after the October Revolution she accused the Soviet leaders of erecting 'a dictatorship, to be sure, but not the dictatorship of the proletariat, however, but only the dictatorship of a handful of politicians'.[21] At roughly the same time Weber declared in a lecture that 'It is the dictatorship of the official, not that of the worker, which, at the present anyway, is on the advance.'[22] With this opponent of dogmatic Marxism she also shared the dismay with the loss of life in war and revolution. While Lenin welcomed the First World War because it portended the collapse of bourgeois society, Luxemburg deplored the terrible misery it wrought; and Weber was similarly shocked by the great suffering during the Russian Revolution.

Ignazio Silone, one of the co-founders of the Italian Communist Party and active in the struggle against fascism, discovered Stalin's lack of scruples when taking part in meetings of the executive of Comintern. He was struck by the incapacity of the Russian leaders to be fair in discussion:[23]

> An adversary in good faith is inconceivable to the Russian
> Communists. . . . What an aberration of conscience this is, for
> so-called materialists and rationalists to uphold absolutely in
> their polemics the primacy of morals over intelligence. To find
> a comparable infatuation one has to go back to the
> Inquisition.

After internal conflicts he left the party. Many experienced the same bitter disillusionment: André Gide, Romain Rolland, Louis Céline, Max Eastman; and later those who fought in the Spanish Civil War: Arthur Koestler, Ernest Hemingway, Stephen Spender, George Orwell, to name but a few.

In the fight against fascism many restrained their attacks on the Soviet Union. Socialist intellectuals everywhere remained silent during the show trials in the 1930s. As late as 1944 Orwell's *Animal Farm* was rejected by several British publishers. Not before the end of the 1940s did people begin to express their disappointment with the communist revolution. When in 1949 David Rousset, until then a committed communist, revealed the existence of the Siberian prison camps in a Paris newspaper, a whole world collapsed for many people. Some concluded that they had been praying to a 'God that failed'. Others stuck to their communist beliefs and were consequently troubled by the dilemma as to how they as the faithful should relate to the corrupted church. Only now the opposition between the functionaries and intellectuals, which had been hinted at in the condemnation of Lukács and Korsch, came out into the open.

Chapter nineteen

The revival of Marxist thought in the 1950s and 1960s

The situation after the Second World War

The aftermath of the First World War saw a revival of interest in Kierkegaard and Nietzsche. Their very pertinent indictment of bourgeois complacency and cultural shallowness was reaffirmed in the existentialism of Jaspers and Heidegger. Existential philosophy emphasized that the task of philosophy, which for a time had been almost forgotten, is 'to catch sight of reality at its origin' (Jaspers) and 'to recapture, to repeat (*wieder-holen*), the beginning of our historical-spiritual existence . . . the beginning must be begun again, more radically' (Heidegger).[1] At the same time Lukács, Korsch, Gramsci and Bloch put forward their new interpretations of Marx's thought. These received unexpected corroboration after the publication of the previously unknown *Economic and Philosophical Manuscripts* in 1932. Marx's early notebooks confirmed that his socialism grew out of the indignation at human alienation in capitalist society. Young Marxist intellectuals were quick to note the similarities between the Marxian concept of alienation and the existentialist search for origins. The first to do so were Herbert Marcuse, a student of Heidegger, in a review of the *Manuscripts*; and Alexandre Kojève, a student of Jaspers, in lectures on Hegel's phenomenology.[2]

After the Second World War Marxist intellectuals were concerned to stress the humanist element in Marxism, thereby countering Soviet despotism and ideology. In this they followed in the footsteps of Lukács and Korsch, and Marcuse and Kojève. In France Sartre and Camus developed a revolutionary Marxist theory which combined the humanism of the young Marx with existentialism. In West Germany the Frankfurt school renewed Marxism by means of the 'negative' dialectic (as we shall see below). Even in Moscow Lukács attempted to preserve Marxist humanism under the Stalinist terror.

Although during the cold war there was often great animosity between intellectuals from different countries, all were united in the effort to dissociate themselves from the vulgar diamat and to preserve the humanist element in Marxism. Among the 'humanist' Marxists one should not count those who were members of the communist parties. Committed humanists were those who — sooner or later — resigned from the party or were expelled from it: Henri Lefèbvre, Maurice Merlau-Ponty and Robert Garaudy in France, Manabendra Nath Roy in India, the poet Aimé Césaire in the West Indies, Ernst Fischer in Austria, Ignazio Silone in Italy, Stephen Spender in Britain; and above all those who never joined the party: Brecht, Benjamin, Horkheimer, Adorno, Sartre; and those intellectuals from Eastern Europe who were active in the short period between the post-Stalinist 'thaw' and the suppression of the Czech experiment of 'socialism with a human face'. Some of them even tried to start a dialogue with Christian theologians.

In the evaluation of the plentiful Marxist literature which has appeared since 1950, we will be concerned mainly with the question of the dependence of art on material forces (in the sections on Marxist aesthetics) and the debate on the status of the dialectic (in the section on the Frankfurt school).

The problem of Marxist aesthetics

For the mechanical conception of dialectical materialism, the diamat, the problem of the relationship between art and society does not exist, since like all forms of consciousness works of art are a reflection of social reality. Marxist intellectuals raised in the tradition of European humanism could of course not be satisfied with this view. Inevitably they were confronted with the same problem that had irritated Marx: great art, although it is dependent on a specific stage of social development, has *intrinsic value* and, in the words of Marx, 'exercises an eternal charm'.[3] It is the general question of intrinsic value — whether the creations of the mind are autonomous of the material conditions of production which becomes problematical for Marxists only in the sphere of aesthetics. Philosophy is in Marxist theory synonymous with the consciousness of material development, religion is a false consciousness, and the political and judicial systems are the expression of class society. But that art possesses a kind of beauty independent of the economic base has never been seriously questioned — not by Marx or Engels, not by Lenin or Trotsky, and certainly not by the academic Marxists.

Marx had left unfinished the manuscript in which he discussed the 'difficulty' of intrinsic value because he could find no satisfactory answer. Engels, Plekhanov, Lenin and Trotsky subsequently studied the problem of art without knowing the contents of this manuscript. Engels hoped to solve the difficulty by demanding that art have a 'tendency'; but he had enough respect for true art to restrict this: the tendency should not be presented crudely and directly but 'must become manifest from the situation and the action themselves without being expressly pointed out'.[4] Lenin had no time for such niceties. He was interested in preparing the way for the revolution and he subordinated art to this goal. Nevertheless, in a letter to Gorky he showed a more profound appreciation of literature than may have been apparent in his political writings.[5] Trotsky and Luxemburg rejected explicitly the notion of art with a tendency and asserted the intrinsic value of art.[6] The first generation of Marxists appreciated, like Marx, the value of art and literature; but they did not have an aesthetic theory which reconciled the particular norms of art with the material base that supposedly determines (or conditions) it.

The materialist aesthetics of Lukács

It was Georg Lukács who first endeavoured to create a synthesis of the 'peculiarity' (*Eigenart*) of the aesthetic and the dependence of the aesthetic on the material base. (His main work is entitled *Eigenart des Ästhetischen*.) He had been taught the concepts of aesthetics by Dilthey, and in his notable early (pre-Marxist) essays he interpreted the history of art in the categories of the Hegelian dialectic. After he had become a Marxist the philosophy of art continued to be the focal point of his thought. His Hegelian background allowed him to see materialism not as a contradiction of art, but the exact opposite, as the concretization of art. According to Lukács, materialism conceives of the creation of artistic forms by the soul, to use the terms of his first essay on aesthetics, *Soul and Form*, as the 'self-creation of man through his own labour' in society.[7] Thus, because of his respect for the imaginative powers of the artist and his Hegelian view of history, Lukács was predestined to formulate a Marxist aesthetics.

As a Marxist, Lukács assumed that art, like any superstructure, is a reflection of society. However, the aesthetic theories developed by him had nothing in common with the banal idea of socialist realism, according to which art reflects reality mechanically. He accepted the work of art as a unique creation of the subjective imagination. Only the subjective, 'anthropomorphic' imagination, called 'the cathartic process' in his later works, transforms realism into art. He purposefully continued the European aesthetic tradition, which had perceived in art the cathartic element (since Aristotle), the reflection of reality (since Plato and Shakespeare), and the unity of subject and object (since Goethe and Hegel). Moreover, he was convinced that materialist aesthetics consummated this tradition.

'Correct' art, he argued, is possible only in periods of 'perfection' (*Vollendung*), when subject and object are in accord. A disturbance in the relationship between subject and object leads to decadence, which is shown in naturalism as the hypertrophy of the object and in artistic formalism as the hypertrophy of spirituality. Decadence (which in his youth he traced to the forlornness of the world) arises during the ideological decline of a class.

Lukács devoted many, often detailed studies to the formulation of what he called 'materialist' aesthetics. But the more one becomes absorbed in his long-winded arguments, the more Marx's difficulty in reconciling the intrinsic value of art with the ideologically false intellectual superstructure becomes apparent in Lukács's work. Marx had been unable to solve the problem, and published only a programmatic declaration (the preface to *Critique of Political Economy*), which has since been dogmatized by his orthodox followers. Lukács, in turn, attempted to resolve it in his book *Probleme der Ästhetik*, first published in 1946. He claimed he could 'divorce particularly clearly true Marxism, the real dialectical world-view, from its cheap vulgarization' by developing Engels's notion of the interaction of base and superstructure.[8] But Lukács realized that the interaction occurs for Engels 'on the basis of economic necessity, which *ultimately* always asserts itself'.[9] It would be mere sophistry if Lukács were to separate true from vulgar Marxism on the basis of this kind of interaction. What he meant was something quite different: he wanted to distinguish, as Weber had done, (true) materialist interpretation of history from (vulgar) materialist dogmatism. Of course Lukács did not credit Weber, who was to all Marxists like a red rag to a bull. As was proper for a good Marxist, he accused Weber of propounding the 'totally meaningless generalities' of bourgeois sociology.[10] We may assume he did so to provide himself with an alibi, or perhaps he preferred to ignore Weber. In any case, many years later, when he was internationally known and could speak openly, he acknowledged his debt to him. 'I do not regret today that I took my first lessons in social science from Simmel and Max Weber.'[11] Only the materialist interpretation of history as suggested by Weber can resolve the dilemma of Lukács's and Marx's materialist aesthetics and make the art of feudal and bourgeois society comprehensible.

Under the suspicious eyes of Stalin and Zhdanov, the party's leading ideologist, Lukács could only very guardedly plead for artistic realism against canonized obscurantist socialist realism. He could make use of one of Lenin's letters to Gorky. Lenin had written:[12]

> I fully and completely agree that in questions of literary
> creations, all books can be useful, and that by extracting the

particular point of view both from your artistic experience and from a philosophy, even idealistic philosophy [a reference to Gorky's work], you may come to conclusions which may be enormously helpful to the Workers' Party.

On the basis of this letter Lukács could argue that[13]

the history of literature proves that if a writer is deeply rooted in popular life, if his writing stems from this intimacy with the most important questions of popular life, he can, even with a 'false consciousness', plumb the real depths of historical truth'.

In other words, realism is true art when the artistic imagination can translate popular life into an adequate aesthetic form. With the authority of Lenin behind him Lukács could define the great pre-socialist literature of Dante, Shakespeare, Cervantes, Goethe, Balzac, Tolstoy and Mann as 'realist' in the accepted orthodox Marxist sense. This is what mattered to him. Occasionally he used the term 'socialist realism' in his work so as to deceive Stalin and Zhdanov. Yet he still drew a distinction between 'realism' and the 'naturalism' of Zola, Hauptmann, Remarque and Mailer. Theirs were certainly 'honest, realistic novels of great aesthetic and ethical merit', he reassured Zhdanov.[14] But, he said explicitly, they lacked the artistic form and stripped life of its beauty. Four years after Stalin's death he admitted that when he had polemicized against 'naturalism' he had meant socialist realism.[15]

As much as Lukács must be praised for preserving the European aesthetic tradition in the dark age of Stalinism, the validity of his aesthetic system could be questioned. Is it adequate for an understanding of great literature? Let us select from his rich work the analysis of Goethe, whom throughout his life he revered as a representative of realism. In the line 'Free people standing on free soil' from Goethe's *Faust* he found confirmation of the proletarian praxis: 'More than thirty years of praxis in the Soviet Union shows – every man stands on free soil with a free people.'[16] However, just like mediocre bourgeois commentators he failed to notice the profound ambiguity of worldly praxis which Goethe expressed in the preceding lines: 'They spoke . . ./ not of a trench but of a grave.' In a similarly simplistic interpretation Lukács found the key to Goethe's meaning in the famous lines at the end: 'He who ever strives and aspires/ we are able to redeem.' Yet in a conversation with Eckermann (which Lukács actually refers to!) Goethe said unequivocally that the key to Faust's salvation lies in the *combination* of human aspirations with, as the following line says, '. . . from above/ the everlasting love coming to aid him'.[17] Did Lukács consciously falsify Goethe's meaning or did he unconsciously misconstrue it in the schizophrenic way so common among Marxists to fit it into his materialism? Goethe also wrote in *Faust* that 'this world is not dumb' only because the love from above reverberates in it. Lukács's realism may tower above the socialist realism of Zhdanov, but *his* world remains dumb.

The interpretation of Mann and Solzhenitsyn suffers from the same flaw. His judgment that 'the world of Thomas Mann is free from transcendental reference' is contradicted by Mann himself in a letter to Anni Löwenstein: 'My presentation derives from the idea of progress predominant in the *Joseph* trilogy, to achieve something with God.'[18] He also did no justice to the work of Solzhenitsyn when he classified it as realism. Solzhenitsyn has never left any doubt about the fact that he pays more attention to the 'eternal' than to the 'topical'.[19] (Even so, it must be said in fairness to Lukács that in his book *Solzhenitsyn* he courageously stood up for a man ostracized in his own country.)

Lukács's materialist aesthetics suffer from the same 'this-worldliness of outlook' he imputed to academic idealist aesthetics. The reflection of reality in art is indeed a central notion in the aesthetic theories of Plato, Goethe, Kafka, and Benjamin. But when they spoke of reflection they did not mean the reflection of this world in the work of art; they meant, rather, the mystical reflection of the divine, which is identical with the truth. Lukács's world-immanent interpretation prevented him from seeing that for the great writers and philosophers the transient is merely a simile.

In addition, his aesthetic concepts are even less suitable to comprehend the formalism and the 'fetishism of spirituality' which he found in Joyce, Valéry, Rilke and Kafka. His judgment of these writers is reminiscent of that of the Nazi aesthetes. It is extenuated only by his tragicomic comment after being imprisoned in an old Transylvanian castle during the Hungarian Revolution of 1956, when he said 'So Kafka *was* a realist!'[20]

To counterbalance these objections it should be mentioned that his analyses of nineteenth-century German, French and Russian novelists are remarkable by any standards. But the principles of his Marxist aesthetics, not his literary criticism, are under scrutiny here. To that extent his criticism of Hegel's idealist aesthetics applies equally to his own work: 'The individual accurate analyses cannot eliminate the contrivances and contradictions which are contained in the system as a whole.'[21]

Again it should be said that pointing out the limitations of Lukács's philosophy of art must not detract from its importance. Its limitations are also the limitations of other philosophers and historians of his age, especially of Dilthey, under whom he studied and whose notion of immanence he subscribed to fully. It was due to his efforts in particular that the earlier crude economic materialism of Marxism was discredited.

Adorno was certainly right when he noted elements of philistinism and dogmatism and double standards in Lukács's writings. But it is unfair to describe him from the secure ivory tower as one who 'is hopelessly pulling at his chains, flattering himself with the belief that their clamour is the march of the world spirit'.[22] All Marxist philosophers think they can recognize the dialectical march of the world spirit. In any case, Lukács showed greater courage than Adorno during the rise of the Nazis. He emigrated to the Soviet Union, whereas Adorno, Marcuse, Brecht and others preferred exile in America.

There lies an element of tragedy over Lukács's life. After Stalin his belief in the 'Great October' was shaken, and towards the end of his life he had lost all hope. After the Russian invasion of Czechoslovakia he disagreed openly with Soviet praxis, which he had once seen as the realization of Goethe's vision of the free people standing on free soil.

Benjamin's so-called dialectical materialism

More original than Lukács's thought is the Marxist literary criticism of Walter Benjamin. Benjamin was influenced by the German *Jugendbewegung*, a movement protesting against the triviality of bourgeois culture. Lukács's *History and Class Consciousness* introduced him to Marxism. As he drew nearer to communism he began studying literature under the aspect of historical materialism.

In the essay *On Some Motifs in Baudelaire* he analysed the 'shock experience' of the writer in the modern city. 'Fear, revulsion, and horror were the emotion which the big-city crowd aroused in those who . . . observed it.'[23] This shock experience corresponds to what the worker ' "experiences" ' at the machine (he illustrated this correspondence with long quotes from *Capital*). Baudelaire manages to 'intercept the shock' in his mystical *Correspondances*. He describes an experience that includes 'ritual elements' and is 'the common property of the mystics'.[24] Although Bergson also attempts to free man from his obsession with time in the concept of 'duration', he is inferior to Baudelaire because as a metaphysical philosopher he suppresses death and is thus denied true historical experience. The experience of ritual is significant because it is the precondition for the representation of beauty. 'In the beautiful the ritual value of art appears.'[25] Baudelaire's lyrical poetry has the form of a 'symbol' (*Chiffre*).[26]

Benjamin employed the Marxist concepts of superstructure and base without trying to constrict the work of art into them. Although he stressed the relevance of his linguistic studies to dialectical materialism, he followed more in the footsteps of Leibniz and Humboldt. He had more in common with his contemporaries the linguist Ernst Lewy and the philosopher Franz Rosenzweig than with other Marxists. A true Marxist could hardly concede, as he did, that 'pure language ... no longer means or expresses anything but is, as expressionless and creative word, that which is meant in all languages'; or that Kafka possessed an 'attentiveness' in which he 'included all living creatures, as saints include them in their prayers'.[27]

The importance of Benjamin does not lie in his Marxist conception of history, as his modern followers have wanted to suggest, but in what he called the 'mystical view of history'. This adopts the Hegelian and Marxist secularization of the biblical story of salvation. But it also incorporates the striving for messianic redemption by giving modern man a task. 'Like every generation that preceded us', he wrote, 'we have been endowed with a *weak* Messianic power' which enjoins us 'to blast open the continuum of history'.[28] For the continuum of history is subject to the eternal and total destiny of nature. The messianic redemption which will blast open this destiny can occur only in the 'present', in the present as understood by the Old Testament: 'for the Jews ... every second of time was the strait-gate through which the Messiah might enter'.[29]

In the early phase of socialism the secular and political movement derived its strength from its messianic ingredient. Benjamin was one of the few who was still (or again) led by a sense of messianic intensity, which in the meantime had been extinguished. His mystical view of history deserves a detailed assessment. In this study a short appraisal must suffice.

It is no coincidence that Benjamin's friends, Horkheimer, Adorno, and Brecht, considered his Marxism out of line. Horkheimer ordered deletions from one of his essays for the journal of the Frankfurt Institute for Social Research on the grounds that, as Adorno admitted, 'Benjamin's use of materialist categories was inadmissible.'[30] Brecht thought that Benjamin had encouraged 'Jewish fascism' in his study of Kafka,[31] but also realized that Benjamin's death — he committed suicide while fleeing from the Nazis — was the first great loss inflicted by Hitler on German literature.

An unorthodox materialist conception of history is also evident in the work of Henri Lefèbvre. An avowed Marxist-Leninist, he nevertheless condemned the transformation of the economic base into an absolute as a 'metaphysical procedure'.[32] He has observed a real interaction between the economic and intellectual spheres; his undogmatic attitude has enriched his numerous instructive studies in the field of agricultural sociology. Joseph Needham's work on the relationship of culture to society in China may also be mentioned in this context.

The studies of Lukács, Benjamin, Lefèbvre and Needham are scientifically important precisely because they go beyond the narrow doctrines of dialectical materialism and Marxism-Leninism in spite of their professed reliance on them.

The Frankfurt school

What did the Marxist intellectuals who were bitterly disappointed by the development of communism in the Soviet Union have to say about the dialectic? Jürgen Habermas, one of the brightest younger Marxist intellectuals, has reviewed the situation and established four historical facts against a theoretical acceptance of Marxism:

1   Political actions can no longer be explained in terms of their dependence on the economic base. The primacy of the base over the superstructure should be recognized as a 'pre-judgment' of historical materialism and as such should be abandoned.

2   In the advanced capitalist countries alienation has lost its economic character since the standard of living has been raised significantly and the wage labour contract 'has divested itself of its undisguised expression, as a relation of power'.

3   The working class has lost its revolutionary class consciousness. 'Every revolutionary theory, under these circumstances, lacks those to whom it is addressed.'

4   The structure of capitalist society is self-regulating by means of the force of 'self-discipline' and is converging with communist society (although it should be noted that the latter 'at times has regressed again from the constitutional rights attained under capitalism to the legal terror of the party dictatorship').[33]

One may wonder what then remains of Marxist theory? For Habermas and the other philosophers of the Frankfurt school (Horkheimer, Adorno, Marcuse), the answer is clear: what remains is the critique of alienation. For although alienation has disappeared in its economic form, it still prevails in the no less dangerous form of man's atrophy and his habituation to a pure consumer life. Alienation has gone so far that modern man is no longer aware of the loss of his humanity and feels content in his alienation. These dangers would not be allayed with the negative utopias of the 'brave new world' type; they can only be exposed in a critique which, as Habermas put it, comprehends the subject dialectically 'in terms of the relations of social praxis ... both within the process of social labour and the process of enlightening the political forces about their goals'.[34] The Frankfurt philosophers contended that because the dialectic comprises an anticipatory understanding of both society as a whole and the meaning of the historical process, it is in a position to criticize alienated society and its false consciousness, its ideology.[35] This critical analysis of society was so fundamental to Horkheimer and Adorno that they called the new Marxist theory 'critical theory' — a term coined by Horkheimer when he selected it as the title for one of his books. Thus even though the neo-Marxists abandoned much of Marxist theory the dialectic once again became the focus of interest.

(Influenced by existentialism, a number of French Marxists — Merleau-Ponty, Lefèbvre and Sartre — also endeavoured to reinterpret the dialectic. But the work of the Frankfurt school is philosophically more important. This is not surprising considering that even before Hegel and Marx dialectical concepts had been introduced into German philosophy by Kant. The French Cartesian philosophical tradition did not know dialectics until Kojève's lectures on Hegel's phenomenology in the 1930s.)

The dialectic, according to the Frankfurt philosophers, has its source in the Kantian spontaneity of the subject, which is the prerequisite for cognition. It was the spontaneity of the subject through which Hegel had traced the dialectical movement from subject to object and through which Marx had discovered that Hegel's dialectical mediation between subject and object left out the factual, that is, society. The materialist dialectic occurs in reality in social labour and the exchange with nature. In the materialist dialectic the subject also remains the transcendental principle, but in contrast to the idealist dialectic it is related to social labour. The materialist dialectic consists of the intervention of the self-critical concept in the reality in which it has its content, in society. As Adorno said, ' "A" is to be what it is not yet' then means: the society of the exchange economy is to be what it not yet is, namely the society of 'free and just barter'.[36]

In falling back on Kant the Frankfurt philosophers could reclaim the dialectic, which had been debased in the Soviet theory of dialectical materialism. But they did not stop here; they also examined the Marxian dialectic. They were the first Marxists to admit that the principle of the primacy of economics is tantamount to a deification of history.

In *Negative Dialectics* Theodor Adorno described two grave consequences of the deification of economic history: firstly, it does not allow an autonomy of the intellectual sphere within the economic sphere, without which there can be neither art nor great philosophy; secondly, it is expected 'to yield historically stringent reasons why the happy end is immanent in history'.[37] Neither of these implications is acceptable. The materialist dialectic is not concluded in a positivity which would be the negation of the negation. The negation, reification, is not eliminated in the actual dialectical movement. 'The concept of freedom lags behind itself as soon as we apply it empirically.'[38] In contradistinction to Marx's dialectic, which ends in a positivity, the true concrete materialist dialectic is a 'negative dialectic' — an insight

Marx himself had anticipated when he abandoned the positive conclusion to the dialectic, the supersession of alienation, in the third volume
of *Capital*.

In so far as the negative dialectic 'will not come to rest in itself as if
it were total', it transcends the inescapably closed and immanent
positive dialectic.[39] 'This is its form of hope.'[40] But the transcendental,
the hope, cannot be represented; only in the process of the dialectical
movement is transcendence possible. The word 'dialectic', which means
language, already points to this aspect. Dialectical thought is not
logical, as Hegel assumed, but linguistic. Dialectics means language as
the 'organon of thought'.[41] In the dialectic 'things in being are read as a
text of their becoming'.[42] The interpretation reveals the essence concealed behind the façade of immediacy. Essence 'can be recognized by
the contradiction between what things are and what they claim to be'.[43]
The interpretation of this contradiction evinces the possibility and hope
for the 'truth content of the deficiency'.[44]

Adorno's negative dialectic has an affinity with the cipher-reading of
Jaspers and Benjamin and the linguistic thought of Rosenzweig and
Lewy. His philosophy is the first serious philosophical attempt to
restore the materialist dialectic as the promise of a free society — no
longer in the immanent supersession of alienation but in utopia and
hope.

The eruption of the opposition between Kant and Hegel in the Frankfurt school

Kant had said that 'the highest good, the kingdom of heaven, cannot be
achieved fully in this life' yet 'the progress towards it is possible and
necessary'.[45] In his utopia Adorno indeed found himself in agreement
with Kant, who 'in his theory of the intelligible . . . registered the constellation of the human and the transcendent as no other philosopher
beside him'.[46] The biblical and Western belief in the coming kingdom of
heaven shines through in both Kant and Adorno. But once Adorno had
restored the Marxian categories to a scientific level after their vulgarization in the reflection theory, the fundamental opposition between Kant
and Hegel reappeared. For Kant the purpose or meaning of history is a
normative idea of practical reason that can be ascertained not in knowledge but in faith. Against this, Adorno endorsed Hegel's rebellion
against the 'regressive and violent aspect of Kantian humility'.[47] He
claimed that the meaning of history is posited and can be ascertained
by the constitutive concept although not as in Hegel and Marx in the
closed dialectic but in the confrontation of the concept (*Begriff*) with
the contingent and untrue reality. Habermas wrote that this procedure

'implies that the "meaning" of history cannot be derived as the idea of practical reason. The structure from which it will be derived must rather be a structure of the socio-historical structure itself, and like this it must be objective'.[48] Thus the subjective interpretation of the meaning of history is purported to be objective. However, the construction of an objective meaning of history is fraudulent, what Kant called *'perversa ratio'*, putting the cart before the horse.[49]

This theoretical question is of the utmost importance for praxis. If the purpose of the dialectical movement is cognizable, then free human initiative is debased. Whether the dialectic is an historical necessity 'about which there is no ... reason to moralise' (Marx); or the 'movement of material bodies' (Trotsky); or the 'blind necessity' of a natural law (Lenin); or the historical movement which rises to consciousness in the proletariat (Lukács); or 'as moving being ... a still undetermined being' (Bloch); or 'not only an advancing process but a retrograde one at the same time' which can be empirically understood and practically carried out (Adorno): invariably the dialectician puts his trust in the dialectic and dismisses the individual's decision as irrational and inconsequential.[50] The clear implication of the Hegelian-Marxist trust in the dialectic and the contempt for morality is that the freedom and activity of man are paralysed. For Kant, Weber and Jaspers, the claim to the knowledge of the meaning and purpose of history – and they believed no less than the Hegelians and Marxists that there is meaning in history – was delusive. They put their trust in the free decision of man. Hence Weber's exasperation at the methodological confusion of the Marxists! Of the Marxist or near-Marxist philosophers, Merlau-Ponty, influenced by Weber, concluded that 'The adventures of the dialectic ... are errors.'[51] Adorno and Horkheimer were honest enough to say that 'Idle waiting does not guarantee what we expect' and that trusting in the dialectic may end in 'doubt'.[52] And in 1969 Habermas wrote that critical theory 'has reinforced political resignation among us younger ones'.[53]

The rift in the Marxist camp between the functionaries and intellectuals has had almost grotesque results. With the politicians the theory fell prey to power, and with the intellectuals the unity of theory and practice became the gauge of philosophy. The communist ruling class restricted itself to the consolidation of power and the economy; esoteric intellectual sects, at least in Western Europe, trusted in dialectical utopias.

The later revisionists

The socialist politicians of the West could gain little from the theories of Marxist intellectuals. Their dilemma, to find an ideology for their praxis, which differed from Soviet praxis, is illustrated in a letter by Enzo Sereni. He wrote to his orthodox Marxist brother:[54]

> It is superfluous to underline that just here from the historical point of view is the greatness of the value of Marxism, which stands the importance of economics in the correct light. But: ... apart from economics, ethics also exist in the world. And woe to him who thinks that there are no ethics, and that they are not capable of 'setting heart on fire'.

British socialists, too, had little sympathy for an amoral dialectic. They felt it necessary to complement Marx's theory with the moral ideal of the early socialists.[55] The German SPD, which had for a long time suffered from the discrepancy between its revolutionary programme and its reformist praxis, summarily cast off its Marxist programme at the portentous 1959 party congress at Bad Godesberg.

After Stalin, even philosophers from Eastern Europe began to move away from the pseudo-Marxist mythology of the dialectic. They demanded an ethical attitude. Leszek Kolakowski, for instance, warned against the danger that in the post-Stalinist era too 'the words "Marxism" and "Marxist" could be turned into instruments for oppression, and that scientific polemic could be replaced by administrative pressure'.[56] When in *The Third Way* Ota Šik outlined a humanist and democratic socialism he did nothing more than repeat Bernstein's revisionism (even if he avoided this word). What courage Kolakowski, Šik, and others showed in putting such revisionist heresies to paper![57] In a similar vein the Yugoslav philosopher Svetozar Stojanović postulated against the 'immature', 'politocratic' and oppressive communism of the Soviet Union a 'mature' and democratic socialism.[58]

Lukács, who had once rejected ethical socialism as petty bourgeois and revisionist, changed his mind after the disillusionment with Soviet praxis. He came to the conclusion that nothing was more essential for socialism than 'the alternative decision of the individual'.[59] To the indignant interjection that this sounded too much like existentialism he retorted: 'this interests me very little'.[60] Shortly before his death in 1971 he even decided that the utopian expectations were harmful because the only thing that mattered (in West Germany) was the consolidation of democracy.[61]

Chapter twenty

The student revolt of the 1960s

America before the protest movement

The United States was not affected by the social revolutionary movements of the nineteenth century. At the time when Marx and Engels agitated for a communist revolution and Disraeli inveighed against the division of the British people into 'two nations', optimism about the future reigned on the other side of the Atlantic. Often still inspired by the puritan ideal of work as an ethical duty, the immigrants found ample opportunities to attain material success in an undeveloped country. But after the civil war a new generation of unscrupulous captains of industry succeeded the devout pioneers. The animating spirit disappeared from the faith; what remained was the confidence in the success of the American way of life. Around the turn of the century the glaring discrepancy between puritan tradition and an emerging materialist attitude came to the notice of and was denounced by individual intellectuals: the sociologist Thorstein Veblen depicted 'conspicuous consumption' and 'conspicuous leisure', and the philosopher William James expressed his contempt for the world of ' "consumer leagues" ' and 'industrialism unlimited' — what today we would call consumer society.[1]

The discomfort with American society grew among the intellectuals. Many of them were encouraged by the prospects offered by the Russian Revolution. 'I have seen the future and it works!', the journalist Lincoln Steffens cried out, and his words met with a lively response.[2] But he and others were soon bitterly disappointed by the Stalinist terror. The McCarthy witch-hunt only exacerbated the feeling of despair. A paralysing disillusionment befell the generation of the 1950s. This was expressed in the reminiscences of ex-communists in the collection *The God that Failed*; in David Riesman's analysis in *The Lonely Crowd* of the supersession of the ' "inner-directed" ' man by the ' "other-directed" ' man who keeps up with the Joneses; in the critical social analyses by C. Wright Mills, William Whyte, and Vance

Packard. Most deprecating was perhaps the playwright Eugene O'Neill, who declared to the press in 1946 that the country had badly administered its rich God-given inheritance; therefore 'We are the greatest failure in history.' In these years the notions of the 'silent majority' and the 'end of ideology', the end of chiliastic hopes, appear. The end of ideology was proclaimed by, among others, the sociologists Edward Shils, Daniel Bell and S.M. Lipset in America, and the historian Hugh Trevor-Roper and the sociologist Franz Borkenau in Europe. It was reiterated in the programmatic introduction to the first volume of the journal *Encounter*. No one at the time thought that the revolutionary fire continued to smoulder under the surface and would break out again within a decade.

The revolutionary student movement

The young generation was not prepared to accept the end of ideology. Admittedly the old revolutionary ideas were run down — so new ideas must change society! In 1962 a small group of dissident students calling themselves Students for a Democratic Society worked out a revolutionary programme in the Port Huron Statement. Initially insignificant, the SDS required a cause with which to make its mark. In the 1960s the civil rights movement and the opposition to the war in Vietnam provided causes. A full-scale rebellion erupted at the Berkeley University campus in 1967, and it spread like wildfire from there to the universities of America, Europe, and Japan.

The political movement also sparked an emotional explosion. As early as the 1920s Negro jazz music had appealed to the emotional life of the white establishment, which for centuries had been frustrated by puritanical values. In *Soul on Ice*, the Black American writer Eldridge Cleaver proclaimed the liberation of the soul and the penis, which had for so long suffered under the white man's defamations and the domination of the brain: the 'Omnipotent Administrator'. The book was received as a revelation and sold several hundred thousand copies. The revolutionary youth finally broke with the old sexual taboos. A radical cultural movement was unleashed as a complement to the revolutionary political movement.

The student activity of the 1960s may be seen as a new wave of the movement that had commenced with the critiques of a few intellectuals around the turn of the century, rose in a second wave with the enthusiasm for the Russian Revolution, and soon afterwards ended in an ebb of resignation. But the new era of the movement lacked a clear purpose. The rebellious students turned against the ruling establishment and the old culture, but no less against the 'perverted' old left, as the

Port Huron Statement said irreverently. In the early revolutionary storm and stress of the 1960s only the negative aspect was expressed in the rejection of the tradition of the older generation and the rejection of communism. This explains the chaotic and diverse aspirations: revolutionary spontaneity against the rigid establishment, natural simplicity against the materialist consumer society, emotion and sex against the cold intellect, drugs against sobriety, the hippy commune against isolation.

Every revolution arouses passions. Even the level-headed Jacob Burckhardt said in praise of crises that 'passion is the mother of great things' and does away with meaningless forms of life.[3] Does it also set free new energies?

Marcuse's alternative

In their rebellion the young found confirmation of their grievances in Herbert Marcuse. At the outbreak of the student revolts this philosopher, who until then had been virtually unknown in America, became overnight one of the intellectual triumvirate, with Marx and Mao, to which the students looked for inspiration.

Marcuse, co-founder of the Frankfurt school, agreed with his colleagues that oppression in modern society exists no longer in an economic way but in a spiritual and intellectual form. Social planning has eliminated poverty but not alienation. The ruling class employs the technological and bureaucratic apparatus not only to increase production but also to manipulate people, to accustom them to the *status quo* and voluntary integration into the labour process. They are contented in the suppression of their drives in accordancy with the ascetic work ethic; they lose their humanity and become passive, 'one-dimensional'.

In *Soviet Marxism* Marcuse argued that Lenin had been forced to sacrifice Marx's humanist ideal to the economic norms of production because the Soviet Union came into being in competition with hostile capitalist states. These norms were then 'canonized' in the Stalinist period.[4] However, he passed over Lenin's suppression of the sailors' uprising and Stalin's show trials, neither of which he could fit into his alibi for the non-realization of humanism in the Soviet Union.

Marcuse called for the 'Great Refusal' against the repressive societies of both East and West. As an alternative he described a humanist society in which people are emancipated from social, political, and spiritual oppression. In *Eros and Civilization* he even defended, against Freud, the possibility of a culture without repressive channelling of drives. But a discussion of what he called 'the old desideratum of hedonism', to think together happiness and truth, lies outside the scope of this study. Suffice it to say that the question arises whether Marcuse here interpreted Epicurean philosophy correctly; whether the striving for sensuous happiness does not betray man's despair about his self, or whether, in the words of Nietzsche, the man who has invented happiness is not in fact 'the most contemptible man . . . the Ultimate Man'.[5]

We are interested here in Marcuse's evaluation of Marx. From the experience that in modern planned societies (both the Eastern communist and the Western welfare states) people still remained intellectually and spiritually oppressed, he concluded that quantitative socialization had not gone far enough. He also conceded that the critical theory of the Frankfurt school was essentially more abstract than he had previously thought. Hence he asked rhetorically: 'Should not the "first phase" of socialism be more and qualitatively other than it was projected in the Marxian theory.'[6] With this demand for a qualitative change of society he led humanist Marxism, which had not advanced beyond a theoretical critique of alienation of modern society, back to praxis.

In order to show the possibility of a qualitative social transformation, Marcuse proceeded from the later Marx's insight into the coexistence of the economic realm of necessity and the true realm of freedom. This conception was idealistic and optimistic, he suggested, because Marx had not perceived the danger of the manipulation of the people through the social planning of the apparatus. But this danger may be obviated by wrenching the apparatus from the hands of the ruling class and putting it in the service of both economically necessary and humanist goals. In this way the dilemma of the later Marx is resolved. The coexistence and separation of the realms of necessity and freedom is not absolute. 'Autonomy over the technical apparatus is freedom *in* the realm of necessity.'[7]

Marcuse's polemic against Weber

Weber had shown that the danger to freedom lies in the apparatus, in the bureaucracy itself. In an attempt to moderate this warning, Marcuse pointed to two supposed fallacies in Weber's analysis. For one thing, Weber is wrong in his 'equation of technical reason with bourgeois-capitalist reason'. The 'fate' of rationalization is not universal, as Weber contended, but unique to capitalist society; and to the extent that it has *become* fate, it can also be 'destroyed' (*aufgehoben*). In a true democracy the apparatus can undergo changes in its own structure, and the people hitherto subjected to the apparatus can master it.[8] However, Marcuse's objection fails to appreciate that the apparatus is a rational means for a specific task. The apparatus may serve the economic inhuman purpose of productivity or it may serve the humane purpose of caring for the sick — in either case it must employ appropriate, i.e. rational, means in order to perform its specific task. Therefore the structure of the apparatus has, irrespective of its function, an 'economically rationalized (and for this very reason ethically irrational) character', as Weber analysed objectively and clearly, or an 'inhuman' character, as Marcuse said emotionally and vaguely.[9] The emotional and indeterminate language obscures the fact that freedom depends not on the structure of the apparatus or its transformation (this is not even possible); rather, it depends on the control, the autonomy, over the apparatus. When Marcuse spoke of 'the combination of centralized authority and direct democracy' as an ideal, he betrayed his total ignorance of how bureaucratic rule actually operates.[10]

Marcuse's second objection is aimed at Weber's method. Weber, he maintained, did not take into consideration the potentiality of a qualitatively different rationality, because his 'positivist, pseudo-empirical sociology, hostile to theory' separates the ideal from science. His value-free analysis boils down to an apologia of the bourgeoisie and a denunciation of the potential alternative. ('Hostile to theory' of course means in Marcuse's parlance hostile to dialectical theory.) The merit of the dialectic lies in its combination of analysis and purpose. 'The "Ought" shows itself in the "Is". The indefatigable effort of conceptual thinking makes it appear.'[11] Thus[12]

> the qualitatively new organization of the realm of necessity,
> upon which the emergence of truly human relationships depends,
> in turn depends on the existence of a class for which the
> revolution of human relationships is a vital need. Socialism is
> humanism in the extent to which this need and goal pre-exist,
> i.e. socialism as humanism has its historical *a priori within*
> capitalist society.

From this passage the reader may judge for himself whether the 'ought', which Weber allegedly denounced, appears in Marcuse. The 'need and goal' appear, but the potentiality of a qualitatively different rationality certainly does not. In default of an empirical investigation of a qualitative transformation of society, the new rationality emerges as a *deus ex machina* from the *a priori* dialectic. In this way Marcuse spoiled the undoubtedly fruitful ideas on the quality of society. Against his will he confirmed Weber's thesis that the 'ought' is obtained fraudulently when it is integral to the analysis of the 'is'. Moreover, the *a priori* dialectic is a regression from Marx's conception of the dialectic, according to which science has to track down the dialectical movement in empirical analysis.

Because he lacked methodological clarity and did not bother to obtain empirical corroboration of his theories, Marcuse mystified the apparatus of capitalist society into 'in the literal sense the subject' and the socialist alternative into a paradise of full control over the apparatus.[13] This double mystification intensifies the historical opposition between capitalism and socialism into a Manichaean dualism of the 'denial of humanity' and the 'equation of socialism and humanism'.[14] Stephen Spender, an outspoken critic of bourgeois values, compared this sociology to the novels of Galsworthy, and recalled D.H. Lawrence's objection to them: 'When one reads Mr Galsworthy's books it seems as if there were not on earth one single human individual. They are all these social beings, positive and negative. There is not a free soul among them.' As Spender pointed out, there is also no such thing as a free soul in the materialist hells of Packard's 'hidden persuaders' and Marcuse's 'one-dimensional man'.[15]

But it must be asked whether those people who are exposed to such extreme totalitarian manipulation that they lose their critical judgment and feel contented in their situation are still able to effect a qualitative transformation of society? Marcuse began to doubt this. In *One-Dimensional Man*, published in 1964, he concluded pessimistically that there is no promise and no sign of success; in *Repressive Tolerance*, published a year later, he advocated violence; and in the preface to *Negations* (1968) he predicted a 'catastrophe'. In this catastrophic situation an intellectual elite would exercise the dictatorship, since the workers, manipulated by the bourgeoisie, have lost their revolutionary impetus. This notion of the dictatorship of the intellectuals (which admittedly he modified subsequently) surely represents a regression into the very denunciation of the alternative Weber had been accused of. Weber emphasized that modern bureaucratization had not yet achieved total domination as it had in China. In the face of the fate of rationalization and bureaucratization he renounced the 'Faustian universality of man'.[16] Goethe and Marx had after all done the same: the former in his later work *Wanderjahre*, subtitled 'the resigned ones', and the latter by his acquiescence in the continued existence of the realm of necessity. They resigned but they did not despair. Whereas for Marcuse night had hopelessly fallen, for Weber it was still day in which man could be active.

Marcuse's simplistic view of society has its roots in the German political romanticism influential in his student days, when many intellectuals — including George, Mann, Sorel, Buber, and Heidegger — spoke out strongly against modern rationalistic civilization. Weber repeatedly reproached the politically romantic German intellectuals for their inability to cope with and aversion to the problems of everyday life. Marcuse's polemic against Weber seems to be a belated, and inadequate, answer to this criticism. When he said of Weber 'He raged against the intellectuals' he did not know why he had raged.[17] How little he understood Weber is shown very clearly in the description of Weber's analysis of labour as the denunciation of the potential alternative; for in *Economy and Society* Weber, following Marx, had condemned in the strongest terms the fact that the worker is forced to sell his labour-power lest he starve.[18]

Scientific analysis and romantic over-simplification are peculiarly interspersed in Marcuse. But during the confused protest movement he at least posed the right questions following on from the later Marx and Weber: the questions about the qualitative transformation of society and the role of the bureaucracy. However unrealistic and banal his answers may have been, the questions should be taken seriously.

What survived of the student movement?

The revolutionary student movement collapsed within two or three years. Nevertheless, in this short time it made a significant impact on political life, quite unlike the German *Jugendbewegung* at the turn of the century, to which it has been compared. Then as now young people voiced their repugnance against the materialist belief in progress and the rationalism of the bourgeoisie, and they were stirred by the romantic longing for simplicity and community. In Germany, the *Jugendbewegung* had been on the whole apolitical and antidemocratic. When those influenced by it engaged in politics, they joined for the most part the antidemocratic extremes of communism and fascism, thereby undermining the Weimar Republic. In the America of the 1960s, however, the young dissidents were heard and noticed. As a result, the revolutionary students — including the militant blacks[19] — switched from violence to responsible activity within the established political institutions. Already de Tocqueville had admired how in America revolutionary ideas and existing institutions correct and balance each other.[20] Gunnar Myrdal experienced the same during his research into the plight of the blacks in America: 'As my duty dragged me through all the serious imperfections of American life related to the Negro problem, I became ever more hopeful about the future.' This confirmed his belief that a moral force survives in the American creed.[21]

So it happened that the protest movement, which had begun with confused ideas and the destruction of university campuses, succeeded in stirring the latent moral force of the American 'silent majority'. Marcuse never recognized this. A few years after the outbreak of the student revolt he was accused, with others, of having imported from Germany the arrogant disdain for the common people. In a remarkable article on the lessons of Watergate, Henry Fairlie observed that 'thinkers such as Emil Lederer, Hannah Arendt, Erich Fromm and Herbert Marcuse, four names out of three hundred, wrote the public out of existence ...; the concern became not how the people should govern themselves, but how they should be governed ... by "governing elites" '.[22]

Just as the initially violent political protest movement in the United States gradually became integrated into the institutional framework and released new energies, the rebellion against a puritanical culture became reintegrated into the intellectual and spiritual tradition and seemed to renew it. Hamilton Fish Armstrong suggested hopefully in an article in *Foreign Affairs* that this infusion could heal the evils of contemporary society 'by leavening the mediocrity of our culture with snatches of unorthodoxy'.[23] The emotional liberation proved particularly fruitful in the field of music, which had flourished in England under the Tudors but had since then been stifled by religious asceticism. Of course some of the chaotic phenomena of the spiritual and cultural revolution survived. Here Hermann Hesse, for whom the young showed such enthusiasm at the time, may be quoted: he warned against the temptation 'to throw ourselves upon some Indian system ... out of despair about our own spiritual situation'.[24]

In Western Europe, on the other hand, the revolutionary youth did not find the path to co-operation in the democratic parties as easily. When in 1970 Jean-François Revel suggested persuasively that 'the new American Revolution has begun' (the subtitle of his book *Without Marx or Jesus*), the revolutionaries of his native France were shocked. He also thought they prevented any social change by insisting on an illusory purity, which was why they found an echo only in esoteric circles.[25] A few years later the young intellectuals were once again roused from their utopian dreams by Solzhenitsyn's revelations about the Gulag camps. As far as one can see, they still keep away from concrete political activity and, like the Frankfurt philosophers, concentrate on theoretical criticism.

Chapter twenty-one

The New Left

New standards of society

The extent to which social thought had changed within a few years is shown in a programmatic declaration by the then president of the Bank of America, Tom Clausen, who argued in 1971 that business had to concern itself with non-business problems, since 'nobody can expect (in the long run) to make profits . . . if the whole fabric of society is being ripped to shreds'.[1] A new belief emerged, a belief that business had a responsibility not only to the traditional profit motive but also to the society in which it operates. This view was diametrically opposed to the economic outlook of the 1950s, when a director of General Motors, Charles 'Engine Charlie' Wilson, could suggest that 'what is good for General Motors is good for America'. The new attitude to the economy made such an impact that in the ninth edition of his standard text on economics Paul Samuelson devoted a special section to 'the inroads made by the new *Weltanschauung*'; and although sceptical of it, he found it 'most exciting'.[2] The new outlook was also evident in Galbraith's proposed 'espousal of non-economic goals, . . . the beauty, dignity, pleasure and durability of life' in the economy; at the same time he dismissed the 'Conventional Wisdom' – the preoccupation with economic growth and profit – as being outmoded.[3] Ezra J. Mishan's book *The Costs of Economic Growth* (1967) caused a stir by asserting that economic growth occurred to the detriment of spiritual and cultural values. The titles of books published in the 1960s may be instanced as indicators of the new mood: *The Coming of Post-Industrial Society* by Daniel Bell, *The Post-Industrial Society* by Alain Touraine, *Arcadie, essais sur le mieux-vivre* by Bertrand de Jouvenel, *Jenseits von Angebot und Nachfrage* by Wilhelm Röpke, *Beyond the Welfare State* by Gunnar Myrdal. Michael Harrington, a committed socialist, also moved away from the dogmatic revolutionary tradition and hoped for the 'emergence of a democratic Left' which would align modern industry with the Western intellectual tradition – 'marry engineering and philosophy'.[4] The new outlook may be summarized as the quest for a world beyond materialism and the rejection of careerism and specialization.

In so far as these new views, which were expressed independently of each other and showed internal differences, shared a new humanist objective and an opposition to both bourgeois economics and Marxist dogma, they will be described in this study as 'New Left', for lack of a better term. They could also be described with some justification as 'neo-conservative', since they reaffirmed the old principle of public welfare against *laissez-faire*. In Europe conservatives and socialists had fought for it against the unrestrained market economy, but they had divided into the dogmatic extremes of right and left (a doctrinaire polarization which was on the whole avoided in America). 'New Left' is here defined by a new approach to society from non-economic goals, and not by a particular political ideology or a specific economic school such as that of the Union of Radical Economists in America. It thereby includes those defenders of capitalism who postulate a moral vision of the common good against crude materialistic individualism.

Precursor of the new economics was John Maynard Keynes. He owes this position not so much to his economic theories as to his fundamental conception of economics. Since as a result of the rising standard of living 'there will be ever larger and larger classes and groups of people from whom problems of economic necessity have been practically removed', he proposed that 'We shall once more value ends above means and prefer the good to the useful.'[5] A similar disillusionment with quantitative technological progress can be found in the later H.G. Wells. His reproach of the Fabians Sidney and Beatrice Webb, called 'Bailey' in the autobiographical novel *The New Machiavelli*, could have been written by a member of the New Left: 'If they had the universe in hand, I know they would take down all the trees and put up stamped green shades and sunlight accumulators.'[6]

Thus even before the student revolt of the late 1960s, a growing number of non-conformist thinkers began to question and so undermine the belief in economic and technological progress. Yet they would not have gained such prominence without the rebellion. Suddenly the public took an interest in the quality of life: in ecology and alternative technologies. Studies investigating these issues, such as *The Limits to Growth* (1972) and *Mankind at the Turning-Point* (1975) sponsored by the Club of Rome, found a strong world-wide echo.

In communist countries the issue of the relationship of economic growth to the quality of life was raised, if only during the short Prague Spring. Radovan Richta set up a project with a team of fifty Marxist scholars; its findings were published, after the forced interruption in 1968, in *Civilization at the Crossroads*. But it was in the countries of the third world that the conflict between the economic-technological sphere and the spiritual-cultural sphere, between modern industry and the old indigenous culture, came to a head. On this topic the Indian novelist Mulk Raj Anand has remarked that the machine will adapt itself to the old consciousness only when 'we notice that the very challenge of technology has forced man everywhere either to face up to his own inner reality or perish'.[7]

The affinity between the New Left and Marx

How do these problems relate to Marx? At a first glance no link is apparent. Nowhere did the workers participate in the student revolts and the movement of the New Left. The politicians and theoreticians of the New Left, Marcuse excepted, probably did not know much about Marx. The New Left and Marx may appear to be worlds apart, yet they have more in common than is perhaps realized. The question about the relationship between business and non-business problems, between economic performance and the quality of life, is no different from the later Marx's question about the relationship between the economic base and the political and intellectual superstructure, between the economic realm of necessity and the true realm of freedom. Marx's idea of human self-realization beyond the realm of necessity is reiterated almost word for word in Galbraith's idea of 'the higher purposes of life . . . *beyond* the reach of economics'.[8] This correspondence is all the more striking since Galbraith did not refer to Marx's work or know it well.

But Marx and the New Left differ radically in the field of praxis. Marx had expected the elevation from the struggle for a bare living to the participation in public and cultural life — what Engels called the 'leap' from the realm of necessity to the realm of freedom. He relied on the dialectical economic movement towards the free society; the dialectic guaranteed the constitution of the new society out of the old. Consequently he prescribed an almost passive role to the working class. The New Left, however, postulated, in effect, the illusionary nature of Marx's expectation. Although for the first time in history wide sections of the population in the economically advanced societies of the West have a legally and materially relatively secure existence, they have not advanced to 'higher activity', but rather content themselves with bread and circuses. The leap predicted by Marx and Engels has not occurred. The New Left picked up the threads at the point where Marx had stopped. It saw a task where Marx had seen a solution. For the New Left the leap was precisely that which Marx had rejected: an ideal that has yet to be put into practice.

Galbraith

This task, 'the espousal of non-economic goals', is at the centre of John Kenneth Galbraith's study *The New Industrial State*, published in 1967. Galbraith analysed the modern economy in order to find a means of fulfilling the task. He even examined — and this is unusual for an American scholar — the new problematic of economics in a special addendum on economic method and the nature of social argument. His analysis reveals the significant economic changes that have occurred in the last seventy years through the emergence of large limited companies, the corporations. Five hundred of these produce half of all goods and services in the United States, and some have a turnover greater than the budget of the federal government. According to Galbraith, the modern corporations differ from earlier capitalist enterprises in the creation of a 'technostructure' (i.e. managers) and the separation of capital ownership and management. Today a firm hoping to sell sophisticated products of technology — a military aircraft for instance — must consider government plans, and vice versa. In this way a 'complex two-way flow of influence' develops between the economy and the state in the arms industry.[9] The marketing corporations and the powerful trade unions act as 'countervailing forces' against the industrial corporations. The corporations are largely independent of market forces because they fix wages in direct negotiations with the unions and are partly self-financing. The state, too, regulates the free market, not only through the big contracts it places with the arms industry but also through its social and financial policies. In addition to these economic changes, changes in expectations have also taken place. The corporation and its employees from a certain income upwards are no longer primarily motivated by pecuniary compensation but by a 'hierarchy of goals' in which the pecuniary motivation recedes in favour of the individual's and the organization's identification with 'some significant social goals'.[10]

The concentration of the means of production and the organization of labour is neither indicative of the transition from the capitalist mode of production to the socialist mode of production (as Marx has thought), nor is it to be regarded as a threat to the free market (as bourgeois economists, Berle and Means in particular, thought). It is the manifestation of a new economic structure between capitalism and socialism. This new structure is preferable to the socialist system because it allows greater freedom and is more successful; it is preferable to the old free market economy because the corporations adapt to accommodate social goals. (One might circumscribe this view with a phrase from Marx, which Galbraith did not quote and perhaps did not know: the corporations are the 'trustees of bourgeois society'.[11]) In this economic structure the state no longer plays a passive role but actively intervenes in the economy by a permanently high level of public expenditure. But it should spend less on the military and more on education, the provision of amenities, health services, and so on. To support the public works, a restriction of consumption through effective taxation is necessary.

Galbraith went even further. He demanded a limitation of profits and growth, in general everything he defined as economic goals. This he justified with the argument that people must be educated to shift their ambitions from economic goals to the non-economic higher goals of life. 'Intellectual preparation will be for its own sake and not for the better service to the industrial system.'[12] But does this preparation not miss the mark? The means necessary to carry out public works and provide the services proposed by Galbraith cannot be extracted from a stagnating economy, except of course by increasing the money supply. He seemed little worried by the fact that the resultant long-term inflation weakens the economy and will ruin morale. This danger was pointed out by other economists. David Riesman, a former advocate of a limitation of production, admitted to have learnt in the twenty years since the publication of his book *The Lonely Crowd* (1950) that in an affluent society production must be continually increased in order to finance social projects.[13] Wilfred Beckerman, whose remark 'In an economy such as that of the United States, . . . leisure is barely moral' Galbraith quoted in support of his argument, has since written a book entitled *In Defence of Economic Growth*.[14]

Galbraith made such economically suspect, even dangerous, demands because for him economic activity is a less meaningful goal than the non-economic goals. The crucial mistake is that he failed to realize that the economy is neither purposive nor meaningful; it is only a means, the indispensable means for the satisfaction of basic needs. Or as Weber put it more precisely, economic action is 'concerned with the satisfaction of a desire for "utilities" '.[15] This definition includes the primitive subsistence economy as well as the modern economy based on profit and accumulation. What matters in this context is that the economy is a *means*, and that Galbraith's idea of the 'Conventional Wisdom' of classical economics in which 'production has to have a goal of pre-eminent importance' is false.[16]

The confusion between means and ends was introduced into economics by Bentham (whom Marx had called 'a genius in the way of bourgeois stupidity'[17]) and Mill. Smith, their predecessor, had established modern economics with the discovery that the pursuance of private interest furthers the interests of society through the interplay of economic forces. For Smith and the other classical economists economic processes are purely empirical processes and in themselves meaningless. But Bentham and Mill gave self-interest meaning by judging it in terms of the principles of utilitarianism. In this way they introduced the pseudo-scientific element into economic theory. With the demand for value-free scientific analysis Weber had intended to counter the intrusion of values, utilitarian or otherwise, into economics. As early as his inaugural lecture he had exposed the 'optical illusion that there are independent economic or "socio-political" ideals in economics'.[18] Yet despite this and other counter-arguments utilitarianism was coupled with an adulterated puritan belief in success — adulterated because stripped of its religious element — especially in the Anglo-Saxon countries. Jevons, Marshall, and their students, accepted it uncritically as the justification of economic action. It brought upon Western civilization, especially American civilization, the odium of vulgar materialism.

The New Left rebelled against this utilitarian and materialistic attitude. But because English-speaking philosophers since Hume had regarded problems beyond those of quantum and number as unverifiable and had therefore neglected them, the specialist scholars were not adequately prepared for the confrontation. It is not coincidental that Samuelson spoke of 'inroads' made by the 'new *Weltanschauung*', when it would have been more correct to say that the new outlook merely recalled to the foreground those 'higher' purposes of life beyond economics. Because Galbraith misunderstood his own intention, he considered it necessary to subordinate profit and growth, as supposedly less important goals, to the non-economic goals *within* economic activity. The chapter on economic method should rather have attempted to eliminate the utilitarian notion of a meaning inherent in economic action, and instead present the economy as mere means.

If a respected economist such as Galbraith did not know how to confront vulgar materialism, it is not surprising that the dilettante writers of the New Left also failed in this respect. The Swedish economist Assar Lindbeck has noted appropriately:[19]

> The New Left has presumably helped to increase interest in issues of principle and ideology and perhaps also the sense of social responsibility in political debate — even though the questions the New Left raises often seem to be more interesting than its answers.

The leap from the realm of necessity to the realm of freedom

Galbraith was certainly right when he said that in the face of the dominant materialist attitude it is important to 'worry about . . . the higher purposes of life when everyone has had a decent meal', and that for the sake of the quality of life consumption should be restricted.[20] The hyperbole evident in his struggle against vulgar materialism may have its roots not only in a confusion about the role of the economy but might also be a consequence of his reformist zeal. Reformers often attempt to establish a perfect society on earth, and in this effort they fail to attain at least the possible. But the New Left is probably not in danger of falling into this trap, if only because it is not dogmatically constricted and has tried to find its way through trial and error.

Essentially, the later Marx and the New Left complement each other. The New Left could learn from Marx that man will always be subject to the economic realm of necessity and that the development of this realm is the precondition for the advance, the 'leap', towards the realm of freedom. The New Left's insistence on the importance of the quality of life is of course beyond argument. Man can never be reduced to *homo oeconomicus*. The worker is not motivated only by pecuniary self-interest; like the manager he has a sense of self-respect and dedication. That is why experiments such as the one at the Swedish motor company Volvo, where monotonous assembly-line work has been replaced by varied group work, are successful. But such experiments do not confirm the existence of Galbraith's 'hierarchy of goals'. Even under the most favourable and dignified conditions the worker works because he *must*, not because he identifies with society. Labour is certainly made easier by additional non-economic incentives, but it remains a bitter must. This is Marx's great insight in the last volume of *Capital*. Free human activity, which for Marx is an end in itself, begins 'where labour which is determined by necessity and mundane considerations ceases'.[21]

Yet the Marxists can also learn something from the New Left. The crucial question is how the leap from the realm of necessity to the realm of freedom is possible. It clearly does not occur by itself, even when its conditions are fulfilled. People must be determined to achieve it and be educated towards it. This realization takes the New Left beyond the Marxists, who still trust in the dialectical movement.

Chapter twenty-two

The Chinese Revolution

Mao

Profoundly impressed by the Russian Revolution, Mao Tse-tung became a communist and adopted the orthodox Soviet version of Marxism. Nevertheless, owing to the special conditions existing in China, Marxism in China acquired a radically different character from Marxism in the Soviet Union or any other communist country. Mao himself symbolized the assimilation of communism to the Chinese past. He combined the qualities of the determined revolutionary with those of the sophisticated intellectual intimately familiar with China's heritage. He spoke the language of the Western Marxists; at the same time he wrote poetry in the classical Chinese style. If we are to understand the special character of Mao's revolution, which reorganized a 3,000-year-old civilization along Western communist lines, it will be necessary to examine briefly Chinese history.

The origin of the Chinese bureaucracy

The course of Chinese history has been determined by the need to control the great rivers. As in other oriental river cultures (Egypt, Mesopotamia, and the Indus Valley), a centralized bureaucracy developed in China to administer the system of canals and govern the people. Once the autocratic bureaucratic state was established, it was never shaken from within; only alien conquerors succeeded in overthrowing the government structure. Hence the stasis of this social formation!

In a newspaper article, 'The British Rule in India' (1853), Marx related the stagnation of Asian history to the fact that 'civilization was too low'. Because in Asia the human mind was constricted within the smallest possible compass, artificial irrigation required the interference of the central government. This he contrasted with the shining example of river regulation in Flanders and Italy through the 'voluntary association' of private entrepreneurs. Life under oriental despotism appeared to him 'undignified, stagnatory, and vegetative', a life deprived of 'all grandeur and historical energies'.[1] In these few sentences Marx grasped the bureaucratic structure of oriental society (he did not go into detail because he was more interested in developments in Western Europe).

The centralized river bureaucracy in China differed from those of Egypt and Mesopotamia in so far as its formation was preceded by 1,000 years of advanced civilization. In the classical cultural epoch, from the ninth to the third century B.C., Confucius and Lao-tse taught (around 600 B.C.), warring vassals ruled, and the emperor exercised only nominal control. But in the third century B.C. the dynasty of Chin overcame its rivals and destroyed the feudal system. The Chin emperors established an absolutist bureaucratic state similar to the European absolutist state at the beginning of the modern epoch. Social upheaval was accompanied by political and intellectual struggle in China no less than in Europe. Confucian teachings and books were proscribed by the new order. But whereas at this stage in Europe the bourgeoisie gained in influence and with it the new secular ideas of the philosophical Enlightenment and political and economic freedom, China remained a peasant society. Confucianism was soon restored. In this process it absorbed elements of mystical Taoism and popular magic. The Han dynasty, which emerged victorious from internal struggles in the first century B.C., introduced entry examinations for the civil service in order to prevent the appropriation of offices and the regression into feudalism. Candidates were tested mainly on their knowledge of Confucian ethics, and so Confucian literati came to monopolize government posts. Over the centuries the examination system became increasingly rigid. Neo-Confucian teachings consequently became an orthodox scholasticism which suffocated cultural life, albeit on a high ethical level. The restoration of Confucianism is the decisive element in Chinese history. It put its stamp on the Chinese bureaucratic state and distinguished it from both the secular modern European state and the undignified — Marx's term is applicable only in these cases — bureaucratic societies of Egypt and Mesopotamia, where the peasants were mere serfs tied to the land and the ruler.

The structure of Confucian society

The transformation of a martial feudal society into a consolidated bureaucratic state, internally pacified and protected from the outside world by the Great Wall (a project of the new administration), gave the Chinese the static and impersonal character which Marx found so contemptible. But it was certainly not undignified. The Chinese God, who in pre-Confucian times had possessed anthropomorphic features, changed into an impersonal 'heaven'. The word *shih*, which had originally meant 'hero', acquired the new meaning of 'civil servant'. The emperor was thought to possess a mandate from heaven to cultivate the *tao*, which may be translated as the 'right way' or the 'great harmony'. *Tao* had both a practical administrative and a ritual and religious significance. The success of the harvest was no less dependent on the maintenance of the dams than on the ethical conduct of the emperor and the mandarins. The Middle Kingdom was part of the heavenly order. Its policies had only one aim: to safeguard the worldly-heavenly peace. The faith in a predestined harmony corresponded to the integration of the individual into the whole, his adaptation to the world, and his pious veneration of authority. For the Chinese the true happiness of man does not lie in the cultivation of the personality but in the dissolution of the personality into the impersonal harmony of the whole.

To the European this regime seems oppressive. But Western notions of individual liberty do not apply in China. Categories of subject, predicate and object do not exist in the Chinese language; nor is there a word for personal freedom, because subjectivism is totally subordinated to collectivism. The Chinese do not see tensions and oppositions in the world, but solidarity and union – the union of *yang* and *yin*, masculine and feminine, heaven and earth, light and dark. The state relates to the people not as a ruler to his subjects but as a father to his children. In times of famine the government protected the peasants; land reforms were occasionally carried out (thus under the Sung dynasty of the eleventh century a portion of the large estates was divided among the peasants). All were in the same way 'under heaven'. Anyone could become a civil servant, at least in principle if not always in practice. For this reason Weber described China as a tolerant 'religious and utilitarian welfare-state'.[2]

Sun's revolution

A revolutionary situation arose not because as in Western Europe a new class formed in the womb of the old productive order, but because the old society collapsed under the pressure from the imperialist powers and a rapid growth of population. External enemies interfered with superior arms in the affairs of the Middle Kingdom and humiliated it. In the eighteenth and nineteenth centuries the peasant population increased approximately fivefold. Many peasants accumulated debts and lost their land. There had been previous occasions when outsiders conquered the country, for example the Mongols in the thirteenth and the Manchus in the seventeenth century. In Chinese eyes, heaven withdrew the mandate from the vanquished emperor at these times and conferred it on the victorious ruler. The peasants had also previously lost their land to creditors and landlords, for example in times of drought. When the peasants rebelled, they had always been offered protection by the central government, and the land would be returned to them through land reforms. However, in the nineteenth century the imperial dynasty proved incapable of defending the empire and protecting the peasantry.

In the 1850s the Taiping Rebellion broke out. (Marx saw this movement correctly as the beginning of the 'revolutionization of the living fossil'.[3]) This peasant rebellion, like the Boxer Rebellion in 1900, was not yet carried by modern Western ideas. It aspired to change the dynasty which in the eyes of the peasants had lost its mandate. The old order would eventually be restored, as the name *tai ping*, 'heavenly kingdom of peace', suggests.

The real revolution occurred fifty years later, when Sun Yat-sen deposed the last emperor in 1911. Sun belonged to the first generation of Chinese intellectuals educated at Western universities. The party he founded, the Kuomintang, championed modernization through Western-style industrialization and democratization. The Japanese had shown in the Russo-Japanese War of 1905 that with Western technology they could defeat a European power.

In India the British effected the social transformation of a stationary and traditional society by setting up a modern administration and educating the intellectual elite to self-rule. But Sun proclaimed a democracy modelled on that of the United States, yet without any preparation. Parliamentary democracy, which in Europe had evolved in the course of centuries from the Greek citizen acting responsibly for the common good and from the Judaeo-Christian tradition of the solitary soul standing before God, could not take root after its transplantation into the very different Chinese soil. European individualism undermined the Confucian security of man without providing a new ethic. As a result, the monarchy was superseded not by democracy but by anarchy, and the new assembly was soon dissolved. The generals became independent and plundered the land. Chiang Kai-shek, the general appointed by Sun and his successor, defeated the war-lords, but he was more interested in the consolidation and extension of his influence than the welfare of the people. Nepotism and corruption paralysed his government.

The only achievement of the Sun government was the reform of the script, which it carried out to facilitate the diffusion of modern education. Written ideographically and in the pronunciation of the classical epoch, the Chinese script was very difficult to master. The reform reduced the more than 3,000 characters to about 800 and aligned the written language more closely to colloquial speech.

Mao's revolution

Communism filled the political and ethical vacuum that arose after the dissolution of the empire. The small group that founded the Chinese Communist Party in 1921 consisted of people who had followed closely the course of the Russian Revolution. After the failure of Sun they took courage from the communist revolution, which had been successful in constructing a new society. The Russian Revolution interested them all the more because its Japanese and British opponents were also their enemies. In the year of the victory over Chiang's forces Mao said at the celebration for the twenty-eighth anniversary of the foundation of the party:[4]

> Under the leadership of Lenin and Stalin, the revolutionary
> energy of the great proletariat and labouring people of Russia,
> hitherto latent and unseen by foreigners, suddenly erupted like
> a volcano, and the Chinese and all mankind began to see the
> Russians in a new light. Then, and only then, did the Chinese
> enter an entirely new era in their thinking and their life. They
> found Marxism-Leninism, the universally applicable truth,
> and the face of China began to change.

But Mao realized that Marxism-Leninism could not be transferred mechanically to China. 'Chinese culture should have its own form.'[5] This has two important implications:

1   Communism in China must gain the support of the peasantry, since China is on the whole an agricultural country. Against strong opposition from within the party and the Russian advisers Mao formed the Red Army from peasant recruits. As early as the 1920s, when the communists were only a small group, he declared confidently that 'Several hundred million peasants will rise like a mighty storm, like a hurricane.'[6]

2   The 'democratic essence' of the 'splendid old culture' created during the long period of Chinese feudal society must be assimilated to Marxism.[7] Mao grasped the old culture's democratic essence as constituted in the equality of all Chinese. The dialectical development in China therefore consists of the abolition of the decadent old feudal ruling class and the entry into a world of the communist ' "Great Harmony" (*tao*) of the people's republic' through the application of scientific socialism.[8] (Note Mao's use of the old concept of *tao*.)

Mao's rise, the many setbacks he suffered, and his final victory, cannot be traced in detail here. He was expelled three times from the party's central committee because of his 'deviation' from the orthodox dogma of the urban and proletarian revolution. He was forced to retreat to the far north-eastern frontier in the Long March to evade Chiang's stronger forces. Nevertheless, the Red Army gained in strength and eventually emerged victorious from the civil war. Mao succeeded because he gained the support of the peasant masses. He did so by presenting to them a form of communism that assimilated Chinese traditions. Mao and his party thus appeared as the legitimate successors to the emperor and his mandarins.

In the provinces conquered by the Red Army a land reform was immediately carried out. For the first time in more than a century the suffering peasants found in the communist commissars an authority which would help them. Cramming courses for the illiterate were started; all who absolved a course were obliged to teach a course themselves. Within a decade 200 million peasants learned to read and write. The programme of mass education earned China world-wide admiration, even during the cold war. But Western observers often did not see that education was connected with communist indoctrination. The simple peasant was all the more receptive to the new theory because in the Chinese view education gives a man the dignity of sophistication. No wonder the peasants flocked to communism! Even intellectuals educated at mission schools and European universities were impressed by the effective and just administration of the communists. Many, including Sun's widow, switched their loyalties from the Kuomintang to the Communist Party. Eventually even some of Chiang's younger generals changed sides and joined the Red Army.

Once the Red Army had gained the confidence of the peasants, Mao began to collectivize agriculture. The programme was carried out not wholly without terror: 'a revolution is not a dinner party' and 'it is necessary to create terror for a while', he noted.[9] But mainly through education the conservative peasants were persuaded that communes were more suited than small parcels of land for the extension of the irrigation works, the cultivation of new land, and the use of new machines (which of course were available only later, after the growth of industry). There can be no doubt that on the whole the peasants participated in the collectivization of their own volition. This can be inferred from the fact that agricultural production increased, while, in contrast, Stalin's violent programme of collectivization cost millions of lives and brought production to an all-time low.

Chapter twenty-three

Maoist orthodoxy

Mao and Stalin

Even though Stalin had rejected Mao's strategy of the peasant revolution and had officially recognized Chiang as the ruler of China at the Yalta conference, Mao surprisingly sided with the Stalinists in the controversy between them and Khrushchev. After Khrushchev's fall he reaffirmed his pro-Stalinist position. During Nixon's visit to Peking in February 1972, the Great Hall of the People (where the Americans were welcomed) was decorated with a large portrait of Stalin. It would be reasonable to link Mao's support for Stalin and criticism of Khrushchev to the Sino-Soviet split, which occurred after Stalin's death. Khrushchev recalled the Russian experts from China to forestall the production of a Chinese atom bomb. And presumably he was also alarmed by renewed Chinese claims to the strategically important west bank of the Amur, an area including the port of Vladivostok. Mao evidently wanted to play off Stalin against Khrushchev, in whom he saw a prophet of imperialism. But supporting Stalin had another, more important reason. Stalin's transfer of power to the centre of the party was the model for Mao. 'Our state is a people's democratic dictatorship', he declared.[1] He organized the party along centralist lines; it was based on unity, discipline, and cadres. Whoever undermined the democratic centralism of the party, as he believed Khrushchev did, was in his eyes a revisionist.

Mao's goal was Stalinist: a system of democratic centralism; but the means were different: not violence but education was to achieve the goal. The difference between the brutal Soviet method and the educative Chinese method is shown, for instance, in the treatment of prisoners in labour camps. Like the emperor before him, Mao justified his rule on the basis of ethics, not Confucian ethics but Marxist ethics. The weapon of the revolution was, consequently, 'not the machine-gun, but Marxism-Leninism'.[2] Already during the civil war he saw his struggle as an 'anti-feudal and cultural revolution'.[3] Quotations from Mao, collected in the famous Little Red Book, were distributed for the political education of the army. (In this political education lay also the secret of the success of technologically inferior North Korean and Vietcong troops.) Mao's precepts were distributed among the masses during the cultural revolution of the 1960s. Several hundred million copies of the book were printed in two years.

The so-called Cultural Revolution, provoked by Mao in 1964, was merely the continuation of revolutionary education. A few years before Mao had noted that 'among students and intellectuals there has recently been a falling off in ideological and political work' and that the bureaucracy was becoming estranged from the people.[4] The Cultural Revolution was to eradicate the remnants of 'feudalism', i.e. Confucianism, and indoctrinate the bureaucracy and the masses with the communist truth. Criticism of the bureaucracy, which Mao encouraged, meant criticism of a merely objective and detached administration and criticism of 'revisionism', i.e. liberalization within the party structure. Like the Confucian mandarins, the communist civil servants were supposed to be educated not so much in the specialized technical disciplines as in the 'correcting mistaken ideas'.[5] Revolutionary committees were set up to instil the revolutionary spirit into party members, administrators and the masses. This cultural revolution was to complete the social revolution.

From the beginning Mao viewed his revolution both as a social transformation and a national liberation movement against imperialism. Unlike Sun, Mao recognized the democratic essence of Chinese culture. By adopting the dialectical science of Marxism from the West and simultaneously appealing to democratic sentiments in the peasantry, Mao and his revolution succeeded where Sun's had failed. Decadent Confucian society was destroyed and the Middle Kingdom flourished again. The victory of the communists in the civil war strengthened the new national self-confidence after a century of humiliation by alien barbarians. The first preface of the Little Red Book postulated that 'Comrade Mao Tse-tung is the great Marxist-Leninist of our era'; a year later the word 'great' was replaced by 'greatest'. The Cultural Revolution began as education in Marxism-Leninism and ended as education in Maoism. The new generation received the Little Red Book as a Chinese Bible.

The structure of Chinese communist society

Western visitors were impressed with what James Reston described as a change of human nature in his reports for the *New York Times* in the summer of 1971. The Chinese worked dedicatedly for minimal remuneration because they were motivated not by material incentives but by Mao's principle of 'subordinating the needs of the part to the needs of the whole'.[6] In 1973 even the Vatican acknowledged in a bulletin that the People's Republic of China, in contrast with the Soviet Union, 'looks towards the mystique of disinterested work for others, to inspiration, to justice'.[7] China accumulated capital for industrial growth without discriminating against certain sections of the population and without the help of foreign investment. But these changes did not portend the transformation into the new man or the free development of the individual Marx had hoped for. The mystical Great Harmony of old changed into the 'scientific' Great Harmony of communist society, and the passive subordination under heaven changed into active commitment to the collective; but the impersonal and authoritarian hierarchy, *da tong*, the 'great togetherness', was preserved. Contents and attitude changed, but not the structure. Where once practical actions were accompanied by Confucian ceremonies, they were now accompanied by quotations from Mao.

The revolutionization of the 'living fossil' recorded by Marx a century before came about as a regeneration through self-reliance. Even before the watershed of Nixon's visit in 1972, observers had noted objectively — partly in admiration, partly in criticism — the uniquely Chinese elements in Chinese communism: the combination of revolution and orthodoxy, Western modernization and Confucian authoritarian government (C.P. Fitzgerald); the 'exemplary fidelity to the universal truth of Marxism-Leninism in its specific Chinese incarnation' (Stuart Schramm, biographer of Mao); the 'Confucianization of Marx' (Alberto Moravia); the preservation of the 'mental superstruction' after the violent revolution (Han Suyin, pseudonym of a doctor and writer born in China and educated at universities in China and Britain).[8]

Strength and weakness of Maoist orthodoxy

In the combination of Chinese tradition and Marxist theory there lies a danger and at the same time a strength. During the Cultural Revolution a young Englishman working in China told the economist Joan Robinson:[9]

> One thing is certain: the collectivization of conscience which in the present anchorless state of society is China's greatest source of danger, will also prove to be her precious heritage and a unique source of strength.

The Western reader is shocked. Is such a thing as a 'collectivization of conscience' possible? Surely conscience speaks only in the individual who is free and responsible, or flees from his freedom and responsibility. But even after the revolution the Chinese citizen does not know the freedom of the individual. He finds his 'conscience' only in the identification with the collective. To this extent the collectivization of conscience can be seen as a strength of the Chinese.

What in China is strength has appeared as intellectual and political immaturity to Western political thought since Locke. Only in China, where the population was accustomed to an authoritarian hierarchy, could the so-called 'system of democratic socialism', which is in fact a system of authoritarian centralism, be celebrated as a regeneration. Mao carried the orthodoxy of Stalin even further when he rejected subjectivism out of hand and declared that 'Not to have a correct political orientation is like not having a soul.'[10]

When the New Left students were flirting with Maoism and Marcuse presented Chinese society as the model for Marxist humanism, they were only betraying their own intellectual confusion. In contrast, Klaus Mehnert, who knows China better than Marcuse, has expressed serious concern about 'the ease with which the attitudes of the Chinese can be manipulated'.[11] The view of China propagated by left-wing intellectuals of the West was often unrealistic, even mere fancy. It may also be noted that the isolation of China during the 1950s and 1960s was partly self-induced, particularly because the first-generation Chinese communist leaders were acutely aware of the dangers of Western science and thought for Marxist orthodoxy.

What does the future hold for China?

At the end of the civil war Mao wrote that China must make 'a greater contribution to humanity' and 'should get rid of great-power chauvinism'; yet he also wrote that 'All wars that are progressive are just.'[12] This last phase is notable because Mao showed what he meant by it: the only time he justified Khrushchev's policies was in the case of the armed intervention in Hungary. One can only hope that beside the centralized bureaucracy the humane and tolerant spirit of the great Confucian and pacifist heritage will — even in altered form — survive the revolution.

Another question for the future concerns the durability of the symbiosis of the Chinese past and Marxism. Until now China has always been able to absorb alien theories and conquerors (e.g. Indian Buddhism and the Mongolians) without losing its individual character. Mao could assimilate communism to the Chinese social formation; but can the scientific elements in Marxism also be reconciled to the Chinese spirit?

China has a long scientific tradition which in some fields surpasses European achievements. Centuries before Europe the Chinese were using the clock, the magnetic compass, the printing press, gunpowder and porcelain, to name but a few scientific and technological achievements. But it was the Western spirit of adventure that made the breakthrough to modern science possible. 'Have courage to use your *own* understanding!' was according to Kant the slogan of the scientific revolution.[13] The intellectual daring of modern science, which questions any frontier and any authority, cannot go together with the Chinese integration into an existing order. Although modern science first flourished on Greek soil, it could still explode the Greek myths of the spherical cosmos. Will it not also destroy the more alien impersonal Great Harmony of China?

Weber and Needham, who both wrote a comparative sociology of China and Europe, did not question China's ability to embrace socialism, but they did stress the contrast between Chinese and modern science.[14] Is it possible that the intrusion of Western science could destroy Chinese culture? By using science as an educational device Mao inadvertently built a time bomb into his orthodoxy. 'Marx, Engels, Lenin and Stalin have taught us that it is necessary to study conditions conscientiously and to proceed from objective reality and not from subjective ideas', he wrote.[15] But he also believed that 'To be subjective means not to look at problems objectively, that is, not to use the materialist viewpoint in looking at problems.'[16] He failed to see that Marx's objectivity requires above all scientific honesty and is hence irreconcilable with any orthodoxy, including the materialist viewpoint when it is shown to be unscientific. Will not a revisionist, combining in himself the qualities of Galilei and Bernstein, emerge from the Marxist school in China — precisely because Mao instructed him to learn from Marx's science? Such philosophical revisionism will certainly not be found in Mao's own generation, perhaps not even in the next. But will the end of China's isolation, foreshadowed by the events of the early 1970s, not create the necessary conditions for its emergence?

Epilogue

Freedom and Fate

The New Left's critique of contemporary bureaucratic industrial society is the latest offshoot of the counter-movement against modern capitalism that has accompanied it since its emergence. The rational character of the economy, to this extent distinct from earlier forms of capitalism, has entailed the domination of man by objects, his own products. It has reduced man to a *homo oeconomicus*. This inhuman character of the economy, described by Marx as 'alienation', was feared and opposed from the beginning: by the eighteenth-century English conservatives represented by Bolingbroke; by the humanists, from More to Goethe; and by the romantics, from Rousseau to Adam Müller and Ruskin. They all attempted, in vain, to turn back the wheel of history. Only socialism perceived the inevitability of the process of rational industrialization sparked off by modern capitalism.

Socialism promised a better society through the socialization of production. Marx was the first socialist to analyse scientifically the emergence of the new society in the interplay of the immanent laws of production. His diagnosis, made more than a century ago, has proved correct. The socialization of production has occurred in practice to a greater or lesser extent. But his promise that alienation hitherto inherent in the production would be overcome has not been fulfilled.

Marx realized in his later years that socialization indeed eliminates the exploitation of the worker but does not achieve what he had hoped for, namely labour as self-realization. In the third volume of *Capital* he showed how free labour, that is, 'the development of human energy which is an end in itself', becomes possible only in the true realm of freedom, which is *detached* from the realm of necessity where man must work to provide for his external needs.[1]

If this realm is to be 'true' and 'an end in itself', in other words not, as until now, a reflection and product of the economic base, what then does its advent depend on? Towards the end of his life Marx recognized a problem here. Earlier he had admitted only the existence of the iron laws of economic development. But the description in volume three of a realm of freedom which begins 'beyond this sphere of labour' and which 'can blossom forth' implies a renunciation of historical necessity.[2] However, Marx did not modify his theory to admit that the realm of freedom is not a necessary result of the transformation of society. Thus there appears a glaring contradiction in his thought: on the one hand he conceded that the new society will remain a realm of necessity; on the other hand he interpreted political praxis merely as the setting free of the elements of the new society.

Is Marx's work not reduced to absurdity in the light of this contradiction? His political praxis certainly is, but his science is not, nor his goal. The *scientific analysis* has after all been vindicated: everywhere a regulated productive order has partly or wholly superseded unrestrained capitalist production. The *humanist goal*, the emancipation of man from the domination by objects, is in the present-day bureaucratically controlled society even more relevant than it was in the society of the free market. But his *political praxis* must fall short of this goal because bureaucratization goes hand in hand with economic socialization. Whoever takes Marx's goal seriously cannot, as Marx did, put his faith in economic developments; he must, in Weber's exhortative words, 'swim "against the stream" of material developments'.[3]

It was a long road for Marx from his youthful vision of humanist socialism, in which the contradiction between necessity and freedom was truly resolved, to his mature realization that in social reality the conflict between the economic requirements of mass society and the free development of the individual had been far from resolved. This is in fact Marx's legacy: to face the conflict openly and master it.

Certainly many will object to this interpretation of Marx. To them one could quote a passage from the *Grundrisse*; in a discussion of the method for arriving at economic laws, Marx wrote that:[4]

> The correct observation and deduction of these laws . . . always leads to primary equations . . . which point towards a past lying behind this system. These indications, together with a correct grasp of the present, then also offer the key to the understanding of the past. . . . This correct view likewise leads at the same time to the points at which the suspension of the present form of production relations gives signs of its becoming — foreshadowings of the future.

A correct grasp of the present, not a mechanical application of the Marxian system, will enable man to cope with the problems of the present and the future. Marx was ahead of his students not in his dogmatic solution but in his constant readiness to measure the vision of the future with the reality of the present.

Those who still have eschatological hopes for a social revolution refuse to accept Marx's realistic assessment. They will cause only harm because they refuse to see reality as it is. The true realm of freedom can never be achieved in this world. It is an ever-disappointed hope, but it must nevertheless remain a tenacious hope (to paraphrase Silone).[5] It will be fruitful in political activity only as an ideal to be aspired to. For the true transformation of society a totally different change must take place as well: the transformation of the individual 'into a different subject', as Marx put it, or 'the revolution of attitudes', as Kant had said before him.[6] This is the old prophetic demand for a return, a turning back, which also inspired Marx. Only these two aspects together, an external social and an internal human transformation, can renew society.

Notes

ABBREVIATIONS

1   of works by Marx (and Engels):

(a) *collections:*

EW	=	Marx, *Early Writings*
FIA	=	Marx, *The First International and After*
MECor	=	Marx and Engels, *Correspondence 1846-1895*
MECW	=	Marx and Engels, *Collected Works*
MEGA	=	Marx and Engels, *Gesamtausgabe*
MESC	=	Marx and Engels, *Selected Correspondence*
MESW	=	Marx and Engels, *Selected Works*
MEW	=	Marx and Engels, *Werke*
R48	=	Marx, *The Revolutions of 1848*
SfE	=	Marx, *Surveys from Exile*

(b) *individual works by Marx:*

Cap. 1 and 2	=	*Capital*, vols 1 − 2 (Penguin)
Cap. 3	=	*Capital*, vol. 3 (Lawrence & Wishart)
Comm. Man.	=	*Manifesto of the Communist Party*, in *R48*
Cr. Doctr. St.	=	*Critique of Hegel's Doctrine of the State*, in *EW*
Cr. Gotha Pr.	=	*Critique of the Gotha Programme*, in *FIA*
Cr. Phil. R.	=	*A Contribution to the Critique of Hegel's Philosophy of Right. Introduction*, in *EW*
Econ. Phil.	=	*Economic and Philosophical Manuscripts*, in *EW*
G. Id.	=	*The German Ideology*, in *MECW* 5
Grundr.	=	*Grundrisse*
Jew. Q.	=	*On the Jewish Question*, in *EW*
Pov. Phil.	=	*The Poverty of Philosophy*, in *MECW* 6

2   of works by Weber:

(a) *collections:*

GPS	=	*Gesammelte Politische Schriften*
Sel. Tr.	=	*Selections in Translation*

(b) *individual works:*

Econ. Soc.	=	*Economy and Society*
'Obj.'	=	*'Objectivity' in the Social Sciences*, in *The Methodology of the Social Sciences*
Parl. Reg.	=	*Parlement und Regierung im neugeordneten Deutschland*, in *GPS*
'Pol. Voc.'	=	*'Politics as a Vocation'*, in *Sel. Tr.*
Prosp.	=	*The Prospects for Liberal Democracy in Tsarist Russia*, in *Sel. Tr.*
'Sci. Voc.'	=	*'Science as a Vocation'*, in *From Max Weber*

Note: When no author is given in a reference, the work referred to is by Marx (and Engels).

NOTES

Prefaces

1 T. Mann, 'Goethe and Tolstoy', *Essays of Three Decades*, p. 173. 'That loftier Germany' he would later call 'the European humanity' (*Politische Schriften* II, p. 165).
2 Lukács, *Conversations*, p. 100.
3 Fabian Society, Annual Report of 1896; Keynes, *The End of Laissez-Faire*, pp. 34f.

Chapter 1   The intellectual setting

1 Goethe, *Dichtung und Wahrheit*, Werke 9, p. 400.
2 Ibid.
3 Goethe, *Maximen und Reflexionen*, Werke 12, p. 518.
4 Goethe, *Schriften zur Literatur*, Werke 12, p. 360.
5 Kant, *Contest of the Faculties*, *Political Writings*, p. 182.
6 Kant, *What Is Enlightenment?*, *Political Writings*, pp. 58-9.
7 Weber noted that 'the internalized devotion to authority . . . has remained an almost ineradicable legacy of unrestrained patrimonial rule in Germany' (*Econ. Soc.* 3, p. 1108); and the Canadian historian J.S. Conway explained the submission of the Christian churches to the 'pagan mythologies' of Nazism in terms of an 'ingrained tradition of pietism' (*The Nazi Persecution of the Churches*, pp. 334-6).
8 Goethe, *Faust*, pt 1, Werke 3, p. 68.
9 Hegel, *History of Philosophy*, I, p. xii.
10 Hölderlin, 'An die Deutschen', *Gedichte*, I, p. 225.
11 Goethe, *Eckermann's Conversations*, 12 March 1828, pp. 543f.
12 Goethe, *Maximen und Reflexionen*, Werke 12, pp. 507f.
13 Goethe, *Eckermann's Conversations*, 11 Oct. 1828, p. 218.
14 Goethe, *Maximen und Reflexionen*, Werke 12, p. 506.
15 Marx to Ruge, March 1843, *EW*, p. 199; Ruge to Marx, March 1843, quoted in *Die Frühschriften*, p. 156.
16 Gervinus, *Geschichte der deutschen Dichtung*, V, p. 814.
17 Quoted in Rapp, *Friedrich Theodor Vischer*, p. 6.

18 Grillparzer, *Studien zur Deutschen Literatur, Werke* 3, p. 802.
19 Heine, *Atta Troll, Werke* 1, p. 336.
20 Heine, *Deutschland. Ein Wintermärchen, Werke* 1, p. 425.
21 Heine to Varnhagen, 3 Jan. 1846, *Werke* 3, pp. 36f.
22 Huch, *Michael Bakunin*, p. 67.

Chapter 2   Marx's philosophical apprenticeship

1   Marx to his father, 10 Nov. 1837, *MECW* 1, pp. 18f.
2   Marx to Ruge, March 1843, *EW*, p. 199.
3   Cieszkowski, *Prolegomena zur Historiosophie*, p. 128.
4   *Cr. Phil. R.*, p. 257.
5   All quotes in this paragraph from *Notebooks on Epicurean Philosophy*, *MECW* 1, pp. 491-3 and p. 498.
6   *Theses on Feuerbach, EW*, p. 423.
7   Mehring, *Karl Marx*, p. 51.
8   Marx to Ruge, 25 Jan. 1843, *MECW* 1, p. 397.
9   Marx to Ruge, 9 July 1842, *MECW* 1, p. 389.
10 Article in the *Rheinische Zeitung*, 16 Oct. 1842, *MECW* 1, pp. 215f. and p. 220.

Chapter 3   Modern capitalism

1   Weber, *The Protestant Ethic*, p. 95 (see also p. 193n.).
2   Defoe, 'Giving Alms no Charity . . .', in *The Shortest Way with Dissenters*, p. 187.
3   The subtitle of Disraeli's novel *Sybil*.
4   Smith, *Wealth of Nations*, I, p. 400; *Theory of Moral Sentiments* (published before his famous text on political economy), p. 184.
5   Smith, *Wealth of Nations*, II, p. 269.
6   Ibid., pp. 263-6.
7   Ricardo, *Principles of Political Economy*, p. 126.
8   Ibid., p. 115.
9   Malthus, *Essay on the Principle of Population* (second edition, 1803), p. 531.
10 Ibid. (Everyman edition), IV, p. 172.
11 Ibid., p. 168.
12 Ibid., pp. 172f.
13 Ibid., p. 260.
14 Quoted in Webb and Webb, *History of Trade Unionism*, p. 60.
15 Burke certainly shared the contemporary idea of natural freedom in politics *and* in the economy (unlike his conservative successors in Germany – Gentz and Adam Müller – and the historicist school of law). But because he was sceptical of the rationality and perfection of man he thought it dangerous to construct a constitution or a society solely on the basis of abstract principles, as the French Revolution had attempted, and insisted that the obsolete organization of the state be taken into account.

Chapter 4   The emergence of socialism

1   Hegel, *Essay on Natural Law*, p. 70.
2   Balzac, *Old Goriot*, p. 68.
3   By the turn of the century the Fabians had rejected the notion of socialism as a panacea to all the evils of human society. Fifty years later, after the socialist parties of the European continent had embraced Marxism, Morgan Phillips, Labour Party delegate at the congress reconvening the Second International (1951 in Frankfurt), declared categorically that his party 'had never accepted the Marxian conception of class conflict'.
4   Although Marx, contrary to twentieth-century usage, did not in principle distinguish between socialism and communism, he preferred the latter term in his political writings (such as the *Communist Manifesto* and the *Critique of the Gotha Programme*) to differentiate his revolutionary programme from reformism. It was Stalin who at the party congress in 1952 first proclaimed the 'transition' from socialism to communism. But this was merely a ploy to detract from the imperfection of his own society. He justified his view by referring to Marx's distinction, discussed in the *Critique of the Gotha Programme* (*FIA*, p. 347), between 'the first phase of communist society', which still has certain characteristics of the old society, and the 'more advanced phase of communist society'. But here Marx was describing two phases *within* communism, not a difference between socialism and communism.
5   Heine, *Lutezia*, *Werke* 3, p. 554.
6   Ruge, *Briefwechsel*, p. 347.
7   From Lenz, *Staat und Marxismus* I, p. 100.
8   *Cap.* 1, p. 95.
9   Grün, *Die soziale Bewegung*, p. 224.
10   Quoted in Newman, *The Life of Richard Wagner*, 2, p. 54.
11   Hess, *Sozialistische Aufsätze*, p. 129 and p. 131.
12   *Comm. Man.*, p. 91.
13   Riehl, *Die bürgerliche Gesellschaft*, pp. 216-17.
14   Goethe, *Wanderjahre*, *Werke* 8, p. 429.
15   Goethe to Zelter, 6 June 1825, *Letters*, p. 463.
16   Keller, *Jeremias Gotthelf*, *Sämtliche Werke* 22, p. 100.
17   Goethe, *Eckermann's Conversations*, 2 April 1829, p. 250.
18   Sombart, *The Quintessence of Capitalism*, pp. 215-16.
19   Mann, *Betrachtungen eines Unpolitischen*, p. 109.
20   *Econ. Phil.*, p. 376 and p. 359.
21   Rosenzweig, *Star of Redemption*, p. 287.
22   Tocqueville, *L'Ancien Régime*, p. 15.
23   Lessing, *Education of the Human Race*, *Laocoön*, p. 286.
24   Trotsky, *Literature and Revolution*, p. 256.
25   Stein, *The History of the Social Movement in France*, p. 280.
26   Weitling, *Die Menschheit, wie sie ist, und wie sie sein sollte*, *passim*.
27   Bakunin, *Sozialpolitischer Briefwechsel*, p. 363.
28   Quoted in Gutman, *Work, Culture and Society*, p. 111.
29   Ragaz, *Von Christus zu Marx*, p. 178 (an allusion to Isaiah 65.17).
30   Quoted in Crossman (ed.), *The God that Failed*, pp. 172-3.
31   Koestler, *Arrow in the Blue*, p. 185. The tragedy is that most of the few hundred young people from Palestine who made the pilgrimage to the land of the Red Messiah were killed.
32   Hess, *Die heilige Geschichte und die Menschheit*, p. 315.

33   *Cr. Phil. R.*, p. 256.
34   Dostoyevsky, *The Idiot*, p. 587.
35   Dostoyevsky, 'My Paradox', *Diary of a Writer* I, pp. 352-3.
36   The following studies spring to mind: Cohn, *The Pursuit of the Millennium*; Talmon, *Political Messianism*; Voegelin, *The New Science of Politics*.
37   Kierkegaard, *Journals* 6, p. 61.
38   Kant, *Critique of Practical Reason*, pp. 224-6.
39   Weber, 'Pol. Voc.'. For a detailed discussion of Weber's views on politics, see ch. 16.
40   Marx to Ruge, Sept. 1843, *EW*, p. 207.
41   Ibid., p. 208.

Chapter 5   The Hegelian dialectic

1   Hegel, *Theologische Jugendschriften*, p. 380 and p. 377.
2   Hegel, *Phenomenology*, p. 295.
3   Goethe, *Westöstlicher Divan*, *Werke* 2, p. 19.
4   Hegel, *Science of Logic*, p. 54.
5   Hegel, *The Logic* (part of the *Encyclopedia*), p. 379.
6   Hegel, *Science of Logic*, p. 50 and p. 706.
7   Kant, *Critique of Practical Reason*, pp. 245-6.
8   Hegel, *History of Philosophy* III, pp. 454f.
9   Hegel, *Science of Logic*, p. 840 (Hegel's italics).
10   Adorno, *Drei Studien zu Hegel*, p. 83.
11   Hegel, *Philosophy of World History*, p. 90.
12   Ibid., p. 75.
13   Hegel, *Phenomenology*, p. 31.
14   Ibid., pp. 455-6.
15   Ibid., p. 56.
16   Ibid., p. 493.
17   Haym, *Hegel und seine Zeit*, p. 4.
18   *G. Id.*, pp. 27f.
19   *Notebooks on Epicurean Philosophy*, *MECW* 1, p. 498.
20   *Cap.* 1, pp. 102-3.
21   Ibid., p. 103; see also Marx to Engels, 14 Jan. 1858, *MECS*, p. 100.

Chapter 6   Feuerbach's inversion of the dialectic

1   Feuerbach, *The Essence of Christianity*, p. xxxvii and *passim*.
2   Feuerbach, *Fragmente zur Charakteristik meines philosophischen Werdegangs*, *Sämtliche Werke* II, p. 388.
3   Feuerbach, *Todesgedanken*, *Sämtliche Werke* I, p. 19.
4   Ibid., p. 12.
5   Feuerbach, *Zur Reform der Philosophie*, *Sämtliche Werke* II, p. 319.
6   The significance of Feuerbach's dialogic thought was not recognized until the 1920s, when several philosophers introduced independently of each other the notion of 'communication' (Jaspers), 'grammatical thought' (Rosenzweig), and 'I and Thou' (Buber), as an alternative to abstract logical thought. The politically committed generation of the pre-1848 period adopted from the concept of love only its political consequence: that is, because man realizes his true essence only in dialogue, in community, he is a

social being, and this should be reflected in the organization of society.
7 Feuerbach, *Zur Reform der Philosophie, Sämtliche Werke* II, p. 235.
8 Ibid., p. 239.
9 Feuerbach, *The Essence of Christianity*, p. 3.
10 Feuerbach, *Briefwechsel und Nachlass* I, p. 90.
11 Feuerbach, *The Essence of Christianity*, p. 87; Kierkegaard, *Journals and Papers* 5, p. 201.
12 Engels, *Ludwig Feuerbach, MESW* III, p. 345.
13 *Cr. Doctr. St.*, p. 73.
14 *Cr. Phil. R.*, p. 244.
15 Marx to Ruge, Sept. 1843, *EW*, p. 209.
16 *Cr. Phil. R.*, p. 257.

Chapter 7   Marx's early communist phase: the realization of the true political community

1 *Cr. Phil. R.*, pp. 249-50.
2 Hegel, *System der Sittlichkeit, Schriften zur Politik*, pp. 473-5.
3 Hegel, *Philosophy of Right*, para. 244.
4 Ibid., para. 246.
5 Hegel, *On the English Reform Bill, Political Writings*, p. 311.
6 Ibid., p. 309.
7 Montesquieu, *Spirit of Laws*, p. 15; he called these intermediate institutions 'pouvoirs intermédiaires'.
8 Hegel, *Philosophy of Right*, para. 289.
9 *Cr. Doctr. St.*, p. 141.
10 Ibid., e.g. p. 116, p. 158, p. 177.
11 Ibid., p. 141.
12 Ibid., p. 196. At the opposite end of the political spectrum, the conservative Julius Stahl uttered the same criticism of Hegel's 'ultra-governmental' theory of the state (*Geschichte der Rechtsphilosophie*, p. 475).
13 Rousseau, *Social Contract*, p. 165.
14 Ibid., p. 175 and p. 243.
15 Ibid., p. 174.
16 Ibid., pp. 247-8 and p. 184.
17 Ibid., p. 177.
18 Rousseau, *Émile*, p. 426.
19 Rousseau, *Social Contract*, p. 267.
20 Ibid., pp. 275-6.
21 Rousseau, *Discourse on Political Economy, Social Contract*, p. 130.
22 Rousseau, *Émile*, p. 243 and p. 277.
23 Rousseau, *Lettres écrites de la montagne, Political Writings*, II, p. 200.
24 Rousseau, *Discourse on Political Economy, Social Contract*, p. 132.
25 Ibid.
26 Rousseau, *Social Contract*, p. 165 and p. 218.
27 Ibid., p. 205.
28 Ibid., pp. 235-6.
29 Kant, Fragments from the *Nachlass, Werke* VIII, p. 624.
30 All quotes in this paragraph from Kant, *Idea for a Universal History, Political Writings*, pp. 45-6.
31 Schiller, *Lykurgus und Solon, Werke* 4, pp. 815f.
32 Quoted in Beik (ed.), *The French Revolution*, p. 286.

33 Heine, *Zur Geschichte der Religion und Philosophie in Deutschland, Werke* 4, p. 121.
34 This point has been argued by, for instance, E.H. Carr (*The Soviet Impact on the Western World*, p. 7), and Jacob Talmon in a monumental study of totalitarianism (*The Origins of Totalitarian Democracy*). Long before these two modern historians, however, Benjamin Constant, in an essay written in 1816 (*Cours de politique constitutionelle*), had traced the despotism of the French Revolution and Napoleon to Rousseau's unrestricted sovereignty. Somewhat later Émile Faguet argued that the concept of popular sovereignty must inevitably lead to democratic despotism and denial of human rights (*La Politique comparée de Montesquieu, Rousseau et Voltaire*, p. 284 and *passim*). And similarly Bernard Groethuysen illustrated the contrast between Rousseau's egalitarian ideal and the ideas of other Enlightenment philosophers (*Philosophie de la Revolution française*).
35 Fichte, *Grundlage der gesamten Wissenschaftslehre, Sämtliche Werke* I, p. 86.
36 Fichte, *Die Grundzüge des gegenwärtigen Zeitalters, Sämtliche Werke* VII, pp. 144-6, and *Grundlage des Naturrechts, Sämtliche Werke* III, para. 17.
37 Grillparzer, *Epigramme, Sämtliche Werke* I, p. 500.
38 Hegel, *Philosophy of Right*, addition to para. 270, p. 284.
39 *Jew. Q.*, pp. 232-3.
40 Ibid., p. 234.
41 *Cr. Phil. R.*, p. 251.
42 Ibid., p. 256.
43 Ibid., p. 257.
44 Ibid.
45 *Jew. Q.*, p. 237.
46 Quoted in Golo Mann, *The History of Germany since 1789*, p. 69. Feuerbach had observed a 'malignant principle' in the Jewish and Christian faiths, in so far as they limit love to the believers; this exclusive love – 'egoism' – of faith he set against the humanism of ancient Greece (*The Essence of Christianity*, p. 252). Feuerbach's generation shared with him the idea of the opposition of faith and philosophy, unlike the earlier humanists (Lessing, Herder, Goethe), who regarded Greece and the Bible as similar and complementary. Feuerbach's opposition to religion and humanism was not intended to be anti-semitic; the later romantics and Marx added the anti-semitic dimension to this idea and identified the Jews with capitalist self-interest in bourgeois society.
47 *Cr. Phil. R.*, p. 251.

Chapter 8   The birth of historical materialism

1 Engels, *Outlines of a Critique of Political Economy, MECW* 3, p. 427.
2 Ibid., p. 432.
3 Preface to the *Critique of Political Economy, EW*, p. 426.
4 Engels, *Ludwig Feuerbach, MESW* 3, p. 361; see also Engels to Bernstein, 14 March 1883, *MESC*, p. 359.
5 *G. Id.*, p. 30.
6 Marx to von Schweitzer, 24 Jan. 1865, *MESC*, p. 151.
7 *Econ. Phil.*, pp. 385f.
8 Ibid., p. 389.

9   *G. Id.*, p. 28.
10 *Econ. Phil.*, p. 281.
11 *Pov. Phil.*, p. 93.
12 Ranke, *Die Epochen der neueren Geschichte*, p. 10.
13 *The Eighteenth Brumaire*, *SfE*, p. 146.
14 *Cap.* 1, p. 92 and p. 102.
15 Hegel, *Philosophy of Right*, addition to para. 189, p. 268.
16 *Comm. Man.*, p. 83.
17 *Pov. Phil.*, p. 162.
18 *Cap.* 1, pp. 101-2.
19 Ibid., pp. 493-4.
20 Ibid., p. 929, p. 91 and p. 92.
21 Marx's law of accumulation states that the capitalist is compelled to
    accumulate and modernize his machines lest he fall behind his competitors.
    It is therefore an inexorable law, since presumably not many capitalists
    would wish to bring about their own economic ruin. 'My standpoint', Marx
    wrote, 'from which the development of the economic formation of society
    is viewed as a process of natural history, can less than any other make the
    individual responsible for relations whose creature he remains, socially
    speaking, however much he may subjectively raise himself above them'
    (*Cap.* 1, p. 92). In other words, in the conditions prevailing in the capitalist
    economy the individual capitalist is compelled to accumulate if he wants to
    compete. This 'must' exposes the immanent character of alienation in the
    modern economy: man is governed by the products of his own hand. Marx
    described properly the law of accumulation as being 'mystified . . . into a
    supposed law of nature' (ibid., p. 771). So when he referred to capital as
    being endowed 'with consciousness and a will' (ibid., p. 739 and *Cap.* 3,
    pp. 289ff.), he did not invoke a metaphysical force but was describing the
    'supposed' law of nature. He did *not* treat the law of accumulation as a law
    of natural science, but showed only that it *operates as if it were one*. The
    individual capitalist can act differently, say, accumulate less and consume
    more, and Marx himself took such factors into consideration. The law of
    gravity, however, stipulates that the apple must *invariably* fall with the same
    acceleration.
        What has been said about the law of accumulation applies to all Marxian
    laws. Weber's point that the laws of economic theory presuppose the
    existence of free will (see p. 114) applies equally to Marx's economic laws.
22 Goethe to Zelter, 6 June 1825, *Letters*, p. 463.
23 Marx to Kugelmann, 27 June 1870, *MESC*, pp. 239f.
24 *Cap.* 3, p. 792.
25 *Grundr.*, pp. 747-51.
26 Marx to Vera Zasulich, 8 March 1881, *MESC*, pp. 339f. Marx must have
    attached great importance to this letter, since he wrote four drafts before
    finally sending it off. These may be found in *MEW* 35, pp. 384ff.

Chapter 9   Economic base and ideological superstructure

1   *Econ. Phil.*, p. 354.
2   *Cap.* 1, p. 284.
3   *Cap.* 3, p. 791.
4   *G. Id.*, p. 420.
5   *The Eighteenth Brumaire*, *SfE*, esp. pp. 148-50.

6   *Cap*. 1, p. 280.
7   Preface to the *Critique of Political Economy*, *EW*, p. 425.
8   Leading article in the *Kölnische Zeitung*, 14 July 1842, *MECW* 1, p. 198.
9   Nietzsche, *Richard Wagner in Bayreuth*, *Werke* IV, 3, p. 48.
10 Feuerbach, *Zur Reform der Philosophie*, *Sämtliche Werke* II, p. 239.
11 *G. Id.*, pp. 418f.
12 Ranke, *Politisches Gespräch*, p. 25.
13 Marx to Weydemeyer, 5 March 1852, *MESC*, p. 69.
14 Ranke, *Weltgeschichte*, p. vii.
15 *Grundr.*, p. 111.
16 Ranke, *Die Epochen der neueren Geschichte*, p. 8.
17 *Grundr.*, p. 111.
18 Preface to the *Critique of Political Economy*, *EW*, p. 424.
19 Marx to Engels, 2 April 1851, *MECor*, p. 36.
20 *G. Id.*, p. 44, and *Theories of Surplus-Value*, 1, p. 401.
21 *Grundr.*, p. 612.
22 Rubel, *Karl Marx*, pp. 297-8.
23 See Paul Lafargue's memoirs in *On Art and Literature*, pp. 138-40.

Chapter 10   Historical sociology

1   *Cap*. 1, p. 292.
2   *G. Id.*, p. 47.
3   *Cap*. 1, p. 474.
4   *Grundr.*, p. 161.
5   Ibid., p. 488 and p. 853.
6   *Econ. Phil.*, p. 354.
7   Ibid., p. 370.
8   *Cap*. 1, p. 92.
9   He did so first in a newspaper article of 1853, 'The British Rule in India' (*SfE*, pp. 303-6), and later in the preface to the *Critique of Political Economy* (*EW*, p. 426).
10 *Cap*. 1, pp. 164-5; *Econ. Phil.*, p. 364.
11 *Cap*. 1, p. 772.
12 *Econ. Phil.*, p. 373.
13 Ibid., p. 377.
14 Ibid., p. 361.
15 *Pov. Phil.*, p. 125.
16 *Comm. Man.*, p. 67.
17 Preface to the *Critique of Political Economy*, *EW*, p. 426.

Chapter 11   Political economy

1   *Cap*. 1, p. 131.
2   Ibid., p. 129.
3   Ibid., p. 130.
4   Ibid., p. 325.
5   Ibid., p. 168.
6   Ibid., p. 325.
7   Ibid., p. 769.
8   Ibid., p. 873.

9   Ibid., p. 730.
10 Ibid., p. 742.
11 Ibid.
12 Ibid., p. 739.
13 *Comm. Man.*, p. 71.
14 Ibid., p. 72 and p. 70.
15 'The British Rule in India', *SfE*, p. 307.
16 *Cap*. 1, p. 739.
17 Ibid., p. 781.
18 Ibid., p. 793.
19 Ibid., p. 798.
20 If only variable capital creates surplus-value, the question arises how it is possible that a capitalist who invests a greater share of variable capital than another capitalist achieves the same rate of profit as his competitor. Marx resolved this apparent contradiction in the third volume of *Capital* with reference to the competition of capitals. Competition ensures that in both cases almost the same quantum is produced; this is called the 'average profit' (*Cap*. 3, p. 179).
21 *Cap*. 3, p. 250.
22 *G. Id.*, p. 24.
23 *Cap*. 3, p. 266.
24 *Cap*. 1, p. 929.
25 *Comm. Man.*, p. 82.
26 *Cap*. 1, p. 929.
27 *Theories of Surplus-Value* 2, p. 118.
28 Böhm-Bawerk, *Capital and Interest*, II, pp. 168-71.
29 *Cap*. 1, p. 325.
30 Ibid., p. 929.

Chapter 12   Towards the new society

1   *Cap*. 1, p. 929.
2   Marx's inaugural address at the First International, *FIA*, p. 81.
3   *The Civil War in France*, *FIA*, p. 213.
4   Address of the Central Committee to the Communist Leagues, *R48*, p. 328.
5   Preface to the new German edition of the *Communist Manifesto*, *MESW* 1, p. 98.
6   *Cap*. 1, p. 92.
7   Preface to the new German edition of the *Communist Manifesto*, *MESW* 1, p. 98.
8   For examples of the 'uncompromising' Marx, see e.g. the address of the Central Committee to the Communist League, *R48*, p. 329, and *The Class Struggles in France*, *SfE*, p. 61; the 'conciliatory' Marx appears in the Amsterdam speech on the Hague Congress of 1872, *FIA*, p. 324.
9   The opposite views are expressed in two letters: Marx to Kugelmann, 12 April 1871, *MESC*, p. 263, and Marx to Domela-Nieuwenhuis, 22 Feb. 1881, *MESC*, p. 338.
10 *Econ. Phil.*, p. 349.
11 *G. Id.*, p. 81.
12 Ibid., p. 49.
13 Mill, *The Principles of Political Economy*, p. 113.
14 *Econ. Phil.*, p. 346.

15   *G. Id.*, p. 88.
16   Ibid., p. 47.
17   *Pov. Phil.*, p. 212.
18   *Theses on Feuerbach*, *EW*, p. 423, and *G. Id.*, p. 78.
19   *G. Id.*, p. 439.
20   *Excerpts from James Mill's 'Elements of Political Economy'*, *EW*, p. 278.
21   *Econ. Phil.*, p. 348 and pp. 349f.
22   *Grundr.*, p. 712 and p. 706.
23   *Cap.* 1, p. 172.
24   *Cap.* 2, p. 212.
25   *Cap.* 3, p. 851.
26   *Cap.* 1, pp. 618-19.
27   *Cap.* 3, pp. 386-90.
28   Ibid., p. 250.
29   Ibid., p. 820.

Chapter 13   Contradictions in Marx

1   *Cap.* 3, p. 825.
2   Ibid., p. 820.
3   Ibid.
4   *Grundr.*, p. 712.
5   Ibid., pp. 711-12.
6   *Theories of Surplus-Value* III, p. 257.
7   *Grundr.*, p. 612.
8   *Results of the Immediate Process of Production*, appendix to *Cap.* 1, p. 1033.
9   *The Civil War in France*, *FIA*, p. 213.
10   *Cap.* 3, p. 820.
11   *Crit. Gotha Pr.*, p. 343.
12   Engels, *Anti-Dühring*, p. 312.
13   See *Crit. Gotha Pr.*, p. 347 (written in 1875), and *Cap.* 3, p. 820. This internal contradiction in Marx's concept of labour has been pointed out by a number of critics, notably Heinrich Popitz (*Der entfremdete Mensch*, p. 160) and Simone Weil (*Oppression and Liberty*, p. 159).
14   For Ernest Mandel, a Trotskyist and a respected scholar, 'factory work would continue to be a *sad necessity*' even in a socialist society. But at the same time he reaffirmed that 'The more that labour in the traditional sense of the word withers away, the more it is replaced by creative *praxis* of all-round developed and socially integrated personalities. The more man frees himself from his needs by satisfying them, the more does "the realm of necessity give place to the realm of freedom" ' (*Marxist Economic Theory* II, p. 686). In a footnote he dismissed Simone Weil's contention that no technology can liberate man from the need for hard work as a 'dark prophecy' which is wholly 'unfounded and unreasonable' (ibid., p. 679). But which is the unfounded and unreasonable view – Weil's pessimism or Mandel's optimism? Weil gained the insight into the continued necessity of labour from her own experience of factory work, which she, a frail intellectual, took upon herself to share the lot of the workers. Mandel, though, devised the transformation of labour into creative praxis in his study, and certainly not on the basis of a scientific analysis.
15   Klaus and Buhr (eds.), *Marxistisch-leninistisches Wörterbuch der Philosophie*

III, p. 1002.
16 This applies especially to a symposium on 'socialist humanism'. A book with this title was first published in 1965 and edited by Erich Fromm. It included contributions by Lucien Goldmann, Mihailo Marković, Adam Schaff, Ernst Bloch, Erich Fromm, Bertrand Russell, Herbert Marcuse, and others.
17 Althusser, *For Marx*, pp. 55ff.
18 Althusser, *Reading Capital*, p. 115.
19 *Cap.* 1, p. 626.
20 Ibid.
21 Bismarck, *Die politischen Reden* X, 26 Nov. 1884, p. 246.
22 *Cap.* 3, p. 437.
23 The validity of the law of the falling rate of profit has been questioned not only by opponents of Marxism but also by some Marxist economists, e.g. Joan Robinson (*An Essay on Marxian Economics*, pp. 35ff.). But Mandel accepted it in his *Marxist Economic Theory* (I, pp. 169ff.).
24 *Cap.* 1, pp. 97f.
25 Ibid., p. 103.
26 1 Corinthians 1, 23. This is a translation from the German. In the Authorized King James Version the verse reads 'But we preach Christ crucified, unto the Jews a stumblingblock, and unto the Greeks foolishness.'
27 Engels's introduction to the new (1895) edition of *The Class Struggles in France, MEW* 7, p. 512. The comment refers to a specific conclusion drawn by Marx, but it applies in general as well.
28 *Econ. Phil. Man.*, p. 382; *Cap.* 1, p. 102.
29 Feuerbach, *The Essence of Christianity*, pp. 187f.
30 Preface to the *Critique of Political Economy*, *EW*, p. 426.
31 *G. Id.*, p. 62.
32 *Crit. Doctr. St.*, p. 174.
33 Heinrich Marx to Karl Marx, 2 March 1837, *CW* 1, p. 670.
34 Goethe, *Eckermann's Conversations*, 2 March 1831, p. 367.
35 Goethe, *Dichtung und Wahrheit*, *Werke* 10, p. 177.
36 Hess, quoted in *MEGA* I, 2, p. 261.
37 Schurz, *Reminiscences* I, pp. 139f.
38 Bakunin, quoted in *MEW* 18, p. 626.
39 Hess, *Briefwechsel*, p. 256.
40 Marx to his father, 10 Nov. 1837, *CW* 1, p. 11 and p. 17.
41 Rosenzweig, *Star of Redemption*, p. 271.
42 Quoted in Braun, *Memoiren einer Sozialistin*, p. 409.

Chapter 14   Consequences of the contradictions

1 Engels, *Anti-Dühring*, p. 157.
2 *Cap.* 1, p. 102.
3 Marx to Engels, 22 June 1867, *MESC*, p. 189.
4 *Cap.* 1, p. 494n.
5 Schumpeter, 'Karl Marx', *Ten Great Economists*, p. 10.
6 Böhm-Bawerk, *Karl Marx and the Close of His System*, p. 101.
7 *Circular against Kriege*, *MECW* 6, p. 35.
8 *Moralising Criticism and Critical Morality*, *MECW* 6, p. 320.
9 *Comm. Man.*, p. 83.
10 *G. Id.*, p. 323.
11 Marx to Engels, 18 June 1862, *MESC*, p. 128, and Marx to Kugelmann,

27 June 1870, *MESC*, p. 238.

12 Engels's speech at Marx's graveside, *MESW* 3, p. 162.

13 *Pov. Phil.*, p. 169; conspectus of Bakunin's *Statism and Anarchy*, *FIA*, p. 335.

14 *Pov. Phil.*, p. 178.

15 Marx to Jenny Lafargue, 11 April 1881, *MECor*, p. 391.

16 These are revealed in the biography by his secretary, Angelica Balabanoff (*Impressions of Lenin*).

17 Lukács, postscriptum (dated 1957) to 'Mein Weg zu Marx', *Schriften zur Ideologie und Politik*, p. 649.

18 Brecht, *Arbeitsjournal* 2, p. 1009.

19 In their book *The Modern Corporation and Private Property* (1932), Berle and Means described the trend towards the separation of private property and control in the modern capitalist corporation, without mentioning that Marx had already seen an intermediate form between the capitalist and socialist mode of production in the separation of capital and factory management. Berle and Means's thesis was generally rejected at the time. Ten years later James Burnham, in *The Managerial Revolution*, concluded on the basis of a comparison of the economic systems of America, Germany, Italy and the Soviet Union that in advanced countries a new form of society was emerging out of the capitalist form, not a socialist society but a 'managerial' social organization, in which neither the owners of capital nor the workers but instead the managers exercised control and determined economic policies. In 1955 the Congress for Cultural Freedom convened a meeting with the aim to examine, above all, the 'simple antithesis "capitalism against economic planning" ' (*The Soviet Economy*, p. 6). The idea of a convergence of the two economic systems has since then been energetically advocated by Galbraith, Tinbergen, Sampedro, Myrdal, the sociologists of the Frankfurt school, and others.
    In the 1970s the convergence theory has gained further ground. Donald M. Morrison wrote in *Time*: 'The capitalist economy may thus eventually take on some features of socialism, just as socialism over the years has adopted some practices of capitalism. . . . [America] is surely strong and diverse enough to accommodate the best features of both systems' (14 Feb. 1972, p. 47). The non-orthodox idea of a convergence of communism and capitalism has been expressed in the Soviet Union by Andrei Sakharov (see especially his essay 'Progress, Coexistence and Intellectual Freedom' in *Sakharov Speaks*).

20 Weber, *Parl. Reg.*, pp. 318f.

21 Weil, *La Condition ouvrière*, p. 9; Horkheimer and Adorno, *Sociologica II*, p. 14; Marcuse, *Reason and Revolution*, p. 439; Jaspers, *Man in the Modern Age* p. 75; Galbraith, *The New Industrial State*, p. 397; Arendt, *The Human Condition*, p. 5; Benjamin, *Charles Baudelaire*, p. 35; Steiner, *In Bluebeard's Castle*, ch. 1 title; Mills, *The Causes of World War Three*, p. 175; Fromm in Fromm (ed.), *Socialist Humanism*, p. 215.

22 Goethe to Schiller, 9 Aug. 1797, *Letters*, p. 261.

23 Schaff, *Marxism and the Human Individual*, pp. 107-8.

Chapter 15   Weber's lifelong dialogue with Marx

1 Weber's *'Obj.'*, p. 103, and 'Socialism', *Sel. Tr.*, p. 256.

2 Weber, 'The National Interest in Imperial Germany', *Sel. Tr.*, p. 265.

3 Quoted in Baumgarten, *Max Weber*, pp. 554f.
4 Ibid., p. 615.
5 Baumgarten, quoted in Schlipp (ed.), *Karl Jaspers*, p. 353.
6 Weber, *Parl. Reg.*, p. 431.
7 Weber, *Urbanisation and Social Structure in the Ancient World*, *Sel. Tr.*, p. 313.
8 Weber, *The Protestant Ethic*, p. 16.
9 Weber, 'The Nature of Social Action', *Sel. Tr.*, pp. 28-9.
10 Weber, *The Protestant Ethic*, p. 181.
11 Weber, *Parl. Reg.*, p. 320.
12 Weber, 'Sci. Voc.', p. 152.
13 Weber, *Prosp.*, pp. 282-3.
14 Quoted in Baumgarten, *Max Weber*, p. 429.
15 Quoted in Mommsen, *Max Weber*, p. 256n.
16 Weber, *Roscher and Knies*, p. 193.
17 Weber here contradicted the positivists and anticipated the work of the Frankfurt school, which also held that historical understanding implies an orientation to a value. Adorno, like Weber, had only contempt for 'the most wretched nitpicking garbed as scientific acribia' of those subject-matter specialists who treat the material as an end in itself and do not place it in a historico-philosophical context (*Negative Dialectics*, p. 301). But despite this fundamental similarity, there also exists a fundamental difference: the Frankfurt school claimed that the value could be apprehended scientifically, which Weber considered impossible.
18 Weber, 'The Nature of Social Action', *Sel. Tr.*, p. 22.
19 Weber, *Roscher and Knies*, p. 194.
20 Weber, *'Obj.'*, p. 98.

Chapter 16 Marx in the light of Weber's clarification of method

1 Weber, *'Obj.'*, p. 68.
2 Simone Weil has expressed the same 'positive' critique of Marx's materialist conception of history. She pointed out that Marx was the first to have the twin idea of society as the fundamental fact and of studying the relationship of force in it (she erroneously assumed that Marx has been the only one to have done this). But having had the idea, Marx rendered it barren. 'The result was a system according to which the relationships of force that define the social structure entirely determine both man's destiny and his thoughts' (*Oppression and Liberty*, p. 171).
3 *The Holy Family*, *MECW* 4, p. 93.
4 Weber, *Prosp.*, p. 282.
5 Weber, *Econ. Soc.* 1, p. 138.
6 Ibid., p. 110.
7 Weber, *Parl. Reg.*, p. 385.
8 Quoted in Mommsen, *Max Weber*, pp. 268f.
9 Weber, *Zwischen zwei Gesetze*, *GPS*, p. 141. This struggle for survival is not Darwinist. Mommsen completely misconstrued Weber's intention when he referred to his 'social Darwinist conceptual system' (*Max Weber*, p. 25). Weber distinguished his own conception of human life as a struggle from Darwin's views, and he considered it a mistake to apply Darwin's theory of the struggle for survival to the social sciences ('Der Nationalstaat und die Volkswirtschaftspolitik', *GPS*, p. 9).

10   Weber, 'Pol. Voc.', p. 214.
11   Goethe, *Belagerung von Mainz*, *Werke* 10, p. 391.
12   Weber, 'Pol. Voc.', p. 214.
13   Ibid.
14   Weber, *Econ. Soc.* 2, p. 515.
15   All quotes in this paragraph from Weber, 'Pol. Voc.', pp. 222-5.
16   Ibid., p. 225.
17   For instance, at the congress of the Deutsche Gesellschaft für Soziologie in honour of the centenary of Weber's birth, eminent sociologists and philosophers debated the topic of 'Max Weber and Power Politics' for a whole day without even mentioning the positive element of Weber's lecture (Stammer (ed.), *Max Weber and Sociology Today*).
18   Berlin, *Four Essays on Liberty*, pp. 1xf.
19   Weber, 'Pol. Voc.', p. 213.
20   Quoted in Baumgarten, *Max Weber*, p. 429.
21   Jaspers, *Hoffnung und Sorge*, p. 318.
22   L. Strauss, *Natural Right and History*, p. 48.
23   Jaspers, *Schicksal und Wille*, p. 33.
24   Weber, *Gesammelte Aufsätze zur Religionssoziologie* I, p. 569.
25   Weber, 'Sci. Voc.', p. 153.
26   Ibid., pp. 154f.
27   Weber, '*Obj.*', p. 57.
28   Quoted in Baumgarten, *Max Weber*, p. 670n and p. 677.
29   Weber, *Econ. Soc.* 2, p. 567.
30   Quoted in Baumgarten, *Max Weber*, p. 670n.
31   Weber, 'Sci. Voc.', p. 142.
32   Quoted in Baumgarten, *Max Weber*, p. 399.
33   Benjamin, *Theologisch-politisches Fragment*, *Schriften* II (1), p. 203.
34   Weber, *Gesammelte Aufsätze zur Soziologie*, pp. 466f. That Weber spoke from personal experience is substantiated by Paul Honigsheim, who often took part in discussions at Weber's home. He noted that Tolstoy and Dostoyevsky 'were, so to speak, actually present' (*On Max Weber*, p. 80). Honigsheim was one of the few, perhaps the only one, to describe Weber as a *homo religiosus*.
35   Weber, '*Obj.*', p. 182 and p. 152.
36   Weber, 'Sci. Voc.', p. 155.
37   Silone, *The Story of a Humble Christian*, p. 26.

Chapter 17   The controversy over the dialectic

1   Engels, preface to *Condition of the Working Class in England*, *MESW* 3, pp. 442-3 and pp. 447-8.
2   Bernstein, *Evolutionary Socialism*, pp. 209f.
3   Lenin, *What Is To Be Done?*, *Selected Works* 1, p. 105.
4   Ibid., p. 117.
5   Lenin, *Materialism and Empirio-Criticism*, pp. 172-4.
6   Lenin, *Aus dem philosophischen Nachlass*, p. 99.
7   Luxemburg, review of Bernstein's *Evolutionary Socialism*, *Rosa Luxemburg Speaks*, p. 83.
8   Quoted in Korsch, *Marxism and Philosophy*, p. 101n.
9   Luxemburg, *The Accumulation of Capital*, p. 164.
10   Bernstein, 'Kritisches Zwischenspiel', *Neue Zeit*, 16/1, p. 749.

11 *The Holy Family, MECW* 4, p. 93.
12 Quoted in Kramár, *Geschichte und Kritik des Bolschewismus*, p. 174.
13 *Das Kapital*, first German edition, p. 763. Marx deleted this comment in later editions after he had met and grown to respect the young Russian revolutionaries.
14 Lenin, *What Is To Be Done?, Selected Works* 1, p. 116 and p. 102.
15 Quoted in Labedz (ed.), *Revisionism*, p. 279.
16 Quoted in Eastman, *Stalin's Russia*, p. 231.
17 Müller, *Hegel*, p. 230.
18 Mehring, *Geschichte der deutschen Sozialdemokratie*, IV, p. 355.
19 Lenin, *State and Revolution, Selected Works* 2, p. 346.
20 Quoted in Baumgarten, *Max Weber*, p. 607.
21 Lenin, *State and Revolution, Selected Works* 2, p. 357.
22 Ibid., p. 335.
23 Ibid., p. 334.
24 Ibid., p. 303.
25 *The Civil War in France, FIA*, pp. 210-11.
26 Lenin, *State and Revolution, Selected Works* 2, p. 299. In their struggle against Stalinism Russian intellectuals relied on this anti-autocratic (though utopian) passage. In Solzhenitsyn's *The First Circle* Stalin says against Lenin: 'This had all been Lenin's fault. . . . "Any cook should be able to run the country" . . . what had Lenin actually meant by this? Did he mean that they should take a day off every week to work in the local Soviet? A cook is a cook, and his job is to get the dinner ready, whereas telling other people what to do is a highly skilled business: it can only be done by specially selected and trained personnel, . . . this personnel could only be entrusted to one pair of hands − the practised hands of the leader' (p. 99).
27 Balabanoff, *Impressions of Lenin*, p. 151.
28 Lenin, *State and Revolution, Selected Works* 2, p. 338.
29 Balabanoff, *Impressions of Lenin*, p. 3.

Chapter 18   Marx's influence on the communists of the second generation

1   Stalin, *Problems of Leninism*, p. 794.
2   Camus, *The Rebel*, p. 185.
3   Djilas, *The New Class*, p. 9.
4   Liberman, 'The Soviet Economic Reform', *Foreign Affairs*, 46/1, p. 63.
5   Stalin, 'Economic Problems of Socialism in the USSR', *The Essential Stalin*.
6   Rosdolsky, *The Making of Marx's 'Capital'*, p. 570.
7   Quoted in Fromm (ed.), *Socialist Humanism*, p. 83.
8   Prucha, 'Marxismus als Philosophie', *Neues Forum*, 167/68, pp. 848f.
9   O. Mandelshtam, 'Fourth Prose', *Selected Essays*, p. 161.
10 N. Mandelshtam, *Hope against Hope*, p. 333.
11 Among these pioneers are the philosopher and chemist Bonifaty Kedrov, the literary critic Angel Davidov, the novelist Vasily Ilyenkov, and the anthropologist Elizaveta Danilova.
12 Lukács, *Theory of the Novel*, p. 152.
13 Lukács, preface to *Balzac und der französische Realismus, Werke* 6, p. 435.
14 Lukács, *History and Class Consciousness*, p. xliii.
15 Ibid., p. 178.
16 Ibid., p. 194 and p. 195; Korsch, *Marxism and Philosophy*, p. 77.
17 Gramsci, *Selections from Political Writings*, p. 309.

18   Korsch, *Marxism and Philosophy*, p. 125.
19   Luxemburg, 'Organizational Questions of Social Democracy', *Rosa Luxemburg Speaks*.
20   Luxemburg, 'The Russian Revolution', *Rosa Luxemburg Speaks*, p. 389.
21   Ibid., p. 391.
22   Weber, 'Socialism', *Sel. Tr.*, p. 260.
23   Quoted in Crossman (ed.), *The God that Failed*, pp. 106f.

Chapter 19   The revival of Marxist thought in the 1950s and 1960s

1   Jaspers, *Philosophy of Existence*, p. 3; Heidegger, *An Introduction to Metaphysics*, p. 39.
2   Marcuse, 'Neue Quellen zur Grundlegung des Historischen Materialismus', *Die Gesellschaft*, 9/8; Kojève, *Introduction to the Reading of Hegel*.
3   *Grundr.*, p. 111.
4   Engels to Minna Kautsky, 26 Nov. 1885, *MESC*, p. 391.
5   Lenin to Gorky, 25 Feb. 1908, *Letters*, p. 265.
6   Luxemburg, *The Spirit of Russian Literature*, *Rosa Luxemburg Speaks*, pp. 341-6; Trotsky, *Literature and Revolution*, pp. 168-70.
7   Lukács, *Die Eigenart des Ästhetischen*, I, *Werke* 11, p. 28.
8   Lukács, *Probleme der Ästhetik*, *Werke* 10, p. 207.
9   Ibid., p. 208 (quoted from Engels to Starkenburg, 25 Jan. 1894, *MESC*, p. 467).
10   Ibid., p. 638.
11   Lukács, *Conversations*, p. 100.
12   Lenin to Gorky, 25 Feb. 1908, *Letters*, p. 265. Lukács refers to this letter in *Realism in our Time*, p. 97.
13   Lukács, *The Historical Novel*, p. 275.
14   Lukács, *Realism in our Time*, p. 101.
15   Lukács, *The Meaning of Contemporary Realism*, pp. 9-10.
16   Lukács, quoted from a speech delivered in 1949 in Berlin, printed in the German edition of *Goethe und seine Zeit*, p. 363.
17   Lukács, *Goethe and his Age*, pp. 215-17. The quotes are from *Faust*, pt two, act 5. For Goethe's interpretation of this passage, see *Conversations with Eckermann*, 6 June 1831, p. 398.
18   Lukács, *The Meaning of Contemporary Realism*, p. 78; T. Mann to A. Löwenstein, 27 Oct. 1945, *Briefe*, p. 455.
19   Solzhenitsyn, *Von der Verantwortung des Schriftstellers*, p. 16.
20   Quoted by F. Bondy in Lukács's obituary, *Die Weltwoche*, 11 June 1971.
21   Lukács, *Probleme der Ästhetik*, *Werke* 10, p. 126.
22   Adorno, 'Erpresste Versöhnung', *Der Monat*, 122, p. 49.
23   Benjamin, *On Some Motifs in Baudelaire*, *Illuminations*, p. 176.
24   Ibid., p. 183.
25   Ibid., p. 184.
26   Ibid., p. 191.
27   Benjamin, 'The Task of the Translator', *Illuminations*, p. 80, and 'Franz Kafka', *Illuminations*, p. 134.
28   Benjamin, 'Theses on the Philosophy of History', *Illuminations*, p. 256 and p. 264.
29   Ibid., p. 266.
30   Adorno, *Über Walter Benjamin*, p. 92.
31   Quoted in Sholem, 'Walter Benjamin', *Neue Rundschau*, 76, p. 19.

32   Lefèbvre, 'De l'explication en économie politique et en sociologie',
     Cahiers Internationaux de Sociologie, xxi, p. 29.
33   Habermas, *Theory and Practice*, pp. 195-8.
34   Ibid., p. 211.
35   Just as Heidegger analysed 'loss of being' (*Seinsvergessenheit*) from the
     standpoint of the anticipatory understanding of being, so the dialectical
     philosophers of the Frankfurt school analysed the 'self-forgetting aspect'
     (*Selbstvergessenheit*) of production from the anticipatory understanding
     of the social goal (Adorno, *Drei Studien zu Hegel*, p. 40). Adorno's strong
     polemic against Heidegger's 'jargon of authenticity' (the title of one of
     Adorno's essays) conceals their agreement that essence *is* cognizable. For
     Adorno it is not the essence of being and existence – what Heidegger called
     the 'existentials' – that is cognizable but the essence of society (*Negative
     Dialectics*, p. 167). It is the possibility of a theoretical cognition of essence
     which is contested by Kant, Weber and Jaspers.
36   Adorno, *Negative Dialectics*, p. 150 and p. 147.
37   Ibid., pp. 321f.
38   Ibid., p. 151.
39   Ibid., p. 406.
40   Ibid.
41   Ibid., p. 56.
42   Ibid., p. 52.
43   Ibid., p. 167.
44   Ibid., p. 373.
45   Kant, *Critique of Practical Reason*, p. 225.
46   Adorno, *Negative Dialectics*, p. 397.
47   Adorno, *Drei Studien zu Hegel*, p. 83.
48   Habermas, 'Literaturbericht zur philosophischen Diskussion um Marx und
     den Marxismus' (1957), *Theorie und Praxis*, p. 311.
49   Kant, *Critique of Pure Reason*, p. 563.
50   Marx to Jenny Lafargue, 11 April 1881, *MECor*, p. 391; Trotsky, *In Defence
     of Marxism*, p. 51; Lenin, *Materialism and Empirio-Criticism*, p. 173; Bloch,
     Das Prinzip Hoffnung, p. 623; Adorno, *Negative Dialectics*, p. 157.
51   Merleau-Ponty, *The Adventures of the Dialectic*, p. 204.
52   Adorno, *Negative Dialectics*, p. 375; Horkheimer, *Critique of Instrumental
     Reason*, p. 4.
53   Habermas, *Protestbewegung und Hochschulreform*, p. 41.
54   Urquhart and Brent, *Enzo Sereni*, pp. 90f.
55   See for instance T.B. Bottomore's contribution in Fromm (ed.), *Socialist
     Humanism*, pp. 372-3.
56   Kolakowski, *Der Mensch ohne Alternative*, p. 51.
57   After the invasion of Czechoslovakia, Sik was forced to flee his homeland
     and Kolakowski was suspended by the University of Warsaw (he has since
     emigrated and moved away not only from orthodox Marxism but even from
     the basic tenets of Marxist theory). In the epilogue of his book *Main
     Currents of Marxism*, written in his new residence, Oxford, Kolakowski
     stresses that Marx's belief in a society without conflict and an economy
     without money have nothing in common with the idea of democratic social-
     ism to which he adheres.
58   Stojanović, *Between Ideals and Reality*.
59   Lukács, 'Zur Soziologie des gesellschaftlichen Seins', *Neues Forum*, 207,
     p. 21, and *Conversations*, p. 130 and p. 138.
60   Lukács, *Conversations*, p. 130.
61   Personal communication from Professor Iring Fetscher.

Chapter 20   The student revolt of the 1960s

1   Veblen, *The Theory of the Leisure Class*, titles of chs 3 and 4; James, 'The Moral Equivalent of War', *Memories and Studies*, p. 276.
2   Quoted in Salisbury, *To Peking – and Beyond*, p. 59.
3   Burckhardt, *Weltgeschichtliche Betrachtungen*, p. 188.
4   Marcuse, *Soviet Marxism*, p. 265.
5   Nietzsche, *Thus Spake Zarathustra*, p. 71.
6   Marcuse, *Negations*, p. xvi.
7   Ibid., p. xx.
8   Quoted in Stammer (ed.), *Max Weber and Sociology Today*, pp. 149-51.
9   Weber, *Econ. Soc.* 2, p. 584.
10 Marcuse, *One-Dimensional Man*, p. 252.
11 Quoted in Stammer (ed.), *Max Weber and Sociology Today*, pp. 134-8.
12 Quoted in Fromm (ed.), *Socialist Humanism*, p. 99.
13 Marcuse, *Negations*, p. xix.
14 See Fromm (ed.), *Socialist Humanism*, p. 106, where Marcuse expresses this dualism most poignantly.
15 Spender, *The Year of the Young Rebels*, p. 106.
16 Weber, *The Protestant Ethic*, p. 180.
17 Marcuse, *Negations*, p. 208.
18 Weber, *Econ. Soc.* 1, p. 111.
19 Sartre was the only European intellectual who could elicit the message of mad fury from Frantz Fanon's *The Wretched of the Earth*. This book, which for many blacks became a Black Bible, idolizes violence not as a means in the political struggle but as the expression of a new self-confidence after centuries of humiliation. This can be gathered from the rhetoric: 'since each individual forms a violent link in the great chain, a part of the great organism of violence which has surged upward in reaction to the settler's violence in the beginning' (p. 73). In contrast to Sartre, Fanon calls for 'cautious political advance' and warns against becoming 'drunk' with violence (p. 136).
20 De Tocqueville, *Democracy in America*, p. 517.
21 Myrdal, preface to the twentieth edition of *An American Dilemma*, p. xxiii.
22 Fairlie, 'The Lessons of Watergate', *Encounter*, 43/4, p. 23.
23 Armstrong, 'Isolated America', *Foreign Affairs*, 51/1, pp. 9f.
24 Hesse, *Betrachtungen, Gesammelte Werke* 10, p. 111.
25 Revel, *Without Marx or Jesus*, p. 58.

Chapter 21   The New Left

1   Quoted in Davenport, 'Bank of America is not for burning', *Fortune*, lxxxiii/1, p. 152.
2   Samuelson, *Economics*, preface to the ninth edition, p. ix.
3   Galbraith, *The New Industrial State*, p. 409.
4   Harrington, *The Accidental Century*, pp. 301-2.
5   Keynes, 'Economic Possibilities for our Grandchildren', *Essays in Persuasion*, p. 372.
6   Wells, *The New Machiavelli*, p. 216.
7   Mulk, 'By mouth or by book', *Times Lit. Sup.*, 12 May 1972, p. 552.
8   Galbraith, *The New Industrial State*, p. 407 (italics JIL).
9   Ibid., p. 316.
10 Ibid., p. 162.

11   *Cap.* 3, p. 226.
12   Galbraith, *The New Industrial State*, p. 399.
13   Riesman, ' "The Lonely Crowd", 20 Years After', *Encounter*, 33/4, p. 39.
14   Galbraith, *The Affluent Society*, p. 139.
15   Weber, *Econ. Soc.* 1, p. 63.
16   Galbraith, *The Affluent Society*, p. 137.
17   *Cap.* 1, p. 759n.
18   Weber, 'Der Nationalstaat und Volkswirtschaftspolitik', *GPS*, p. 16.
19   Lindbeck, *The Political Economy of the New Left*, p. 100.
20   Galbraith, *The New Industrial State*, p. 407.
21   *Cap.* 3, p. 820.

Chapter 22   The Chinese Revolution

1   'The British Rule in India', *SfE*, pp. 303-6.
2   Weber, *The Religion of China*, p. 136.
3   'Chinesisches', article in *Die Presse*, 7 July 1862, *MEW* 15, p. 514.
4   Mao, *People's Democratic Dictatorship*, *Selected Works* IV, p. 413.
5   Mao, *On New Democracy*, *Selected Works* II, p. 381.
6   Mao, 'Report on an Investigation of the Peasant Movement in Hunan'
      (1927), *Selected Works* I, p. 23.
7   Mao, *On New Democracy*, *Selected Works* II, p. 381.
8   Mao, *People's Democratic Dictatorship*, *Selected Works* IV, p. 414.
9   Mao, 'Report on an Investigation of the Peasant Movement in Hunan'
      (1927), *Selected Works* I, p. 28 and p. 29.

Chapter 23   Maoist orthodoxy

1   Mao, *Correct Handling of Contradictions*, *Selected Works* V, p. 387.
2   Mao, *People's Democratic Dictatorship*, *Selected Works* IV, p. 412.
3   Mao, *On New Democracy*, *Selected Works* II, p. 381.
4   Mao, *Correct Handling of Contradictions*, *Selected Works* V, p. 405.
5   Mao, *Quotations*, para. 24.
6   Mao, *Quotations*, p. 243.
7   Quoted in *Time*, 30 April 1973, p. 97.
8   Fitzgerald, *The Birth of Communist China*, ch. 6; Schramm, *Mao Tse-tung*,
      p. 316; Moravia, *The Red Book and the Great Wall*, p. 39; Han, *Asia Today*,
      p. 24.
9   Quoted in Robinson, *The Cultural Revolution in China*, p. 30.
10   Mao, *Correct Handling of Contradictions*, op. cit., p. 405.
11   Mehnert, *China Returns*, p. 237.
12   Mao, *Quotations*, p. 180 and p. 59.
13   Kant, *What is Enlightenment?*, *Political Writings*, p. 54.
14   See Weber, *Religion of China*, and Needham, *The Grand Titration*, especially
      the essay 'Science and Society in East and West'.
15   Mao, *Quotations*, pp. 233f.
16   Ibid., p. 217.

Epilogue

1   *Cap*. 3, p. 820.
2   Ibid.
3   Weber, *Prosp.*, p. 282.
4   *Grundr.*, pp. 460f.
5   Silone, *The Story of a Humble Christian*, p. 26.
6   *Grundr.*, p. 712; Kant, *What is Enlightenment?*, *Political Writings*, p. 52.

Bibliography

1 Marx and Engels collections:

Collected Works. London, 1965—.
Correspondence 1846-1895, trans. D. Torr. London, 1934.
Gesamtausgabe, ed. D. Rjazanov/V. Adoratskij. Frankfurt-Berlin, 1927-32.
On Art and Literature. New York, 1947.
Selected Correspondence, trans. I. Lasker, 2nd ed. Moscow, 1965.
Selected Works, 3 vols. Moscow, 1970.
Werke. Berlin, 1956—.

2 Works by Marx:

Capital, vol. 1, trans. B. Fowkes. Harmondsworth, 1976.
Capital, vol. 2, trans. D. Fernbach. Harmondsworth, 1978.
Capital, vol. 3. London, 1974.
Early Writings. Harmondsworth, 1975.
The First International and After. Harmondsworth, 1974.
Die Frühschriften. Stuttgart, 1964.
Grundrisse, trans. M. Nicolaus. Harmondsworth, 1973.
The Revolutions of 1848. Harmondsworth, 1973.
Surveys from Exile. Harmondsworth, 1973.
Theories of Surplus-Value, 3 vols. London, 1969-72.

3 Other works:

Adorno, Theodor W. *Drei Studien zu Hegel*. Frankfurt, 1963.
Adorno, Theodor W. 'Erpresste Versöhnung', *Der Monat*, 122, Nov. 1958, pp. 37-49.
Adorno, Theodor W. *The Jargon of Authenticity*, trans. K. Tarnowski and F. Will. London, 1973.
Adorno, Theodor W. *Negative Dialectics*, trans. E.B. Ashton. London, 1973.
Adorno, Theodor W. *Über Walter Benjamin*. Frankfurt, 1970.
Althusser, Louis. *For Marx*, trans. B. Brewster. London, 1969.
Althusser, Louis. *Reading Capital*, trans. B. Brewster. London, 1965.
Arendt, Hannah. *The Human Condition*. Chicago, 1958.
Armstrong, Hamilton F. 'Isolated America', *Foreign Affairs*, 51/1, Oct. 1972, pp. 1-10.

Bakunin, Michail. *Sozialpolitischer Briefwechsel mit Herzen und Ogarjew*, trans. B. Minzès. Stuttgart, 1895.

Balabanoff, Angelica. *Impressions of Lenin*, trans. I. Cesari. Ann Arbor, 1964.

Balzac, Honoré de. *Old Goriot*, trans. E. Marriage. London, 1948.

Baumgarten, Eduard. *Max Weber: Werk und Person*. Tübingen, 1964.

Beckermann, Wilfred. *In Defence of Economic Growth*. London, 1974.

Beik, P.H., ed. *The French Revolution*. London, 1971.

Bell, Daniel. *The Coming of Post-Industrial Society*. London, 1974.

Benjamin, Walter. *Charles Baudelaire: A Lyric Poet in the Era of High Capitalism*, trans. H. Zohn. London, 1973.

Benjamin, Walter. *Illuminations*, trans. H. Zohn. London, 1973.

Benjamin, Walter. *Schriften*. Frankfurt, 1972–.

Berle, Adolf A. and Means, Gardiner, C. *The Modern Corporation and Private Property*. New York, 1932.

Berlin, Isaiah. *Karl Marx*, London, 1939.

Berlin, Isaiah. *Four Essays on Liberty*. London, 1969.

Bernstein, Eduard. *Evolutionary Socialism*, trans. E.C. Harvey. New York, 1961.

Bernstein, Eduard. 'Kritisches Zwischenspiel', *Neue Zeit*, 16/1, 1898, pp. 740-51.

Bismarck, Otto von. *Die politischen Reden*. Stuttgart, 1914.

Blanc, Louis. *Organisation du travail*. Paris, 1840.

Bloch, Ernst. *Das Prinzip Hoffnung*. Frankfurt, 1954-9.

Böhm-Bawerk, Eugen von. *Capital and Interest*, 3 vols, trans. G.D. Huncke and H.F. Sennholz. South Holland, III., 1959.

Böhm-Bawerk, Eugen von. *Karl Marx and the Close of His System*, trans P.M. Sweezy. New York, 1949.

Braun, Lily. *Memoiren einer Sozialistin*. München, 1922.

Brecht, Bertolt. *Arbeitsjournal*, 2 vols. Frankfurt, 1973.

Buonarotti, Filippo. *Conspiration pour l'égalité dite de Babeuf*, 2 vols. Paris, 1957.

Burckhardt, Jacob. *Weltgeschichtliche Betrachtungen*. Stuttgart, 1969.

Burnham, James. *The Managerial Revolution*. London, 1942.

Camus, Albert. *The Rebel*, trans. A. Bower. London, 1953.

Carr, E.H. *The Soviet Impact on the Western World*. London, 1946.

Cieszkowski, August von. *Prolegomena zur Historiosophie*. Berlin, 1838.

Cleaver, Eldridge. *Soul on Ice*. London, 1969.

Cohn, Norman. *The Pursuit of the Millennium*. London, 1957.

Congress for Cultural Freedom. *The Soviet Economy*, by R. Aron, *et al.* London, 1956.

Constant, Benjamin. *Cours de politique constitutionelle*. Paris, 1861.

Conway, John S. *The Nazi Persecution of the Church 1933-45*. London, 1968.

Croce, Benedetto. *What is Living and What is Dead in the Philosophy of Hegel*, trans. D. Ainslie. London, 1915.

Crossman, Richard, ed. *The God that Failed*. London, 1950.

Davenport, John. 'Bank of America is not for burning', *Fortune*, lxxxiii/1, Jan. 1971, pp. 91-3 and p. 152.

Defoe, Daniel. *The Shortest Way with the Dissenters and other Pamphlets*. Oxford, 1927.

Disraeli, Benjamin. *Sybil*. London, 1927.

Djilas, Milovan. *The New Class*. London, 1957.

Dostoyevsky, Fyodor Mikhail. *The Diary of a Writer*, 2 vols, trans. B. Brasol. London, 1949.

Dostoyevsky, Fyodor Mikhail. *The Idiot*. Harmondsworth, 1955.

Eastman, Max. *Stalin's Russia and the Crisis in Socialism*. London, 1940.
Engels, Friedrich. *Anti-Dühring*, trans. E. Burns. London, 1934.

Faguet, Émile. *La Politique comparée de Montesquieu, Rousseau et Voltaire*. Paris, 1902.
Fairlie, Henry. 'The Lessons of Watergate', *Encounter*, 43/4, Oct. 1974, pp. 8-29.
Fanon, Frantz. *The Wretched of the Earth*, trans. C. Farrington. London, 1965.
Feuerbach, Ludwig. *Briefwechsel und Nachlass*, K. Grün, ed. Leipzig-Heidelberg, 1874.
Feuerbach, Ludwig. *The Essence of Christianity*, trans G. Eliot. New York, 1957.
Feuerbach, Ludwig. *Sämtliche Werke*. Stuttgart, 1903-11.
Fichte, Johann Gottlieb. *Sämtliche Werke*. Berlin, 1845.
Fitzgerald, C.P. *The Birth of Communist China*. Harmondsworth, 1964.
Fromm, Erich, ed. *Socialist Humanism*. London, 1967.

Galbraith, John K. *The Affluent Society*. Boston, 1958.
Galbraith, John K. *The New Industrial State*. Boston, 1967.
Gervinus, Georg Gottfried. *Geschichte der deutschen Dichtung*, 5 vols, 5th ed. Leipzig, 1971-4.
Goethe, Johann Wolfgang. *Eckermann's Conversations with Goethe*, trans. R.O. Moon. London, 1950.
Goethe, Johann Wolfgang. *Elective Affinities*, trans. E. Mayer and L. Bogan. Chicago, 1963.
Goethe, Johann Wolfgang. *Letters from Goethe*, trans. M. v. Herzfeld and C.M. Sym. Edinburgh, 1957.
Goethe, Johann Wolfgang. *Werke*. Hamburg, 1949–.
Gramsci, Antonio. *The Modern Prince and other writings*, trans. L. Marks. London, 1957.
Gramsci, Antonio. *Selections from Political Writings*, trans. J. Matthews. London, 1977.
Grillparzer, Franz. *Sämtliche Werke*. München, 1960–.
Groethuysen, Bernard. *Philosophie de la Révolution française*, 2nd ed. Paris, 1956.
Grün, Karl. *Die soziale Bewegung in Frankreich und Belgien*. Darmstadt, 1845.
Gutman, Herbert G. *Work, Culture and Society in Industrializing America*. New York, 1976.

Habermas, Jürgen. 'Literaturbericht zur philosophischen Diskussion um Marx und den Marxismus' (1957), in *Theorie und Praxis*. Frankfurt, 1963.
Habermas, Jürgen. *Protestbewegung und Hochschulreform*. Frankfurt, 1969.
Habermas, Jürgen. *Theory and Practice*, trans. J. Viertel. London, 1974.
Han, Suyin. *Asia Today*. Montreal, 1969.
Harrington, Michael. *The Accidental Century*. New York, 1965.
Haym, Rudolf. *Hegel und seine Zeit*. Berlin, 1957.
Hegel, G.W.F. *Essay on Natural Law*, trans. T.M. Knox. Philadelphia, 1975.
Hegel, G.W.F. *History of Philosophy*, 3 vols, trans. E.S. Haldane and F.S. Simson. London, 1892-5.
Hegel, G.W.F. *Lectures on the Philosophy of World History*, trans. H.B. Nisbet. Cambridge, 1975.
Hegel, G.W.F. *The Logic of Hegel*, trans. W. Wallace. Oxford, 1892.
Hegel, G.W.F. *The Phenomenology of Spirit* trans. A.V. Miller. Oxford, 1977.
Hegel, G.W.F. *The Philosophy of Right*, trans. T.M. Knox. Oxford, 1952.
Hegel, G.W.F. *Political Writings*, trans. T.M. Knox. Oxford, 1964.

Hegel, G.W.F. *Schriften zur Politik und Rechtsphilosophie*, ed. G. Lasson. Leipzig, 1923.
Hegel, G.W.F. *Science of Logic*, trans. A.V. Miller. London, 1969.
Hegel, G.W.F. *Theologische Jugendschriften*, ed. H. Nohl. Tübingen, 1907.
Heidegger, Martin. *An Introduction to Metaphysics*, trans. R. Manheim. New Haven, 1959.
Heine, Heinrich. *Werke*. Frankfurt, 1968.
Hess, Moses. *Briefwechsel*, ed. E. Silberner. The Hague, 1919.
Hess, Moses. *Die heilige Geschichte und die Menschheit*. Stuttgart, 1837.
Hess, Moses. *Sozialistische Aufsätze 1841-47*. Berlin, 1921.
Hesse, Hermann. *Gesammelte Werke*. Frankfurt, 1966–.
Hilferding, Rudolf. *Das Finanzkapital*. Wien, 1910.
Hölderlin, Friedrich. *Sämtliche Gedichte*, ed. D. Lüders. Frankfurt, 1970.
Honigsheim, Paul. *On Max Weber*, trans. J. Rytina. New York, 1968.
Horkheimer, Max. *Critique of Instrumental Reason*. New York, 1974.
Horkheimer, Max and Adorno, Theodor W. *Sociologica II*. Frankfurt, 1962.
Huch, Ricarda. *Michael Bakunin und die Anarchie*. Frankfurt, 1923.

James, William. *Memories and Studies*. New York, 1911.
Jaspers, Karl. *Hoffnung und Sorge*. München, 1965.
Jaspers, Karl. *Man in the Modern Age*, trans. E. and C. Paul. London, 1951.
Jaspers, Karl. *Philosophy of Existence*, trans. R.F. Grabau. Philadelphia, 1971.
Jaspers, Karl. *Schicksal und Wille*. München, 1967.
Jouvenel, Bertrand de. *Arcadie, essais sur le mieux-vivre*. Paris, 1968.

Kant, Immanuel. *Critique of Practical Reason*, trans. T.K. Abbot. London, 1883.
Kant, Immanuel. *Critique of Pure Reason*, trans. N.K. Smith. London, 1929.
Kant, Immanuel. *Political Writings*, trans. H.B. Nisbet. Cambridge, 1971.
Kant, Immanuel. *Werke*, ed. G. Hartenstein. Leipzig, 1867-8.
Keller, Gottfried. *Sämtliche Werke*. Erlenbach-Zürich, 1926–.
Keynes, John Maynard. *The End of Laissez-Faire*. London, 1926.
Keynes, John Maynard. *Essays in Persuasion*. London, 1931.
Kierkegaard, Søren. *Journals and Papers*, 7 vols, trans. H.V. and E.H. Hong. Bloomington, 1967-78.
Klaus, Georg and Buhr, Manfred, eds. *Marxistisch-leninistisches Wörterbuch der Philosophie*, 3 vols. Leipzig, 1970.
Koestler, Arthur. *Arrow in the Blue*. London, 1952.
Kojève, Alexandre. *Introduction to the Reading of Hegel*, trans. J.H. Nichols Jr. New York, 1946.
Kolakowski, Leszek. *Der Mensch ohne Alternative*. München, 1960.
Kolakowski, Leszek. *Main Currents of Marxism*. 3 vols, Oxford, 1978.
Korsch, Karl. *Marxism and Philosophy*, trans. F. Halliday. London, 1970.
Kramář, Karel. *Geschichte und Kritik des Bolschewismus*. München, 1925.

Labedz, Leopold, ed. *Revisionism*. London, 1962.
Labriola, Antonio. *Essays on the Materialist Conception of History*, trans. C.H. Kerr. Chicago, 1903.
Lefèbvre, Henri. 'De l'explication en économie politique et en sociologie', *Cahiers Internationaux de Sociologie*, xxi, 1956, pp. 19-36.
Lenin, Vladimir Ilyich. *Aus dem philosophischen Nachlass*. Berlin, 1954.
Lenin, Vladimir Ilyich. *Letters of Lenin*, trans. E. Hill and D. Mudie. London, 1937.
Lenin, Vladimir Ilyich. *Materialism and Empirio-Criticism*, 4th ed. Moscow, 1964.

Lenin, Vladimir Ilyich. *Selected Works*, 3 vols. Moscow, 1967.
Lenz, Friedrich. *Staat und Marxismus*, 2 vols. Stuttgart, 1922-4.
Lessing, Gotthold Ephraim. *Laocoön and other Prose Writings*, trans. W.B. Rönnfeldt. London, 1895.
Liberman, Yevsei. 'The Soviet Economic Reform', *Foreign Affairs*, 46/1, Oct. 1967, pp. 53-63.
Lindbeck, Assar. *The Political Economy of the New Left*. New York, 1971.
Lukács, Georg. *Conversations with Lukács*, ed. T. Pinkus. Cambridge, Mass., 1975.
Lukács, Georg. *Goethe and his Age*, trans. R. Anchor. London, 1968.
Lukács, Georg. *The Historical Novel*, trans. H. and S. Mitchell. London, 1962.
Lukács, Georg. *History and Class Consciousness*, trans. R. Livingstone. London, 1971.
Lukács, Georg. *The Meaning of Contemporary Realism*, trans. J. and N. Mander. London, 1963.
Lukács, Georg. *Realism in our Time*, trans. J. and N. Mander. New York, 1971.
Lukács, Georg. *Schriften zur Ideologie und Politik*. Neuwied/Rhein, 1967.
Lukács, Georg. *Soul and Form*, trans. A. Bostock. London, 1974.
Lukács, Georg. *Solzhenitsyn*, trans. W.D. Graf. London, 1969.
Lukács, Georg. *Theory of the Novel*, trans. A. Bostock. London, 1971.
Lukács, Georg. *Werke*. Neuwied/Rhein, 1962–.
Lukács, Georg. 'Zur Soziologie des gesellschaftlichen Seins', *Neues Forum*, 207 I/II, Feb.-March 1971, pp. 19-22.
Luxemburg, Rosa. *The Accumulation of Capital*, trans. A. Schwarzschild. New Haven, 1951.
Luxemburg, Rosa. *Rosa Luxemburg Speaks*, ed. M.-A. Waters. New York, 1970.

Malthus, Thomas. *An Essay on the Principle of Population*, 2 vols in one. London, 1973.
Mandel, Ernest. *Marxist Economic Theory* 2 vols, trans. B. Pearce. London, 1968.
Mandelshtam, Nadezhda. *Hope Against Hope*. London, 1971.
Mandelshtam, Osip. *Selected Essays*, trans. S. Monas. Austin, 1977.
Mann, Golo. *The History of Germany since 1789*, trans. M. Jackson. London, 1968.
Mann, Thomas. *Betrachtungen eines Unpolitischen*. Berlin, 1919.
Mann, Thomas. *Briefe 1937-1947*. Frankfurt, 1963.
Mann, Thomas. *Essays of Three Decades*, trans. H.T. Lowe-Porter. New York, 1929.
Mann, Thomas. *Politische Schriften*, 2 vols. Frankfurt, 1968.
Mao Tse-tung. *Quotations from Chairman Mao*. Peking, 1965.
Mao Tse-tung. *Selected Works*. Peking, 1961–.
Marcuse, Herbert. *Eros and Civilization*. New York, 1962.
Marcuse, Herbert. *Negations*, trans. J.J. Shapiro. Boston, 1968.
Marcuse, Herbert. 'Neue Quellen zur Grundlegung des Historischen Materialismus', *Die Gesellschaft*. ix/2, 1932, pp. 136-74.
Marcuse, Herbert. *One-Dimensional Man*. London, 1964.
Marcuse, Herbert. *Reason and Revolution*, 2nd ed. London, 1955.
Marcuse, Herbert. 'Repressive Tolerance', in Robert Wolff *et al.*, *A Critique of Pure Tolerance*. Boston, 1969.
Marcuse, Herbert. *Soviet Marxism*. London, 1958.
Meadows, Donella, *et al. The Limits to Growth*. London, 1972.
Mehnert, Klaus. *China Returns*. London, 1972.

Mehring, Franz. *Geschichte der deutschen Sozialdemokratie*, 2nd ed. Stuttgart, 1903.
Mehring, Franz. *Karl Marx*, trans. E. Fitzgerald. London, 1936.
Merleau-Ponty, Maurice. *The Adventures of the Dialectic*, trans. J. Brien. London, 1974.
Mesarović, Mihajlo and Pestel, Eduard. *Mankind at the Turning-Point*. London, 1975.
Mill, John Stuart. *Principles of Political Economy*. Harmondsworth, 1970.
Mills, C. Wright. *The Causes of World War Three*. London, 1959.
Milosz, Czeslaw. *The Captive Mind*, trans. J. Zielonko. London, 1953.
Mishan, Edward Joshua. *The Costs of Economic Growth*. London, 1967.
Mommsen, Wolfgang. *Max Weber: Gesellschaft, Politik und Geschichte*. Tübingen, 1974.
Montesquieu, Charles de Secondat. *Spirit of Laws*, trans. T. Nugent. London, 1949.
Moravia, Alberto. *The Red Book and the Great Wall*, trans. R. Strom. London, 1968.
Mulk, Raj Anand, 'By mouth or by book', *Times Literary Supplement*, 12 May 1972, p. 552.
Müller, Gustav. *Hegel*. Bern, 1959.
Myrdal, Gunnar. *An American Dilemma*, 20th anniversary ed. New York, 1962.
Myrdal, Gunnar. *Beyond the Welfare State*. New Haven, 1960.

Needham, Joseph. *The Grand Titration*. London, 1969.
Newman, Ernest A. *The Life of Richard Wagner*, 4 vols. New York, 1965.
Nietzsche, Friedrich. *Thus Spake Zarathustra*, trans. R.J. Hollingdale. London, 1969.
Nietzsche, Friedrich. *Werke*. Berlin, 1967–.

Orwell, George. *Animal Farm*. London, 1945.
Orwell, George. *Nineteen Eighty-four*. London, 1949.

Packard, Vance. *The Status Seekers*. New York, 1959.
Pannekoek, Antonie. *Lenin as Philosopher*. New York, 1948.
Popitz, Heinrich. *Der entfremdete Mensch*. Basel, 1953.
Proudhon, Pierre-Joseph. *What Is Property?*, trans. B. Tucker. London, 1970.
Prucha, Milan. 'Marxismus als Philosophie menschlicher Existenz', *Neues Forum*, 14, 1967, pp. 845-50.

Ragaz, Leonard. *Von Christus zu Marx – Von Marx zu Christus*. Wernigerode/Harx, 1929.
Ranke, Leopold von. *Die Epochen der neueren Geschichte*. Berlin, n.d.
Ranke, Leopold von. *Politisches Gespräch*. München, 1924.
Ranke, Leopold von. *Weltgeschichte*, 5th ed. Leipzig, 1896.
Rapp, Adolf. *Friedrich Theodor Vischer und die Politik*. Tübingen, 1911.
Revel, Jean-François. *Without Marx or Jesus*, trans. J.F. Bernard. New York, 1971.
Ricardo, David. *The Principles of Political Economy and Taxation*. Harmondsworth, 1971.
Richta, Radovan *et al. Civilization at the Crossroads*, trans. M. Šlingová. White Plains, 1969.
Riehl, Wilhelm H. *Die bürgerliche Gesellschaft*, 4th ed. Stuttgart, 1856.
Riesman, David. *The Lonely Crowd*. New Haven, 1950.

Riesman, David. ' "The Lonely Crowd", 20 Years After', *Encounter*, 33/4,
Oct. 1969, pp. 36-41.
Robinson, Joan. *The Cultural Revolution in China*. Harmondsworth, 1969.
Robinson, Joan. *An Essay on Marxian Economics*. London, 1942.
Röpke, Wilhelm. *Jenseits von Angebot und Nachfrage*. Erlenbach bei Zürich, 1966.
Rosdolsky, Roman. *The Making of Marx's 'Capital'*, trans. P. Burgess.
London, 1977.
Rosenzweig, Franz. *Star of Redemption*, trans. W.W. Hallo. New York, 1971.
Rousseau, Jean-Jacques. *Émile*, trans. B. Foxley. London, 1911.
Rousseau, Jean-Jacques. *Political Writings*, ed. C.E. Vaughan. Cambridge, 1915.
Rousseau, Jean-Jacques. *The Social Contract and Discourses*, trans. G.D.H.
Cole, new ed. London, 1973.
Rubel, Maximilien. *Karl Marx*. Paris, 1957.
Ruge, Arnold. *Briefwechsel*. Berlin, 1886.

Sakharov, Andrei D. *Sakharov Speaks*. New York, 1974.
Salisbury, Harrison E. *To Peking – and Beyond*. London, 1973.
Samuelson, Paul. *Economics* , 9th ed. New York, 1973.
Schaff, Adam. *Marxism and the Human Individual*, trans. O. Wojtasiewicz.
New York, 1970.
Schiller, Friedrich. *Sämtliche Werke*. München, 1958–.
Schlipp, Paul, ed. *Karl Jaspers*. Stuttgart, 1957.
Schramm, Stuart. *Mao Tse-tung*. Harmondsworth, 1967.
Schumpeter, Joseph. *Ten Great Economists*, trans. R. Aris. London, 1952.
Schurz, Carl L. *The Reminiscences*, 3 vols. New York, 1907.
Sholem, Gershom. 'Walter Benjamin', *Neue Rundschau*, 76, 1965, pp. 1-21.
Sik, Ota. *The Third Way*, trans. M. Sling. London, 1976.
Silone, Ignazio. *The Story of a Humble Christian*, trans. W. Weaver. London,
1970.
Smith, Adam. *An Inquiry into the Nature and Causes of the Wealth of Nations*.
London, 1910.
Smith, Adam. *Theory of Moral Sentiments*. Oxford, 1976.
Solzhenitsyn, Aleksandr. *The First Circle*, trans. M. Guybon. London, 1968.
Solzhenitsyn, Aleksandr. *One Day in the Life of Ivan Denisovich*, trans. R.
Parker. London, 1963.
Solzhenitsyn, Aleksandr. *Von der Verantwortung des Schriftstellers*. Zürich,
1969.
Sombart, Werner. *The Quintessence of Capitalism*, trans. M. Epstein.
New York, 1915.
Spender, Stephen. *The Year of the Young Rebels*. London, 1969.
Stahl, Friedrich Julius. *Geschichte der Rechtsphilosophie*. Heidelberg, 1856.
Stalin, Jozef V. *The Essential Stalin*, ed. B. Franklin. London, 1973.
Stalin, Jozef V. *Problems of Leninism*. Moscow, 1953.
Stammer, Otto, ed. *Max Weber and Sociology Today*, trans. K. Morris.
Oxford, 1971.
Stein, Lorenz von. *The History of the Social Movement in France 1789-1850*,
trans. K. Mengelberg. Totowa, N.Y., 1964.
Steiner, George. *In Bluebeard's Castle*. London, 1971.
Stojanović, Svetozar. *Between Ideal and Reality*, trans. G.S. Sher. New York,
1973.
Strauss, David Friedrich. *The Life of Jesus Critically Examined*, ed. P. Hodgson.
London, 1973.
Strauss, Leo. *Natural Right and History*. Chicago, 1965.

Talmon, Jacob L. *The Origins of Totalitarian Democracy*. London, 1952.
Talmon, Jacob L. *Political Messianism*. London, 1960.
Tocqueville, Alexis de. *L'Ancien Régime*, trans. M.W. Patterson. Oxford, 1956.
Tocqueville, Alexis de. *Democracy in America*, trans. H. Reeve. London, 1946.
Touraine, Alain. *The Post-Industrial Society*, trans. L.F.X. Mayhew. London, 1971.
Trotsky, Lev D. *In Defence of Marxism*. New York, 1942.
Trotsky, Lev D. *Literature and Revolution*, trans. R. Strunsky. Ann Arbor, 1960.

Urquhart, Clara and Brent, Peter L. *Enzo Sereni: A Hero of Our Time*. London, 1967.

Veblen, Thorstein. *The Theory of the Leisure Class*. New York, 1899.
Voegelin, Eric. *The New Science of Politics*. Chicago, 1952.

Webb, Sidney and Webb, Beatrice. *History of Trade Unionism*. London, 1920.
Weber, Max. *Economy and Society*, 3 vols, eds G. Roth and C. Wittich. New York, 1968.
Weber, Max. *From Max Weber: Essays in Sociology*, trans H. Gerth and C.W. Mills. London, 1948.
Weber, Max. *Gesammelte Aufsätze zur Soziologie und Sozialpolitik*. Tübingen, 1920-1.
Weber, Max. *Gessamelte Aufsätze zur Soziologie und Sozialpolitik*. Tübingen, 1924.
Weber, Max. *Gesammelte Politische Schriften*. Tübingen, 1958.
Weber, Max. *The Methodology of the Social Sciences*, trans. E.A. Shils and H.A. Finch. New York, 1949.
Weber, Max. *The Protestant Ethic and the Spirit of Capitalism*, trans. T. Parsons, 2nd ed. London, 1976.
Weber, Max. *The Religion of China*, trans. H. Gerth. Glencoe, 1951.
Weber, Max. *Roscher and Knies: The Logical Problems of Historical Economics*, trans. G. Oakes. New York, 1975.
Weber, Max. *Selections in Translation*, ed. W.G. Runciman, trans. E. Matthews. Cambridge, 1978.
Weil, Simone. *La Condition ouvrière*. Paris, 1951.
Weil, Simone. *Oppression and Liberty*, trans. A. Wills and J. Petrie. London, 1958.
Weitling, Wilhelm. *Die Menschheit, wie sie ist, und wie sie sein sollte*, 2nd ed. Bern, 1845.
Wells, H.G. *The New Machiavelli*. London, 1911.
Wilson, Edmund. *To the Finland Station*. London, 1941.
Whyte, William H. *The Organization Man*. London, 1957.

Index